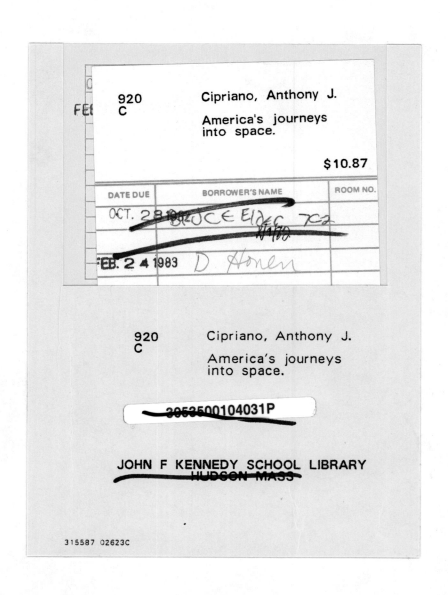

920
C

Cipriano, Anthony J.

America's journeys
into space.

$10.87

DATE DUE	BORROWER'S NAME	ROOM NO.
OCT. 28	BRUCE ELDER	7C2
FEB. 2 4 1983	D. Honen	

discard

America's Journeys into Space

America's Journeys into Space

The Astronauts of the United States

PORTRAITS BY

William Joffe Numeroff

TEXT BY

Anthony J. Cipriano

Foreword by Gordon Cooper

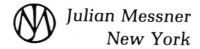

Julian Messner
New York

Drawing "Cast of Characters" (slightly abridged) from *Carrying the Fire* by Michael Collins. Copyright © 1974 by Michael Collins. Reproduced with the permission of Farrar, Straus & Giroux.

Photos courtesy of National Aeronautics and Space Administration

Library of Congress Cataloging in Publication Data

Cipriano, Anthony J
    America's journeys into space.

    Includes index.
    SUMMARY: Presents biographical sketches of American astronauts from Alan Shepard to Vance Brand and discusses the various space programs in which these men have participated.
    1. Astronautics—United States—Juvenile literature. 2. Astronauts—United States—Biography—Juvenile literature. [1. Astronauts. 2. Astronautics] I. Numeroff, William Joffe. II. Title.
TL789.8.U5C56   629.4′092′2 [B] [920] 79-10254
ISBN 0-671-33020-9

This book is dedicated to the memory of
ROBERT H. GODDARD and all those with the
VISION, the ENERGY, and the COURAGE to explore.

Robert Hutchings Goddard / 1882–1945

Contents

Acknowledgments

THE PORTRAITS in this book are part of a growing collection dedicated to Dr. Robert H. Goddard, the father of modern rocketry. The project, which currently numbers 175 portraits, was started in 1957 when the space age was in its infancy. I wanted to record the faces of the people who were in the forefront of the expanding age of science.

The list of thirty-two names suggested by Dr. Arthur Holly Compton from his book, *Atomic Quest,* was expanded as the scope of the collection grew. I am indebted to the many people who helped to guide me through the maze of names associated with each discipline and helped in other ways to keep the collection growing.

I would like to express special appreciation to the following: Mrs. Esther C. Goddard, wife of the rocket pioneer, for her generous help ever since my first visit to the "old, white house with geraniums in window boxes" in 1961; Dr. Wernher von Braun; Dr. Eugene Emme, Chief Historian NASA (Ret); Shirley Thomas, author of the eight-volume series, *Men of Space;* Prof. Lloyd Motz, Columbia University, Department of Astronomy; Col. Walter H. Flint, USAF (Ret); Don Eppert, USA Corps of Engineers, Cape Canaveral (Ret); Maj. James Sparks, USAF (Ret); Ivy Edmonds, M/Sgt. USAF Office of Information, Edwards AFB, Calif. (Ret); Astronaut Deke Slayton; Lee Saegesser, NASA Historian; Edmond C. Browne; Jules Warzybok; Sister M. Fidelma, Curator of the Cardinal Spellman Philatelic Museum, Weston, Mass., who recognized the historical significance of the collection and arranged for its first full-scale showing in 1966; American Institute of Physics, Public Relations Division; Les Gaver, NASA Office of Public Information; Office of the Secretary of the Air Force, N.Y., Office of Information; American Museum, Hayden Planetarium; and a special tribute to my wife, Florence, who kept her feet on the ground and the family together while my head was in space.

WILLIAM JOFFE NUMEROFF

MY INTENTION in writing this history was in some way to express my gratitude to the people of our country's space program. In twenty short years they managed an incredible expansion of the human experience beyond our planet.

Their true gift to history was the reassurance to Mankind—collectively and as individuals—that there are still dreams to be had and that we continue to possess the greatness to realize them. If this work imparts but a small portion of my admiration, I will have succeeded in my mission.

I want to thank Frederic C. Durant III, Director of Astronautics, National Air and Space Museum (NASM) for his helpful suggestions on part of this book. I also am greatly indebted to my good friend Colonel Walter H. Flint, Curator of Astronautics, NASM, who guided my early efforts and shares my enthusiasm for the Space Program. My thanks also to Col. Lynn A. Breece, USAF (Ret), who contributed valuable research material. I would also like to single out Lee Saegesser, NASA Historian, Gregory Kennedy, and Walter J. Dillon, Assistant Curators of Astronautics (NASM), who made important research contributions. I am also grateful to Alex P. Nagy, Assistant Director of Public Affairs, NASA, for being kind enough to read my manuscript and offer suggestions. I am indebted to Theresa Lahm for contributing her time to type part of the manuscript.

Lastly, I want to pay an affectionate tribute to my wife, Vikki, for the endless hours of typing and the love and understanding she and my daughter Jillian showed me when I couldn't be with them.

ANTHONY J. CIPRIANO

Foreword

IN THE quiet moments during the rest periods of my Mercury and Gemini space flights, I remember looking at the earth, drifting silently by below me, and wondering what the future held for Man in space. There were so many unknowns and so much to learn then. If, however, there were any doubts about President Kennedy's goal of safely landing astronauts on the moon before the end of the sixties or of the ability of Man to sustain his presence in space, they were decisively laid to rest by the skill, determination, and dedication of the men and women of America's Space Program.

America's Journeys into Space is a journey back to what were some of the most significant moments in our country's history and, for me, the most memorable years of my life. William Numeroff's artistry and Anthony Cipriano's narrative vividly capture the glow of those years.

Bill's vintage portraits summon up the images of my fellow astronauts for us as Dr. Cipriano vividly recreates the drama of Americans pushing ahead determinedly into space. The story unfolds as it happened, and in precise and nontechnical language, Dr. Cipriano interprets what transpired through the perspective of history. Mankind's journey into space was not a sidetrip of history. We evolved into space for the very good reason that giants from every nation and every generation came forth with the important contributions to human knowledge that brought us there.

Dr. Cipriano envisions an enlightened Man, driven by a curiosity that has been a moving force throughout history, choosing to continue his venture into space in search of further enlightenment.

America's Journeys into Space, engenders the love and fascination for space exploration that inspired its creation and inspired my own journeys into space.

Gordon Cooper
Col. USAF (Ret)
Astronaut

Prologue: The Continuation of a Dream

IT WAS 2:30 in the afternoon and the two men stood silently, their eyes carefully appraising the results of the morning's labor. The cold air probed like icy fingers at their bundled clothing, but their thoughts were on the fragile steel-tubing framework that stood before them. Fully assembled, it looked like a child's jungle gym, not like something belonging to the future.

The scene was Effie Ward's farm in Auburn, Massachusetts, and the small rocket that Robert Hutchings Goddard and his assistant were about to launch was to provide mankind with a revolutionary instrument of exploration and make the space age inevitable.

On that day, March 16, 1926, Goddard flew his 10¼-pound rocket a total distance of 184 feet, demonstrating for the first time the feasibility of liquid-fueled rocket propulsion. To Goddard, a modest man with soaring dreams, the door to the exploration of space was now open. He spent the rest of his life quietly working toward the fulfillment of that vision.

Robert Goddard died in 1945, but the dream he had carried with him throughout his life was passed on to a new generation, as it had been passed on to him by the scientists of generations past—by Galileo, Copernicus, Kepler, Newton, and others.

Thirty-two years after Goddard's historic test flight, a giant rocket called Jupiter C bearing America's first satellite, Explorer I, stood poised to carry the United States into the space age alongside the Soviet Union. At 10:48 P.M. on that January 31, 1958, Jupiter roared into the darkness of space on an adventure that has changed man's views of himself for all time.

The launch effort for Explorer I was awesome in scale in comparison to Goddard's earlier attempts, but it was the same principle of liquid-fueled propulsion that gave life to both rockets.

Explorer I was launched as the contribution of the United States to the worldwide scientific research program known as the International Geophysical Year. Its discovery of the earth-girdling Van Allen radiation belt was the most significant scientific discovery of that year and of the decade to follow. Before the fiery end of Explorer I on its reentry into the earth's atmosphere, March 31, 1970, the United States was to launch 1,042 major probes into the upper atmosphere and outer space. Astronauts would circle the earth and walk the moon.

Tiros weather observation satellites were among the earliest space probes. Tiros I was launched on April 1, 1960, to begin television monitoring of the earth's weather systems from space. Transit I-B, launched April 13, 1960, first demonstrated the feasibility of the use of satellites as navigational aids. Today a vastly superior network of satellites is being assembled to guide airliners and ocean-going ships of all nations with pinpoint accuracy.

Landsat satellites are monitoring the natural resources of the earth, while communication satellites ringing the planet make possible the instantaneous transmission of telephone, radio, and television signals.

Planetary spacecraft—Pioneers, Mariners, Rangers, Surveyors, and Vikings—have explored the solar system outwards to the planet Jupiter. The miracle of two Viking robot spacecrafts landing themselves without direct human guidance, on the 240-million-mile-distant planet Mars to search for life is another dream come-true step in our quest to find out who we are and where we came from.

As the inventions of mankind probed deeper and deeper into the vastness of space it became inevitable that man himself would seek to establish his own presence there. The initial voyagers were the astronauts. This book is about them.

AJC
June 1978

2

Project Mercury

THE CHALLENGE of flight is as old as the history of mankind itself. Mythology, religion, and literature dating back thousands of years are replete with fanciful accounts of winged creatures, devices of flight, and winged gods. In one of the earliest recorded accounts, the Greek savant, Lucian of Samosata, in his *Vera Historia* (A.D. 160) tells the story of an imaginary flight to the moon and relates how the angry gods ordered Hermes, the Greek counterpart of the Roman god Mercury, to deposit the bold human intruder, Mennipus, unceremoniously back on earth.

Less than 2,000 years later, less than 300 lifetimes by today's living standards, man has not only developed the capability of flight, he is now crossing the heavens. With seemingly routine precision, man has set foot on the moon.

The first steps in that journey were taken in 1958. In October of that year, a project was organized for the purpose of placing a man in orbit around the earth to observe his reactions and capabilities in the weightlessness of space flight, and to test the system for safe recovery of pilot and craft.

In discussing the problem of spacecraft *reentry* and the safe return of man to earth, the esteemed pioneer in aeronautical science, Theodore von Karman, spoke of Mercury, as had Lucian of Samosata. The messenger of the gods with his winged sandals and helmet is one of the most familiar of the ancient gods and was symbolically an appropriate name for the manned satellite program.

On Wright Brother's Day, December 17, 1958, fifty-five years after the famous flights at Kitty Hawk, North Carolina, T. Keith Glennan (NASA's first Administrator) announced in Washington that the manned satellite program would be called Project Mercury.

The decision to use test pilots to fly the Mercury spacecraft was made by President Eisenhower during the Christmas holidays of 1958. NASA (the National Aeronautics and Space Administration), the civilian authority which directs our country's space program, quickly formulated the following seven criteria for candidate selection:

1. Age less than 40 years old
2. Height not greater than 5 feet 11 inches
3. Excellent physical condition
4. Bachelor's degree or equivalent
5. 1,500 hours total flying time
6. Graduate of test pilot school
7. Qualified jet pilot

After a review of the records of 508 eligible candidates in early 1959, 69 test pilots were asked to report to Washington for final screening. On April 9, 1959, the final selection was officially announced and the names of Alan Shepard, Virgil Grissom, John Glenn, Scott Carpenter, Walter Schirra, Gordon Cooper and Donald Slayton were written into the history books. They would be America's first astronauts, named in the tradition of the legendary Greeks who searched for the Golden Fleece and who were called Argonauts.

By early 1961, a dozen preliminary tests of the Mercury spacecraft and escape systems had shown that the craft was reliable and that its test passengers (monkeys) could be recovered unharmed. Two manned suborbital (ballistic flights) and four manned orbital missions were soon to follow.

The Mercury flights demonstrated the ability of the astronaut to control the spacecraft as efficiently as he would in a high-performance aircraft through all phases of the mission. They proved him invaluable not only in controlling the spacecraft and overcoming mechanical malfunctions, but also in dealing with the unanticipated. The original seven Mercury astronauts took man into a "new ocean" where he could carry on in the tradition of his ancestors—to discover and explore.

Alan Bartlett Shepard, Jr.

Birthplace	East Derry, New Hampshire
Date of Birth	November 18, 1923
Height	5′ 11″
Weight	160 lbs.
Eyes	Blue
Hair	Brown
Marital Status/Wife	Louise
Daughters	Laura and Juliana
Recreational Interests	Golf, waterskiing, ice skating
Service Affiliation	Lt. Commander, U.S. Navy
Flight Record	5,700 hours (3,700 in jet aircraft). Logged 216 hours 57 minutes in two space flights, of which 9 hours 17 minutes were spent walking on the lunar surface in extravehicular activity (EVA).
Education and Training	Bachelor of Science degree from U.S. Naval Academy in 1944, flight training at Corpus Christi, Texas, and Pensacola, Florida. Received his wings in 1947. Attended U.S. Navy Test Pilot School at Patuxent River, Maryland (1950), later becoming an instructor there. Afterwards, he attended Naval War College at Newport, Rhode Island, graduating in 1957.
Astronaut Career	He was chosen with the first group of astronauts, "the Original Seven," on April 9, 1959, and was awarded the Congressional Space Medal of Honor, two NASA Distinguished Service Medals and the NASA Exceptional Service Medal. On May 5, 1961, he became America's first man in space. It was a suborbital flight on board the Mercury capsule *Freedom 7*. He became backup pilot for *Faith 7* before

being grounded for an inner ear ailment. Shepard stayed with the astronaut corps and was designated Chief of the Astronaut Office in 1963, with responsibility for monitoring the control of all activities involving NASA astronauts. This included monitoring the development and implementation of programs for training space flight personnel, and furnishing pilot evaluations of the design, construction, and operations of spacecraft systems and related equipment. Shepard also helped in overall mission planning and selecting experiments to be carried out in space.

He underwent a successful ear operation and was restored to flight status on May 7, 1969 and became commander of the Apollo 14 mission, flown January 31–February 9, 1971. He was accompanied on man's third lunar landing mission by Stuart A. Roosa (command module pilot) and Edgar D. Mitchell (lunar module pilot). Shepard and Mitchell landed their LM (lunar module) *Antares* in the hilly upland Fra Mauro region and Shepard became the fifth man to walk on the moon. They spent 33 hours on the lunar surface, 9 hours 17 minutes of which were spent walking during extravehicular activities.

Shepard resumed his duties as Chief of the Astronaut Office in June 1971, serving in this capacity until April 1974. He retired from NASA and the Navy with the rank of Rear Admiral in July 1974 to enter private business.

Mercury-Redstone 3: The Flight of Freedom 7

May 5, 1961

At 9:34 A.M. EST on May 5, 1961, in full view of a television audience of 45 million people, Alan B. Shepard was dramatically lifted into space and became America's first astronaut. Seconds after the slim Redstone rocket carrying Shepard and his *Freedom 7* Mercury spacecraft roared off its launch pad at Cape Canaveral, Mercury Control and millions of Americans heard the historic transmission; "Ahh, Roger; lift-off and the clock is started. . . . Yes, Sir, reading you loud and clear. This is *Freedom 7*. The fuel is Go . . . 1.2 G . . . cabin at 14 psi . . . oxygen is Go. *Freedom 7* is still Go!"

America's first man in space was in flight only 15 minutes and 22 seconds and was weightless only a third of that time due to the suborbital ballistic nature of the flight. Shepard attained an altitude of 116.5 miles and a maximum speed of 5,180 miles per hour. He landed 9.2 miles from the prime recovery ship, the aircraft carrier *Lake Champlain*, at a point 302 statute miles down the Atlantic Missile Range

from his Cape Canaveral launch site. Shepard was subjected to acceleration forces as high as 6 G (six times his body weight) at lift-off, and 11 G on reentry into the atmosphere. Recovery helicopters transported the undamaged spacecraft and its exuberant commander to the *Lake Champlain*. When greeted on board the flight deck Shepard exclaimed, "It's a beautiful day. Boy, what a ride!"

The numeral 7 was included by Shepard in naming his spacecraft *Freedom 7* because of the fact that his was capsule No. 7 on booster rocket No. 7, and because his flight would be the first of an expected series of seven flights. The numeral 7, however, soon became more strongly associated with the original seven astronauts and, for that reason, included in the call sign for each of the remaining Mercury missions.

Shepard's performance also established the tradition of dedication, engineering excellence, and impeccable professionalism that was to underscore each successive astronaut mission.

Virgil Ivan Grissom

Birthplace	Mitchell, Indiana
Date of Birth	April 3, 1926
Height	5' 7"
Weight	155 lbs.
Eyes	Brown
Hair	Brown
Marital Status/Wife	Betty
Sons	Scotty, Mark
Recreational Interests	Hunting, fishing, skiing, boating
Service Affiliation	Captain, U.S. Air Force
Flight Record	4,600 hours (3,500 in jet aircraft); 100 combat missions (F-86's) in Korea; 5 hours 9 minutes logged in two space flights.
Education and Training	Bachelor of Science, Mechanical Engineering, Purdue University. Earned his wings in 1951, studied aeronautical engineering at the Air Force Institute of Technology, Wright-Patterson Air Force Base, Ohio, in August 1955; Test Pilot School at Edwards Air Force Base from October 1956 to May 1957; returned to Wright-Patterson as a test pilot assigned to the fighter branch.
Astronaut Career	Grissom was chosen with the first group of astronauts, "the Original Seven," was awarded the Congressional Space Medal of Honor (posthumously), two NASA Distinguished Service Medals and the NASA Exceptional Service Medal. He was the second American astronaut to make a space flight, flying the Mercury spacecraft *Liberty Bell 7* on July 21, 1961, on a suborbital mission. On March 23, 1965, he served as command pilot on the first manned Gemini flight (Gemini III), was backup command pilot for Gemini VI, December 1965, and commander of what would have been Apollo 1. Lt. Colonel Grissom perished in the Apollo 1 fire during a training exercise at Launch Pad 34 at Cape Kennedy on January 27, 1967.

Mercury-Redstone 4: The Saga of Liberty Bell 7

July 21, 1961

The twice-postponed launch of Virgil I. "Gus" Grissom into space was nearing realization. For months preparation had been made with painstaking care, and the experience gained from Shepard's previous flight was already evident in the modifications that were worked into Grissom's spacecraft and flight routine.

Freedom 7 had been an unqualified success but this moment was no less dramatic. "T minus 5–4–3–2–1. . . . We have ignition. . . . We have lift-off!" The words of Mercury Control were quickly becoming familiar terminology to millions of fascinated Americans who watched the manned launches.

Lift-off of the Redstone rocket occurred perfectly at 7:20 A.M. (EST) on July 21, 1961. Grissom and his *Liberty Bell 7* spacecraft were placed on the same suborbital path ridden by Alan Shepard two months earlier. (Grissom had chosen his call sign *Liberty Bell 7* because of the similarity of shape between his capsule and America's symbol of freedom.)

A new trapezoidal window (replacing the two smaller side ports of *Freedom 7*) and a less crowded flight schedule enabled Grissom to spend more of his five minutes of weightlessness viewing landmarks with unexpected clarity. This demonstration of man's visual abilities in space was a welcome sign for the upcoming Mercury orbital flights; it meant that the pilot tasks would be simplified considerably, because in the weightlessness of space flight there are no ups or downs, and any visual reference point is a great help in establishing capsule orientation. Grissom also assumed complete manual control of his capsule earlier in the flight than Shepard had, and he tested his craft not merely in one axis of movement but in three—yaw, pitch, and roll—while for a time employing a new steering control system.

Liberty Bell 7's reentry and descent were flawless and splashdown occurred in the Atlantic Ocean 2.3 miles from the prime recovery ship, the carrier U.S.S. *Randolph,* despite strong winds that blew the capsule 6 miles off target.

A faulty circuit caused a premature release of the hatch and *Liberty Bell 7* flooded and sank in 2,800 fathoms during recovery operations. Astronaut Grissom swam clear and was rescued unharmed. Despite the loss of the capsule, Grissom's flight reaffirmed and added to the medical and technical data gained by Shepard and set the stage for John Glenn's historic first American orbital flight.

Grissom is hoisted safely aboard the recovery helicopter after his successful flight in *Liberty Bell 7*.

John Herschel Glenn, Jr.

Birthplace	Cambridge, Ohio
Date of Birth	July 18, 1921
Height	5′ 10½″
Weight	168 lbs.
Eyes	Green
Hair	Red
Marital Status/Wife	Anna Margaret
Daughter	Carolyn Ann
Son	John David
Recreational Interests	Boating, waterskiing
Service Affiliation	Lt. Colonel, U.S. Marine Corps
Flight Record	5,455 hours (1,900 in jets); 59 combat missions (F4U's) in World War II; 63 combat missions (F-86's) in Korea. In July 1957 he set a transcontinental speed record during the first such flight to average supersonic speed between Los Angeles and New York in 3 hours 23 minutes (in an F8U jet aircraft). Logged 4 hours 55 minutes in one space flight.
Education and Training	Bachelor of Science, Engineering, Muskingum College, entered Naval aviation cadet program in March 1942, graduating with a commission in the Marine Corps in 1943. From June 1948 to December 1950, he was an instructor in advanced flight training at Corpus Christi, Texas, then of amphibious warfare training at Quantico, Virginia. After Korea, he attended Test Pilot School at the Naval Air Test Center, Patuxent River, Maryland. Assigned to Fighter Design Branch of Navy

Bureau of Aeronautics in Washington, November 1956–April 1959, simultaneously attending University of Maryland.

Astronaut Career Glenn was chosen with the first group of astronauts in 1959. He was awarded the NASA Distinguished Service Medal and served as backup pilot for Shepard and Grissom before his own flight on February 20, 1962, in the Mercury spacecraft *Friendship 7*. He was the first American astronaut to orbit the earth. In January 1963, Glenn was assigned to Project Apollo planning, specializing in the design and development of the spacecraft and flight control system. He retired from NASA and the Marine Corps as a Colonel in 1964 to go into private business and enter politics. He was elected U.S. Senator from Ohio in November 1974.

Mercury-Atlas 6: The Glory of Friendship 7

February 20, 1962

The United States was not ready to commit a man to an orbital, around-the-world flight until the effectiveness of the onboard life-support system, the worldwide Mercury tracking system, and the protective heat shield had been satisfactorily demonstrated. The heat shield was especially important for astronaut safety because of the incredible speeds attained gaining orbit insertion and during the plunge of the craft into the atmosphere on reentry—speeds as high as 17,500 mph. Shepard and Grissom had reached velocities of almost 5,200 mph.

The successful first orbital flight test of a robot astronaut, a black box called a "crewman simulator," on September 13, 1961, had been a confidence builder, but NASA officials felt that an astronaut should not be risked in the first real checkout of the life-sustaining "environmental control system" on an orbital mission of long duration. It wasn't until the successful flight and recovery of the chimpanzee named Enos (a Greek word for *man*) on the second full orbital test of a Mercury capsule on November 29, 1961, that NASA readied Mercury-Atlas 6 for the flight of Lt. Col. John H. Glenn, Jr.

It was fitting that the entire Glenn family became involved in naming the flight *Friendship 7*; no other flight, with the possible exception of the Apollo 11 moon landing, would draw the interest of so many Americans—an estimated 100 million TV viewers. When *Friendship 7* rose up from Launch Pad 14 at 9:47 A.M. EST on February 20, 1962, the nation's spirit rose with it. To many Americans, the Russian challenge had finally been answered. We had arrived!

This was the first manned mission to employ the powerful Atlas D booster rocket and it placed Glenn in a perfect position and speed to "coast" into orbit around the earth. This is referred to as the "orbital insertion window" and Glenn's speed was within a few feet per second of the desired rate. The Goddard Space Flight Center computers in Maryland, monitoring Glenn's entry into orbit, pronounced *Friendship 7* good enough for 100 orbits. Obviously relieved, Mercury Operations entered into the flight log, "9:52 . . . we are through the gates."

During the early part of orbit number 1, Glenn tested the astronaut's potential as a spatial navigator by visually tracking the spent rocket booster nearby, making depth and distance determinations. This and other experiments were interrupted just prior to orbit number 2 when the jets controlling the yaw (side-to-side) movements began acting up, pushing the capsule out of proper orientation. In resorting to manual controls and the semiautomatic "fly-by-wire" system to control the capsule's attitude, Glenn demonstrated the value of having an astronaut on hand to overcome mechanical difficulties.

No sooner had Glenn begun dealing with the control problems, when a potentially serious problem was noted at Mercury Control. As *Friendship 7* passed over the Cape, ground instruments were indicating that the heat shield had loosened. This later proved to be a false reading but caused great concern during the remainder of the mission. Glenn initiated the critical reentry sequence with the firing of the retrorockets on schedule as he neared the coast of California on orbit number 3. As deceleration commenced, Glenn radioed the Cape, "That's a real fireball outside."

A little more than 4 hours and 33 minutes had

transpired since launch, and the engineers, technicians, physicians, recovery personnel, as well as fellow astronauts, sat transfixed at their consoles in Mercury Control and in the tracking stations and recovery ships ringing the world. Glenn was at the height of the heating period of reentry, during which time voice communications are normally lost for four and a half minutes in what is termed "an ionization blackout." The radar tracking units provided the only indication that all was well, as Glenn and the nation passed through the most dramatic and critical moments in all of Project Mercury.

At 2:43 P.M. EST Glenn safely splashed down in the Atlantic, 40 miles short of the primary recovery ship, the carrier U.S.S. *Randolph,* and within sight of the secondary recovery ship, the destroyer U.S.S. *Noa.* Twenty minutes later a tired but satisfied Glenn was taken aboard the *Noa* and welcomed into the hearts of all Americans as their hero of the hour.

Astronaut John Glenn photographed in the weightlessness of space by an automatic camera on board *Friendship 7.*

Donald Kent Slayton

Birthplace	Sparta, Wisconsin
Date of Birth	March 1, 1924
Height	5′ 10½″
Weight	165 lbs.
Eyes	Blue
Hair	Brown
Marital Status/Wife	Marjory
Son	Kent
Recreational Interests	Hunting, fishing, markmanship
Service Affiliation	Captain, U.S. Air Force
Flight Record	6,250 hours (4,075 in jet aircraft); 63 combat missions in World War II (in B-25's and -26's). Logged 217 hours 28 minutes in one space flight.
Education and Training	Entered Air Force as aviation cadet, receiving his wings in April 1943. B-25 instructor for one year after World War II. Left Air Force to enter University of Minnesota, earned Bachelor of Science degree in Aeronautical Engineering in 1949. Worked two years for Boeing Aircraft Corporation before being recalled to active duty in 1951 with Minnesota Air National Guard. In June 1955 attended USAF Test Pilot School at Edwards Air Force Base, California, where he remained as a test pilot from January 1956 until April 1959.
Astronaut Career	He was chosen with the first group of astronauts in April 1959 and was awarded three NASA Distinguished Service Medals and a NASA Exceptional Service Medal. He was chosen command pilot for Mercury-Atlas 7 but was removed from flying status due to a heart murmur. He resigned his commission as an Air Force

Major in November 1963, but continued as an active member of the astronaut team, becoming Director of Flight Crew Operations until February 1974 when he was selected as docking module pilot for the last flight ever of an Apollo spacecraft—the Apollo-Soyuz Test Project. From December 1975 through November 1977, Slayton directed the Space Shuttle program through a series of critical manned powerless landing tests of the Space Shuttle orbiter, *Enterprise*, prior to the planned launch of the Space Shuttle in 1979.

He is currently Manager of Orbital Flight Testing in NASA's Johnson Space Center in Houston.

The Case of Deke Slayton

March 15, 1962

Donald "Deke" Slayton and Wally Schirra, pilot and backup pilot respectively, for Mercury-Atlas 7 (MA-7), had been training side by side with Glenn and his backup pilot, Carpenter, since the team announcements were made following the successful Mercury-Atlas 5 flight of the chimp, Enos.

On March 15, 1962, shortly after Glenn's successful flight in *Friendship 7*, came the sudden announcement from NASA that Scott Carpenter would replace Slayton as the pilot for MA-7 due to the discovery that Slayton had an "erratic heart rate." The condition was discovered by the astronauts' physician, Dr. William Douglas, when the astronauts first rode the centrifuge at the Navy's Aviation Medical Acceleration Laboratory at Johnsville, Pennsylvania, in August 1959. After consultation with the chief of cardiology at Philadelphia Naval Hospital, Slayton and Douglas were assured that the condition, known as idiopathic atrial fibrillation—occasional irregularity of a muscle at the top of the heart, caused by unknown factors—was of no consequence and should not influence Slayton's eventual choice as a flight astronaut.

While still under close medical observation for the two years he was an astronaut, Slayton's performance had earned him a pilot's slot for the second orbital Mercury mission. Deke, as well as his fellow astronauts, knew how precarious a thing is "perfect health," and with less than six months to go before launch it came as no surprise to insiders when the meticulous NASA Administrator James Webb referred Slayton's case to a group of three nationally eminent cardiologists. Their conclusion was that if a flight-trained astronaut was available who did not present any medical unknowns, he should replace Slayton on the mission.

Of the original team of astronauts, Slayton had been considered the "test pilot's test pilot," largely because of his overwhelming experience and flight time. Never abandoning the hope that he might still make a space flight, Slayton stayed on and distinguished himself as Coordinator of Astronaut Activities, commencing September 1962; and became Director of Flight Crew Operations in November of 1963.

Malcolm Scott Carpenter

Birthplace	Boulder, Colorado
Date of Birth	May 1, 1925
Height	5′ 10½″
Weight	160 lbs.
Eyes	Green
Hair	Brown
Marital Status	Divorced, subsequently remarried
Daughters	Kristen Elaine, Candace
Sons	Marc Scott, Robyn Jay
Recreational Interests	Skin diving, archery, skiing
Service Affiliation	Lieutenant, U.S. Navy
Flight Record	3,500 hours (700 hours in jet aircraft). Served with Patrol Squadron 6 in Korean War. Logged 4 hours 56 minutes in one space flight.
Education and Training	Bachelor of Science degree, Aeronautical Engineering, University of Colorado. Entered Navy in 1949, flight training at Pensacola, Florida, and Corpus Christi, Texas. Entered Navy Test Pilot School at Patuxent River, Maryland, in 1954.
Astronaut Career	He was one of the original seven astronauts chosen on April 9, 1959. Carpenter was awarded the NASA Distinguished Service Medal. Prior to his flight in *Aurora 7,* he served as backup pilot for John Glenn on the first American manned orbital flight. Assigned to monitor the design and development of the lunar module in January 1963, he served temporarily as Executive Assistant to the Director of the Manned Spacecraft Center, Houston, Texas. Took leave of absence from NASA during spring and summer of 1965 to participate in Sealab II Project for the Navy as training officer for the crew and officer-in-charge of the submerged diving teams during the operation. He remained at a depth of 205 feet for 30 days and was awarded the Navy's Legion of Merit for his work on the project. A motorbike accident in Bermuda removed him from flight status in 1964.

Resigned from NASA in 1967, retired with rank of Commander from the Navy on July 1, 1969, and is self-employed in private business.

Mercury-Atlas 7: The Flight of Aurora 7

May 24, 1962

When he learned in March of 1962 that he would fly the next Mercury mission, MA-7, Scott Carpenter chose the name *Aurora 7,* "because I think of Project Mercury and the open manner in which we are conducting it for the benefit of all as a light in the sky. Aurora also means dawn—in this case the dawn of a new age." Coincidentally, in his youth, Carpenter had lived at the corner of Aurora and Seventh Avenues in Boulder, Colorado.

Much had been learned from the flight of John Glenn, and the early morning hours of launch day found the Mercury team carrying out the preparations for *Aurora 7* with renewed confidence. The ground fog surrounding the Cape during the night quickly dispersed as the sun began to rise and at 7:45 A.M. EST, after the smoothest countdown to date of a manned American mission, *Aurora 7*—"the dawn"—rose triumphantly off the pad. An estimated 40 million TV viewers watched astronaut M. Scott Carpenter retrace the path of John Glenn.

The flight plan was basically a duplication of Glenn's, lasting for three orbits—4 hours and 56 minutes—at altitudes as high as 166 miles above the earth.

Carpenter had experienced an unexpectedly quiet lift-off with only slight vibration and reported the onset of weightlessness as pleasant. Like Glenn, he felt no sensation of speed even though he knew he was traveling at an orbital speed of 17,549 mph. As the capsule swung around from the nose-forward position, Carpenter was amazed that he felt no sensation of turning (angular motion).

Soon he had his first awe-inspiring view of the earth, which he described as "an arresting sight." Like Glenn, he began checking for visual reference points for navigation and used the nearby booster rocket in estimating spatial depth in space.

Near dusk of his first "45-minute day," Carpenter began to feel increasingly warm. Despite adjustments to his suit-temperature knobs, a continuing elevation in temperature caused concern. At one point in the flight his body temperature was recorded at 102° F.

Carpenter tested foods specially packaged for the weightlessness of space, observed the properties of fluids in the gravity-free environment, and took photographs and photometric readings of the stars.

Carpenter's heavy schedule of experiments and manual capsule maneuvering exercises seriously taxed his ability to perform and resulted in a higher than anticipated fuel expenditure. By the end of orbit 2, *Aurora 7*'s supply of control fuel was down to an alarming 42 percent. The status of his fuel supply made it necessary for *Aurora 7* to undertake a long period of drifting flight during the third orbit.

Results from this fuel-conserving procedure that Carpenter was forced to employ were to be most useful in planning rest and sleep periods for astronauts on the longer manned missions of the future. Even at this early stage of manned space flight, the thoroughness of NASA in planning each mission was paying dividends. (Later, in the Apollo 13 mission, it would result in the safe return of three astronauts from a near catastrophe in deep space.)

As he passed the Hawaii tracking site on his third and last orbit, Carpenter brought his drifting spacecraft back to life and began reentry procedures. Unwittingly, Carpenter drew fuel from both his manual and semiautomatic systems at once and had barely enough control fuel to execute the last critical movement during reentry. *Aurora 7*'s fuel tanks ran empty between 80,000 and 70,000 feet and for the second manned mission in a row the Project Mercury team as well as the nation held its breath.

The last communications from Carpenter before the anticipated blackout period for radio signals were difficult, since he had to force his breath to make himself understood. As the deceleration forces of gravity neared their peak, it became difficult for the pilot even to squeeze words out.

Again, telemetered signals received at the Cape and on San Salvador predicted a safe reentry. Carpenter rode out still more severe oscillations until 25,000 feet, when he fired the drogue parachute mortar cartridge.

When splashdown occurred at 12:41 P.M. EST,

Carpenter was out of radio contact, 280 statute miles beyond the targeted prime recovery ship, the aircraft carrier U.S.S. *Intrepid*. His condition was unknown to Mercury Control and to the world until he was picked up by a recovery helicopter from *Intrepid* after spending three hours on board a life raft in the Atlantic Ocean.

The spacecraft was recovered by the destroyer U.S.S. *Pierce*.

Mercury Atlas-7 roars into life, carrying Astronaut Carpenter aboard Aurora 7.

Walter Marty Schirra, Jr.

Birthplace	Hackensack, New Jersey
Date of Birth	March 12, 1923
Height	5' 10"
Weight	185 lbs.
Eyes	Brown
Hair	Brown
Marital Status/Wife	Josephine
Daughter	Suzanne
Son	Walter Marty, III
Recreational Interests	Sports cars, waterskiing, music, skiing, hunting, sailing
Service Affiliation	Lt. Commander, U.S Navy
Flight Record	4,300 hours (3,300 in jet aircraft); 90 combat missions (F-84 E's) in Korea. Logged 295 hours 14 minutes in three space flights (no EVA).
Education and Training	Bachelor of Science from U.S Naval Academy in 1945, flight training at the Naval Air Station, Pensacola, Florida. Took part in development of Sidewinder Missile at the Naval Ordnance Training Station, China Lake, California; was project pilot for development of F7U3 Cutlass aircraft. Attended Naval Air Safety Officer School at the University of Southern California and completed test pilot training at the Naval Air Test Center, Patuxent River, Maryland.
Astronaut Career	Schirra was chosen with the first group of astronauts on April 9, 1959. He was awarded two NASA Distinguished Service Medals and two NASA Exceptional Service Medals. Before his first space flight on October 3, 1962, in the Mercury spacecraft *Sigma 7*, Schirra was backup pilot for *Aurora 7*. Chosen backup com-

mand pilot of Gemini III, he was command pilot for Gemini VI on December 15–16, 1965, and performed the first rendezvous of two manned maneuverable spacecraft, a space "first" for the U.S.A. He was the first astronaut to be brought aboard recovery ships twice while inside the spacecraft (Mercury and Gemini). With him on Gemini VI was astronaut Thomas P. Stafford. Schirra also was the commander of Apollo 7, the first manned flight of the third-generation spacecraft, and he became the only astronaut ever to fly all three "families" of spacecraft— Mercury, Gemini, and Apollo. He retired from NASA and the Navy with the rank of Captain in July 1969 to go into private business.

Mercury-Atlas 8: The Textbook Flight of Sigma 7

October 3, 1962

Walter Schirra's selection of the call sign *Sigma 7* was an excellent choice for what was considered to be an engineering flight—a mission designed to thoroughly evaluate the Mercury spacecraft systems. Sigma is an engineering symbol for summation, and in selecting it Schirra also felt he honored "the immensity of the engineering effort" behind him.

In the early dawn of October 3, 1962, as Schirra slipped neatly into his spacecraft, he noticed an automobile ignition key hanging from the hand controller safety latch and a smile slipped across his face. The ground crew had provided this little diversion for Wally to ease the tension that naturally built up in every astronaut during the rigorous preflight checkout of pilot and spacecraft preceding launch.

The countdown proceeded with clockwork precision and at 7:15 A.M. EST *Sigma 7* lifted off smoothly, carrying astronaut Schirra on a space flight that would earn him the reputation of a "textbook pilot."

At lift-off, the Atlas booster climbed slowly at first, then accelerated rapidly as the rocket thrust built. Both spacecraft and booster broadcast vital data to stations on the ground which then relayed them to the giant computers at Goddard Space Flight Center, at Greenbelt, Maryland. At Goddard the computers compared that information with the flight plan programmed for *Sigma 7* and flashed a Go signal to the Mercury Control Center at Cape Canaveral after it was determined that Schirra was safely on course.

The huge Atlas rocket engine shut down as planned after a five-minute burn and the spacecraft separated cleanly from the launch vehicle. Schirra's speed was 15 feet per second faster than planned, sending him higher (176 miles) and faster (17,557 miles per hour) than any other astronaut had gone or would go during Project Mercury.

Once in orbit, Schirra switched on his spacecraft control system to the semiautomatic "fly-by-wire" system and began a slow cartwheel movement to bring forward the blunt end of the capsule holding the heat shield. With his spacecraft properly oriented, Schirra took the long-awaited first look out his window at the magnificent scenery passing below him. At this time he also devoted some time to tracking the spent booster rocket which was still in view. (In the postflight debriefing, he expressed the opinion that rendezvous with another vehicle in space appeared to be possible if the pilot were provided with precise data on his position.)

Schirra was able to perform most of the planned scientific experiments with ease, encountering only minor difficulties with a slight rise in suit temperature. A substantial amount of time during the six orbits of *Sigma 7* was spent in "drifting flight" with all the maneuvering systems off. Schirra did not find this phase of the flight unpleasant and he had no problems whenever it was decided to regain manual control of the craft. The random motions were within acceptable limits during the drifting phase of flight and this fact, coupled with Schirra's ability to conserve control fuel, was a milestone in paving the way for longer missions.

John Glenn, who was assigned to flight monitoring duty at a California tracking station, had a two-minute conversation with Schirra just before the fifth orbit, which was broadcast live over radio and TV. After six flawless revolutions, Schirra flew *Sigma 7* to a smooth landing in the Pacific Ocean within 4.5 miles of the target area and within full view of the prime recovery ship, thé aircraft carrier U.S.S. *Kearsarge*, 9 hours and 14 minutes after launch. The accuracy of the landing prompted the exhilarated Schirra to radio, "I think they're gonna put me on the number 3 elevator" of the carrier.

The success of this flight prompted project officials to cancel a second six-orbit mission in favor of a longer flight of 18 or more orbits. With the speech made by President John F. Kennedy three weeks before, on September 12 at Rice Stadium, fresh in everyone's mind, the U.S. effort in space proceeded with new vigor and the pace quickened.

No man can fully grasp how far and how fast we have come. The exploration of space will go ahead, whether we join it or not. . . . It is one of the great adventures of all time, and no nation which expects to be the leader of other nations can expect to stay behind in the race for space. . . . We intend to be first . . . to become the world's leading spacefaring nation.

We set sail on this new sea because there is new knowledge to be gained and new rights to be won, and they must be won and used for the progress of all people. For space science, like nuclear science and all technology, has no conscience of its own. Whether it will become a force for good or ill depends on us, and only if the United States occupies a position of preeminence can we help decide whether this new ocean will be a sea of peace or a new, terrifying theater of war.

Astronaut Cooper on board recovery ship *Kearsarge.* His *Faith 7* spacecraft is in the background.

Leroy Gordon Cooper, Jr.

Birthplace	Shawnee, Oklahoma
Date of Birth	March 6, 1927
Height	5′ 8″
Weight	150 lbs.
Eyes	Blue
Hair	Brown
Marital Status	Divorced, remarried
Daughters	Camala, Janita
Recreational Interests	Car racing, flying, hunting, fishing, photography
Service Affiliation	Major, U.S. Air Force
Flight Record	5,000 hours (3,000 hours in jet aircraft). Logged 222 hours 15 minutes in two space flights.
Education and Training	Bachelor of Science degree, Aeronautical Engineering, at Air Force Institute of Technology in 1956, having earlier received an Army commission after three years at the University of Hawaii and transferring his commission to the Air Force (1949). Attended Experimental Flight Test School at Edwards Air Force Base, California, graduating in 1957 and remaining as a test pilot.
Astronaut Career	One of the original seven astronauts, Cooper was awarded the NASA Distinguished Service Medal and the NASA Exceptional Service Medal. He was backup pilot for the Mercury *Sigma 7* flight. His first space flight was in the Mercury spacecraft *Faith 7* on May 15–16, 1963, making him the first American astronaut to spend more than a day in space. As command pilot of the eight-day, 120-revolution Gemini V mission, which began on August 21, 1965, Cooper established a new space endurance record of 190 hours 56 minutes. He also became the first man to make a second orbital flight. He later served as backup command pilot for Gemini XII and Apollo 10. He retired from NASA and the Air Force with the rank of Colonel, in July 1970 to go into private business.

Mercury-Atlas 9: Faith 7 Fulfills a Promise

May 15, 1963

Before the brilliant success of *Sigma 7*, those more familiar with the newly acquired art of manned space flight did not imagine that the first generation of spacecraft called Mercury, would have the potential to complete an 18-orbit, one-day mission. The performance of Schirra and *Sigma 7* erased all those doubts and on November 9, 1962, the senior staff at the Manned Spacecraft Center in Houston announced preparations for a 22-orbit flight. Cooper chose the call sign *Faith 7* mentioning "my trust in God, my country, and my teammates" as his motivation.

On May 15, 1963, at 13 seconds past 8:04 A.M. EST, after a delay of one day, Mercury-Atlas 9 lumbered upward the 2 inches that signified lift-off and began a journey that would mark the end of Project Mercury. If Cooper was successful, there would be no need to further test this first-generation spacecraft.

Faith 7 settled into an orbital flight path so close to the one planned that the differences were measured in tenths of a mile and hundredths of a degree, prompting Alan Shepard, the backup pilot for this mission, to report to Cooper "All of our monitors down here are overjoyed. Everything looks beautiful."

Faith 7 was performing beyond all expectations and the jubilant Cooper pursued his assigned tasks with relish. The primary goal of this flight was to test how man, not machine, performed on long-duration space flights. Cooper carefully followed all the medical experiments including the ingestion of food and water. He also conducted a navigational test utilizing a 5½-inch lighted sphere and took measurements of radiation.

On orbit 19, Cooper noticed his first potential problem when a light on the instrument panel falsely indicated that the automatic control system had initiated reentry. On the next two orbits it became apparent that the problem of *Faith 7* went deeper than a malfunctioning light. Cooper first lost all attitude readings and shortly thereafter completely lost electrical power in the automatic control system.

With one orbit to go, Cooper calmly prepared for a manually controlled reentry. All the complicated procedures of the next 15 minutes were performed exactly as planned. The astronaut coolly placed *Faith 7* in perfect position for its fiery plunge through the atmosphere and held it there for 12 minutes as friction-generated temperatures of up to 3,000 degrees F. ate away at his heat shield and the forces of gravity pressed in on him, making his body feel almost eight times its actual weight.

The 6-foot-diameter drogue parachute released as planned at about 20,000 feet, slowing down and stabilizing the craft. At about 10,000 feet the 63-foot-diameter main parachute was deployed and a plastic, air-filled bag extended itself 4 feet below the heat shield to cushion the shock of landing.

Splashdown occurred in the Pacific Ocean 34 hours and 20 minutes after lift-off just 4 miles from the prime recovery ship, the aircraft carrier *Kearsarge*. As had Schirra, Cooper quipped jokingly that he too had "missed that third elevator" upon landing.

As with Glenn's mission, an astronaut had been on hand to save the flight from possible failure, and with the usefulness of human guidance firmly established, NASA went forward with plans to provide the astronauts with a spacecraft of greater maneuverability. On to Project Gemini!

Project Gemini

THE WEEK after Project Mercury was officially terminated, the Soviet Union launched Vostok V, carrying cosmonaut Valeriy F. Bykovskiy into orbit, and two days later Vostok VI, carrying the first woman to fly in space, Valentina V. Tereshkova. Both flights returned to earth on June 19, 1963, completing 81 and 48 orbits, respectively, without any apparent attempt to bring the two craft closer together in joint maneuvers.

At the time, the flights seemed of little significance other than the fact that both were in orbit at the same time. It wasn't until much later, when Tereshkova married a cosmonaut from an earlier Vostok flight, Andriyan Nikolayev, and gave birth to a normal healthy baby, that the meaning of Vostok VI became clearer. Fears of genetic damage from exposure to cosmic radiation during space flight had been convincingly laid to rest.

Of equal significance, perhaps, Vostoks V and VI signaled the end of an era. The heroic age of solo space exploration ended in June of 1963. The next manned Soviet effort in space began on October 12, 1964, with the launch of the first of a new series of multiman spacecraft, the Voskhod I. And in 1965, the United States launched its new series of twin-piloted, more maneuverable Gemini spacecraft.

Project Gemini received its name shortly after December 11, 1961, when NASA laid down the guidelines for the development of a two-man spacecraft to succeed Mercury. Alex P. Nagy from NASA's Office of Manned Space Flight proposed naming the then "Mercury Mark II" program after the mythological twins Castor and Pollux, the patron gods of voyagers. On January 3, 1962, NASA announced acceptance of Nagy's proposal and the title "Gemini"—the Latin word for "twins" and for the third constellation of the zodiac—became official.

Mercury began with the astronaut being little more than a passenger carried by a fully automatic space flight system. By the time Project Gemini had arrived, the astronaut had been elevated to a key role in the operation of the spacecraft system. Gemini was designed for man to *fly!*

Except for its doubled size, lack of an escape tower, and a pair of sunken viewports, the Gemini spacecraft outwardly looked very similar to the Mercury capsule. A glimpse inside, however, showed it to be far more sophisticated than its predecessor.

Unlike Mercury, many Gemini components were located outside the crew compartment, arranged in easily removable units that facilitated maintenance and checkout procedures. Added equipment included a docking apparatus for coupling with another vehicle in space and a computerized guidance and control system sophisticated enough to accomplish the high degree of maneuverability and accuracy in navigation needed for rendezvous and docking with another orbiting space vehicle. An improved radar system was added to assist in tracking during rendezvous operations.

Gemini was being developed as NASA looked forward to the Apollo moon landings, and a system of embarking to the lunar surface in a small lander carried by a moon-orbiting mother ship sounded more feasible than a direct earth-to-moon landing. In ten manned missions, Gemini would develop the rendezvous and docking techniques to be used later in the Apollo missions and establish the groundwork whereby the astronauts could use the stars to navigate. Early estimates of the round-trip travel time of the future Apollo missions to the moon were at least seven days, and the advanced life-support systems designed for Gemini would have to exceed that mark by a comfortable margin before any manned lunar expeditions could be attempted.

To accomplish the immense task before them, the NASA officials of Project Gemini needed more pilots. In preparations for the manned Gemini launches that were to begin in March of 1965, a second group of astronauts, Group II, was chosen on September 17, 1962. The requirements were changed slightly, with the age bracket lowered to 35 and the required educational experience broadened to include degrees in the physical or biological sciences as well as engineering. The candidate had to have "experience as a jet test pilot, having attained experimental flight test status through the military services, the aircraft industry, or NASA, or having graduated from a military test pilot school. Preference will be given to those presently engaged in flying high-performance aircraft." This latter modification opened the selection process to civilians. Of the nine men selected, two were civilians—Neil Armstrong and Elliot See. In addition, there were four from the Air Force—Major Frank Borman, Capt. James McDivitt, Capt. Thomas Stafford, and Capt. Edward White II. The Navy was represented by Lt. Charles "Pete" Conrad, Jr., Lt. Commander James Lovell, and Lt. Commander John Young.

Gemini was not yet two years old when the astronauts of Group III were selected on October 18, 1963. Other changes in the qualifications were made for this third group of candidates. The age limit was lowered to 34. Candidates were required to have only 1,000 hours of jet pilot time or to have attained experimental flight test status in the manner of the Group II astronauts. The change in flying time allowed for increased emphasis on academics rather than flight experience and opened the field to pilots other than test pilots. Fourteen men were selected, eight of whom had advanced degrees; all were jet pilots. Four candidates from that group of fourteen would fly before Project Gemini was completed—Navy Lt. Eugene Cernan and Lt. Commander Richard Gordon, Jr., Air Force Captain Mike Collins, and Major Edwin "Buzz" Aldrin, Jr. Air Force Capt. Charles Bassett II was assigned as pilot to fly on Gemini IX but was killed in the crash of his jet aircraft before making a space flight. The remaining nine would go on to assignments in Project Apollo.

Mercury had shown that for periods of weightlessness lasting up to a day, a man could perform in his spacecraft and readapt quickly upon his return to earth without any harmful effects. The astronauts of Gemini would go one step further, demonstrating convincingly that a man could not only function in weightlessness and survive, but that he could "live" in that state for days at a time (a two-week mission was flown), and fly through space with the same freedoms he enjoyed in earth's skies. Most importantly, it showed that man was capable of safely reaching the moon.

Astronauts Young and Grissom check out their Gemini III spacecraft during a test at Complex 19.

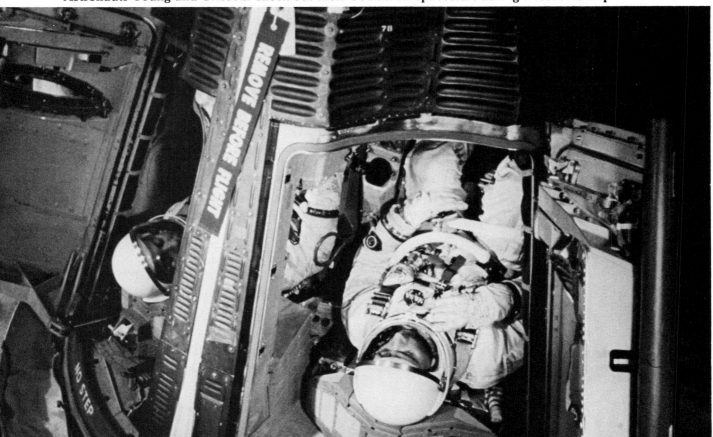

John Watts Young

Birthplace	San Francisco, California
Date of Birth	September 24, 1930
Height	5′ 9″
Weight	165 lbs.
Eyes	Green
Hair	Brown
Marital Status	Divorced, subsequently remarried
Daughter	Sandy
Son	John
Recreational Interests	Jogging
Service Affiliation	Lt. Commander, U.S. Navy
Flight Record	7,700 hours flying time. In 1962, set world time-to-climb records (3,000- and 25,-000-meter altitudes) in the Navy F-4B Phantom jet fighter. Logged 533 hours 33 minutes in four space flights, of which he spent 20 hours 14 minutes walking on the lunar surface (EVA).
Education and Training	Bachelor of Science degree in Aeronautical Engineering with highest honors from the Georgia Institute of Technology in 1952, entering U.S. Navy after graduation. Sent to flight school in 1953. After training at the U.S. Navy Test Pilot School in 1959, he was assigned to the Naval Air Test Center for three years.
Astronaut Career	Chosen with the second group of astronauts, September 17, 1962. Received two NASA Distinguished Service Medals, two NASA Exceptional Service Medals, and the Johnson Space Center Certificate of Commendation. He served as pilot with command pilot Gus Grissom on the first manned Gemini flight on March 23,

1965. Served as backup pilot for Gemini VI, command pilot for Gemini X, and command module pilot for the Apollo 10 mission which buzzed the moon and set the stage for the historic Apollo 11 landing. In his fourth space flight he was spacecraft commander of Apollo 16 with Thomas K. Mattingly (command module pilot) and Charles M. Duke, Jr. (lunar module pilot) and became the ninth man to walk on the moon. Also served as backup spacecraft commander for Apollo 17. Young remained active as an astronaut, having been assigned, in January 1973, to the Space Shuttle Branch of the Astronaut Office, which provided operational and engineering support for the Space Shuttle program. In January 1975 he was assigned temporarily as Chief of the Astronaut Office, replacing Deke Slayton who was assigned to fly the Apollo-Soyuz Test Project. After 25 years of active military service he retired from the Navy with the rank of Captain on September 30, 1976. In March of 1978 he was assigned as spacecraft commander of the Space Shuttle's first orbital flight test (OFT) and with Robert L. Crippen will perform the currently planned two-day mission sometime in mid-1979.

Gemini III: "The Unsinkable Molly Brown"

March 23, 1965

Progress in Gemini had been slow during the first two years of the program. The experience gained in Mercury led to many innovations in the program, and in 1962 it seemed that every one of those areas was running into problems that were costly in terms of time and money. The paraglider landing system and the pilot ejection seats would not stabilize in flight. The fuel cells that had replaced the batteries used earlier in Mercury as a more efficient and long-lasting power source were giving trouble. The Air Force effort to modify a launch vehicle more powerful than the Mercury-Atlas rocket was running into problems. The Titan II rocket, which was to be used to launch the two-man Gemini spacecraft, developed longitudinal vibrations ("pogo effect") too severe for manned space flight. Even the target vehicle for the orbiting spacecraft, the Atlas-Agena rocket, presented design problems. By 1963 the program had fallen a year behind schedule.

As 1964 dawned, however, the worst of Gemini's problems were behind. The first spacecraft, the unmanned Gemini I, was already at the Kennedy Space Center (Cape Canaveral was renamed in November of 1963 by President Lyndon Johnson). The flight of Gemini I on April 8, 1964, qualified the Titan II rocket for use as a manned launch vehicle, and Gemini II's unmanned flight on January 19, 1965, confirmed the integrity of the heat shield and the readiness of a fully equipped spacecraft for manned space flight.

It was against this background that NASA prepared Gemini-Titan III for the final hurdle—a manned, three-orbit qualification test. The crew, veteran astronaut Virgil "Gus" Grissom and rookie John W. Young, nicknamed their spacecraft *Molly Brown* after the Broadway musical comedy *The Unsinkable Molly Brown*. This was a facetious reference to the sinking of Grissom's Mercury capsule in the Atlantic Ocean shortly after splashdown. (After this Gemini mission, NASA would allow only numerical designations for future missions, announcing that "all Gemini flights should use as official spacecraft nomenclature a single easily remembered and pronounced name.")

Grissom and Young were assisted in their mission training by a backup crew consisting of the experienced Walter Schirra as commander and rookie Thomas P. Stafford, who had become an astronaut at the same time as Young.

On March 23, 1965, at 9:24 A.M. EST, Gemini-Titan III (GT-III) was lifted smoothly into orbit. Lift-off was so smooth, in fact, that neither Grissom nor Young felt anything. The only indications that their mission had begun were the clock on the instrument panel, which started running, and the comforting announcement by Cap Com (capsule communicator) astronaut Gordon Cooper, "You're on your way, *Molly Brown.*"

Five and a half minutes after launch, the second-stage engine shut down, the spacecraft separated from its launch vehicle, and Grissom fired the jet-like aft thrusters to place GT-III into an orbit ranging from a high at one end (apogee) of 140 miles to a low (perigee) of 100 miles.

About 20 minutes into the first orbit, just as they were passing beyond the mid-Atlantic tracking station on the Canary Islands, Young noticed a quick drop in the oxygen pressure gauge of the environmental control system. A fast check showed that several other gauges were giving odd readings, and Young reasoned correctly that the real trouble was in the instrument power supply. As he switched from primary to secondary power, the dials returned immediately to their normal positions. The whole epi-sode, from the moment Young first spotted the problem to its proper solution, took 45 seconds and was a clear indication that the intense preflight program that NASA required of each assigned astronaut was paying off.

As Gemini III passed over Texas, nearing its first complete orbit, Grissom and Young became the first astronauts to steer their craft in flight. Firing their forward and aft thrusters a carefully timed 75 seconds, they cut the speed of the spacecraft by 3.3 mph, dropping their spacecraft into a nearly circular orbit. During the second revolution three-quarters of an hour later, Grissom again fired the thrusters of the maneuvering system. This time he tested the craft's

Gemini III spacecraft being hoisted aboard the recovery ship USS *Intrepid* with flotation collar still in place.

translational capability, much like a car's ability to change lanes from side to side on a highway. In this case, Grissom and Young's highway was the orbital plane of the spacecraft, and they were able to effect a minute change of one-fiftieth of a degree, allowing an astronaut for the first time to shift his orbiting spacecraft over to a new point above the earth. On the third pass the crew completed the planned fail-safe maneuver, firing their thrusters for two and a half minutes, dropping their perigee (lowest altitude) to 45 miles. This insured safe reentry even if the retro rockets failed to work during this first manned test of the Gemini reentry system.

After four and a half hours of space flight, Grissom and Young separated the adapter section from their spacecraft (reentry module) and armed the automatic retrofire switch. After a successful burn, the four-rocket retro package was jettisoned and Gemini III began her fiery plunge through the atmosphere, heat shield forward.

One last test was conducted with the spacecraft communications system as *Molly Brown* passed through the "ionization zone" or radio blackout of reentry. At an altitude of 55 miles, Young turned on the automatic water expulsion system which ejected water in timed pulses for the next two and a half minutes. This counteracted the ionization radio blackout, and the ground stations were able to pick up the craft's radio signals.

Grissom and Young landed in the Atlantic 52 statute miles short of their goal, the aircraft carrier *Intrepid*. After riding *Molly Brown* in the long Atlantic swells for 30 minutes, Young remarked "That was no boat!"

As far as her major objectives—testing spacecraft maneuverability, life-support systems reliability, and safe, controlled reentry—Gemini III was a complete success. The time of testing was over. Gemini was ready for its role in the manned space flight program.

The first manned Gemini-Titan launch vehicle leaves the pad at Cape Kennedy (GT-3).

James Alton McDivitt

Birthplace	Chicago, Illinois
Date of Birth	June 10, 1929
Height	5' 11"
Weight	155 lbs.
Eyes	Blue
Hair	Brown
Marital Status/Wife	Patricia
Daughters	Ann, Kathleen
Sons	Michael, Patrick
Recreational Interests	Handball, hunting, golf, swimming, waterskiing, boating
Service Affiliation	Captain, U.S. Air Force
Flight Record	4,400 hours flying time (3,500 hours in jet aircraft); 145 combat missions during Korean War (F-80's, F-86's). Logged 338 hours 57 minutes in two space flights (no EVA).
Education and Training	Bachelor of Science in Aeronautical Engineering from the University of Michigan in 1959, graduating first in his class. After joining the Air Force in 1951 he served as a combat pilot during the Korean War. He graduated from the U.S. Air Force Experimental Test Pilot School and later trained at the U.S. Air Force Aerospace Research Pilot School. He served at Edwards Air Force Base, California, as an experimental test pilot.
Astronaut Career	He was chosen in the second group of astronauts on September 17, 1962. He received the NASA Distinguished Service Medal and the NASA Exceptional Service Medal. His first space flight was as command pilot with Ed White for Gemini

IV, a 62-orbit, four-day mission that began on June 3 and ended on June 7, 1965. McDivitt also served as spacecraft commander for Apollo 9, March 3–13, 1969. This was the third manned flight in the Apollo series and the second to be launched by the mammoth Saturn V rocket. The ten-day flight accomplished the first comprehensive earth-orbital qualification tests of a "fully configured Apollo spacecraft." McDivitt and astronaut Russell Schweickart flew the lunar (module) lander for the first time during this mission, performing critical lunar-orbit rendezvous simulations and docking with fellow crewman Dave Scott piloting the Apollo 9 command spacecraft.

On June 25, 1969, McDivitt was named Manager for Lunar Landing Operations in the Apollo Spacecraft Program Office, being responsible for landing site selection and mission planning, as well as setting requirements for spacecraft modifications to enhance its performance on the future lunar landing missions.

In August 1972, he retired from NASA and the Air Force as a Brigadier General to go into private business.

Gemini IV astronauts White and McDivitt receive congratulatory phone call from the President aboard their recovery ship USS *Wasp*.

Edward Higgins White II

Birthplace	San Antonio, Texas
Date of Birth	November 14, 1930
Height	5′ 11″
Weight	175 lbs.
Eyes	Brown
Hair	Auburn
Marital Status/Wife	Patricia
Daughters	Bonnie, Lynn
Son	Edward
Recreational Interests	Squash, handball, swimming, golf, photography
Service Affiliation	Captain, U.S. Air Force
Flight Record	4,236 hours flying time (3,046 hours in jet aircraft). Logged 97 hours 56 minutes in one space flight, 21 minutes of which he spent in America's first spacewalk (EVA).
Education and Training	Bachelor of Science degree from the United States Military Academy, West Point, in 1952; a Master of Science degree in Aeronautical Engineering from the University of Michigan in 1959. Received flight training in Florida and Texas following graduation from West Point. In 1959 he attended the Air Force Test Pilot School at Edwards Air Force Base, California, and was later assigned to Wright-Patterson Air Force Base, Ohio, as an experimental test pilot with the Aeronautical Systems Division, his duties including piloting flight tests for research and weapons systems development, writing technical engineering reports, and submitting recommendations for improvement in aircraft design and construction.
Astronaut Career	He was chosen with the second group of astronauts on September 17, 1962. He received the NASA Exceptional Service Medal. His first space flight was as pilot

for Gemini IV along with James McDivitt (spacecraft commander), during which he became the first American to walk in space. The mission lasted four days, from June 3 to June 7, 1965, making 62 orbits of the earth. White was named backup command pilot for Gemini VII. He had been named command module pilot for the ill-fated Apollo 1, in which he died in a flash fire during a ground test at the pad on January 27, 1967. Apollo 1 was an honorary name applied to the space craft after the fire. Its original designation was AS-204.

Gemini IV: A Stride in Space

June 3–7, 1965

Gemini IV, like its predecessor Gemini III, had been scaled down in terms of its mission goals. Again, the planned duration of the mission was shortened—from seven to four days of orbiting time—and the practice rendezvous tests were deferred for the second time to a future mission. Still, Gemini IV would not be denied the spectacular. Included in the crew announcement for Gemini IV during a press conference on July 27, 1964, was the possibility that one of the crew members might open the hatch of the spacecraft and stick his head outside during the mission.

This would be the first flight for McDivitt, aged 35, and White, 34, and it was to be historic in the annals of American space flight. The men had known each other since college and had been in the same class at Air Force Test Pilot School. Their backups, Frank Borman and James Lovell, both 36, had met first during their initial testing at NASA. All four were new-comers, or second-generation astronauts.

On March 18, 1965, during the Voskhod II mission, Soviet cosmonaut Aleksey A. Leonov, became the first human to walk in space. Now, on June 3, 1965, McDivitt and White sat patiently in their spacecraft, perched 100 feet above Launch Pad 19, atop their Titan II launch vehicle, waiting to show the world their country's space program was not far behind.

The launch operations crew was beginning to show its mastery of manned-launch preparations and at 10:16 A.M. EST, after a minor delay, Gemini IV climbed smoothly upward to the delight of the first worldwide TV audience to view a manned launch. Twelve European nations were able to view the scene live via the Early Bird satellite. The prospect of a spacewalk and the first use of the new Mission Control Center in Houston created a level of public interest in Gemini IV never again matched in the Gemini program.

As Gemini IV reached its elliptical orbit (101 miles at the perigee and 175 miles at the apogee), space-craft commander McDivitt turned the ship around to look for the trailing spent booster rocket. Both McDivitt and White made separate estimates of its distance but they were unsuccessful in several attempts to close the distance between the booster and themselves. With half their load of fuel gone, the Gemini IV crew broke off their futile chase of the booster target.

Playing catch-up in orbit is an altogether different challenge from running up in a straight line to an earthly target. As Gemini IV increased speed, it also gained altitude, moving into a higher orbit than the target.

The effects of speeding up and slowing down in or-bital space flight are seemingly paradoxical. Like a racer running on a circular track, moving higher means you are now running on the outside lane, which gives you a longer distance to travel than the runner on the shorter inside lane. If both run at the same speed the outer, or "higher," contestant falls behind. Simply put, according to the physical laws governing objects in orbit, speeding up will move you higher towards the slower "outside lanes," and slowing down will move you lower towards the faster "inside lanes."

Now that the rendezvous attempts were over, White began preparing for his spacewalk (EVA), while McDivitt read a checklist of things for him to do. First, White put together his Hand-Held Maneu-vering Unit, a 7½-pound space gun powered by two bottles of compressed oxygen which would allow him maneuverability during his walk in space. Next,

Astronaut White performing the U.S. space program's first spacewalk during the Gemini IV mission.

he pulled out the umbilical package and mounted suit connectors for the tether that would keep him from floating away from the spacecraft, and finally he donned the emergency oxygen chestpack. By this time, the astronauts were well into orbit number 2 and it was decided to wait until orbit 3 for the walk attempt, allowing White a needed rest.

During the rest period, McDivitt and White ran another check on hose connections and suit integrity. EVA preparations were completed as Gemini IV passed over the Indian Ocean. As it neared Carnarvon, Australia, the cabin was depressurized and White opened the stubborn door with a hard push.

Although the Russian cosmonaut Leonov had not shown ill effects from his spacewalk three months earlier, there was more than a trace of tension in Mission Control as White began to move from the safety of his spacecraft into what was still a big unknown—the vacuum of space. Once the hatch was opened, White rose easily from the spacecraft. He carefully installed a camera to record his movements as he slowly floated into the void of space. No spacecraft walls protected White now, just the thin skin of his G 4-C EVA suit. Had those ladies, the seamstresses at the David Clark company in Worcester, Massachusetts, sealed every seam air tight with their little glue pots? Was the suit strong enough to withstand the 7-mile-per-second bombardment of space dust that the scientists and engineers had predicted? Would White become disoriented floating in space? If so, could he recover sufficiently to get back inside the spacecraft? There were many such questions going through the minds of astronauts and ground controllers alike, and no one was going to breathe easily for the next 20 minutes until White was safely tucked back into a securely latched, airtight spacecraft.

As it turned out, both White and his EVA equipment performed well. With a short burst from his hand-held space gun, White cleared the hatch and propelled himself upward and away without imparting any motion to the spacecraft.

With a gold-coated face shield to protect his eyes from the unfiltered glare of sunlight in space, White proceeded to explore the vicinity of his spacecraft to the limits of his 25-foot gold-braided tether and his oxygen lifeline. Using the space gun he traveled about 5 meters but wound up higher above the spacecraft than he wanted to be. As he floated freely he felt a tendency to move in all directions at once (roll, pitch, and yaw). Moving carefully to avoid an uncontrolled tumbling, he tugged on the tether, pulling himself aft and high above the spacecraft adapter at the rear of the cabin. Realizing that he had positioned himself dangerously close to the thrusters that McDivitt was firing to steady the craft, White propelled himself forward over the top of the ship and out beyond its nose. He used the space gun for two pitchovers and two body turns, stopping himself easily each time with bursts from the gun. To his disappointment, the bottle of compressed oxygen fueling the gun soon ran out.

If there was any anxiety on White's part at the beginning of his spacewalk it had completely disappeared by now. He felt completely at ease, relishing his role as the first American human satellite, almost to the point of rapture.

As Gemini IV and its human satellite passed over California, White began to describe the spectacular panorama passing literally below his feet, broadcasting his feelings to both Mission Control and, via radio link-up, live to the world.

Tension increased at Mission Control when it appeared that White and now McDivitt were becoming mesmerized by their dream-like space ballet. The spacewalk was exceeding the planned time limit, and with darkness fast approaching, Mission Control firmly ordered McDivitt, "Tell him to get back in." As McDivitt relayed the message, White was heard to say, "It's the saddest moment of my life." With those words the reluctant White struggled back to the safety of Gemini IV and closed the door on the most dramatic chapter of the Gemini space program.

McDivitt and White drifted through space, watching the capsule's systems and making observations; they completed 11 experiments during the remainder of their four days in space.

Gemini IV returned safely to earth on June 7, 1965, splashing down in the Atlantic and missing its target, the recovery aircraft carrier *Wasp*, by 50 statute miles. A NASA information specialist who had seen Cooper stagger after his Mercury flight was amazed to see White do a jig step on the carrier deck after being weightless for four days. The doctors in charge of the astronauts' safety were obviously relieved. The Gemini IV crew's performance paved the way for the longest space flight yet—the mission of Gemini V.

Charles "Pete" Conrad, Jr.

Birthplace Philadelphia, Pennsylvania

Date of Birth June 2, 1930

Height 5′ 6½″

Weight 145 lbs.

Eyes Blue

Hair Blond

Marital Status/Wife Jane

Sons Peter, Thomas, Andrew, Christopher

Recreational Interests Golf, swimming, waterskiing, automobile racing

Service Affiliation Lieutenant, U.S. Navy

Flight Record More than 6,000 hours flying time (more than 4,800 in jet aircraft). Logged 1,179 hours 38 minutes in four space flights, of which 7 hours 46 minutes were spent walking on the lunar surface during Apollo 12, and 4 hours 59 minutes during two spacewalks on Skylab 2. Total EVA time of 12 hours 45 minutes.

Education and Training Bachelor of Science in Aeronautical Engineering from Princeton University in 1953. Entered the U.S. Navy upon graduation, becoming a naval aviator. Attended Navy Test Pilot School at Patuxent River, Maryland, assigned as Project Test Pilot to Armaments Test Division there after graduation. Also served as flight instructor and performance engineer at the Test Pilot School.

Astronaut Career He was chosen with the second group of astronauts on September 17, 1962. Received two NASA Distinguished Service Medals and two NASA Exceptional Service Medals. In 1978 he received the Congressional Space Medal of Honor. His first space flight was as pilot, with veteran astronaut Gordon Cooper as command pilot, for Gemini V. The eight-day, 120-orbit flight of Gemini V began on August 21 and ended on August 29, 1965, after establishing a space endurance record of

190 hours 56 minutes and covering an orbital distance of 3,312,993 statute miles. (If you recall, Cooper established the Mercury space endurance record of 34 hours 20 minutes in 22 orbits.) Conrad later served as backup command pilot for Gemini VIII, command pilot for Gemini XI, backup commander for Apollo 9.

Conrad was spacecraft commander of Apollo 12, November 14–24, 1969. With him on man's second lunar landing mission were veteran astronaut Richard F. Gordon (command module pilot) and Alan L. Bean (lunar module pilot). Conrad and Bean accomplished the first precision lunar landing, placing their lunar module *Intrepid* down at a point in the moon's Ocean of Storms within walking distance (600 feet) of the U.S. spacecraft Surveyor III which had landed at that spot 31 months earlier. Conrad became the third person to walk on the moon's surface.

As commander of Skylab 2, Conrad performed a 3-hour 23-minute spacewalk (EVA), during which he and astronaut Joseph Kerwin deployed the jammed solar panel wing of Skylab to save his mission from failure and make it a viable space home and workshop for the succeeding Skylab 3 and 4 crews.

Conrad resigned from NASA and retired from the U.S. Navy as a Captain on February 1, 1974, to go into private industry.

The USS *Dupont* accomplished a space first when it retrieved 17 feet of Gemini-Titan V's first stage.

Gemini V: The Third Cautious Step

August 21–29, 1965

Gemini IV had served as a training ground for pilots, flight controllers, and evaluators alike, setting the style not only for Gemini V but for all the remaining Gemini flights and for future Apollo flights as well. The few reservations about the harmful effects of prolonged weightlessness on the astronauts had begun to fade, and a longer, eight-day mission was planned for Gemini V to deal with the riddle of orbital rendezvous and docking. On only the third manned flight of the Gemini spacecraft, NASA cautiously reached out toward the design limits of Gemini.

On Saturday, August 21, 1965, at exactly 9:00 A.M. EST, Cooper and Conrad became the third Gemini team in five months to be launched into space. Kennedy Space Center was beginning to take on the appearance of a well-run air terminal as the precision launch team of Project Gemini closed in on its goal of *five manned launches for 1965!*

The launch began with the usual smooth ride, reaching orbital insertion at an orbital perigee of 101 statute miles altitude with an orbital apogee at 216 statute miles altitude.

Due to the mission's length, Cooper intended to operate the fuel cells, which had yet to prove themselves, at the lowest possible pressure level to power the craft. However, Conrad immediately noticed a dip in cell pressure. It should have risen when Conrad flipped on the oxygen heater, but to his dismay the needle continued to plunge.

At about this time, 2 hours and 13 minutes into the flight, Cooper had commenced the planned rendezvous tests by ejecting the rendezvous pod (a small instrumented target) and turning on his craft's radar. The astronauts began tracking their target when they noticed that adjustments to the heater still had not raised the oxygen pressure in the fuel cells.

By now Gemini V was out of communications range with ground control and Cooper had to make a decision. Having never seen a fuel cell working at the low pressure it was now reading, Cooper reluctantly powered down his craft. Without electrical power rendezvous with the pod was now impossible. Vi-

sions of an early mission termination crossed the minds of both astronauts as they waited to get within radio range of Flight Director Christopher Kraft.

Kraft knew they had enough battery power for reentry even if the fuel cells failed completely; NASA policy had always been to double and sometimes triple the safety systems of every spacecraft. What the Flight Director didn't know was how much time would be left to get Gemini V to a safe reentry zone if the problem could not be solved.

The oxygen pressure finally stabilized during the fourth orbit and Kraft was assured the "back-up" batteries were good for 13 hours. About the same time, Mission Control learned that the low-pressure fuel cell tests it had hurriedly requested from the St. Louis facility were going well; a solution was at hand. Cooper and Conrad could fly for at least one day.

As a new team came on duty at Mission Control, astronaut Edwin E. Aldrin, a rendezvous specialist, worked with a Mission Planning and Analysis Division team to improvise some practice maneuvers that would "simulate" rendezvous with the lost pod if the electrical power could be salvaged.

The fuel cell problem soon was solved and, with power back on, the tired crew placed their craft in drifting flight, taking a needed rest at the end of their first cliffhanging day.

By the third day Cooper and Conrad had settled into a smooth working routine. They worked steadily on the 17 onboard experiments and, using both ground and spacecraft computations, Cooper was able to simulate rendezvous maneuvers, bringing his spacecraft precisely to the positions Kraft had asked for. This was the first checkout of the complete maneuvering system and, considering how close they had come to an aborted mission two days earlier, the two astronauts again demonstrated the value of a manned as opposed to a robot spacecraft.

Gemini V carried the same medical experiments as Gemini IV with the addition of M-1, Cardiovascular Conditioning (conditioning of the heart and blood system) and M-9, Human Otolith Function (a delicate mechanism of the human ear). After the flight, no appreciable medical changes were noted in the astronauts. The inflatable leg cuffs worn by Conrad in the M-1 experiment pressurized automatically two minutes out of six in order to stimulate blood movements and exercise the valve-like tissue flaps in the veins of the legs. In the weightlessness of space, the tissue flaps in the veins, which normally help the blood supply fight its way uphill to the heart against the pull of gravity, become lazy. Upon the astronauts' return to earth, their sluggish response to the gravity-induced rush of blood to the legs can cause a temporary loss of blood pressure in the brain and loss of consciousness. The time needed to recover normal body responses varies.

Conrad's pulse rate returned to normal more quickly and he lost 4 percent less plasma volume (the liquid part of blood minus the blood cells) than did Cooper. Due to the limited data available on these body changes, no medical conclusions were made, although Conrad felt the cuffs would be useful on longer missions. Both astronauts had lost more cal-cium than the Gemini IV crew, but the principal investigator, Pauline Beery Mack, was unwilling to predict a trend since "a form of physiological adaptation may occur in longer space flight."

The landing area for Gemini V was shifted due to the movement of Hurricane Betsy, and splashdown occurred without incident on the morning of August 29, 1965, 80 statute miles short of the Atlantic recovery area and the recovery aircraft carrier *Lake Champlain.*

Gemini V had flown an impressive 190 hours 55 minutes 14 seconds, and the astronauts' physician, Dr. Charles Berry, awaited their arrival aboard the carrier with considerable anxiety. Two days later, to Dr. Berry's relief, the medical responses of both men were almost back to normal.

The medical people were learning a great respect for the human body, and the rookie Conrad was to learn enough from his ride with the gritty Cooper to distinguish himself as the commander of the Gemini XI, Apollo 12, and the first manned Skylab mission.

Gemini V Astronauts Conrad and Cooper on board their recovery ship USS *Lake Champlain.*

Frank Borman

Birthplace	Gary, Indiana
Date of Birth	March 14, 1928
Height	5' 10"
Weight	163 lbs.
Eyes	Blue
Hair	Blond
Marital Status/Wife	Susan
Sons	Fredrick, Edwin
Recreational Interests	Hunting, waterskiing
Service Affiliation	Major, U.S. Air Force
Flight Record	More than 5,500 hours flying time (more than 4,500 hours in jet aircraft). Logged 477 hours 36 minutes in two space flights (no EVA).
Education and Training	Bachelor of Science degree from the United States Military Academy at West Point in 1950, graduating eighth in his class. He entered the Air Force upon graduation, receiving pilot training at Williams Air Force Base, Arizona. Received a Master of Science degree in Aeronautical Engineering from the California Institute of Technology at Pasadena in 1957, whereupon he became an instructor in thermodynamics and fluid mechanics at West Point. Subsequently, he attended the USAF Aerospace Research Pilot School, graduating in 1960. He remained there as an instructor until 1962.
Astronaut Career	He was chosen with the second group of astronauts on September 17, 1962, and received the NASA Exceptional Service Medal. Borman was backup command pilot for Gemini IV and his first space flight was as command pilot with James

Lovell on the longest manned space flight up to that time, 330 hours 35 minutes on Gemini VII, December 4–18, 1965. During that flight, Gemini VII participated in the first rendezvous of two manned maneuverable spacecraft with Gemini VI on December 15, 1965.

On his second space flight, December 21–27, 1968, Borman was the commander of Apollo 8, the second manned Apollo mission. With command module pilot James Lovell and lunar module pilot William Anders (making his first space flight), he became one of the first humans to visit another heavenly body. The flight was especially remembered for the astronauts' readings from the Book of Genesis on Christmas Eve as Apollo 8 circled the moon.

In May 1969, Borman became Field Director of the Long-Term Space Station Program at NASA.

He resigned from NASA and the Air Force with the rank of Colonel on July 1, 1970, to head a commercial airline.

Astronauts Lovell and Borman en route to their Gemini VII launch vehicle.

James Arthur Lovell, Jr.

Birthplace	Cleveland, Ohio
Date of Birth	March 25, 1928
Height	5′ 11″
Weight	170 lbs.
Eyes	Blue
Hair	Blond
Marital Status/Wife	Marilyn
Daughters	Barbara, Susan
Sons	James, Jeffrey
Recreational Interests	Golf, swimming, handball, tennis
Service Affiliation	Lt. Commander, U.S. Navy
Flight Record	More than 4,407 hours flying time (more than 3,000 hours in jet aircraft). Logged 715 hours 6 minutes in four space flights (no EVA).
Education and Training	Attended the University of Wisconsin for two years, then received a Bachelor of Science degree from the United States Naval Academy in 1952. Following graduation from Annapolis he received flight training, later getting a four-year tour as a test pilot at the Naval Air Test Center, Patuxent River, Maryland, where he served as Program Manager for the F4H weapon system evaluation.
Astronaut Career	He was chosen with the second group of astronauts on September 17, 1962. He received the Presidential Medal for Freedom in 1970, two NASA Distinguished Service Medals, and two NASA Exceptional Service Medals. His first space flight was as pilot with command pilot Frank Borman on Gemini VII after he and Borman served as backup crew for Gemini IV. The Gemini VII flight began on December 4, 1965, and lasted 14 days (330 hours 35 minutes), making it the longest manned space flight up to that time. Other firsts were the first rendezvous of two manned maneuverable spacecraft (with Gemini VI), and the longest multi-manned space flight. He served as backup command pilot for Gemini IX and was

assigned command of Gemini XII with pilot Edwin Aldrin. The mission began on November 11, 1966, and this four-day, 59-orbit flight brought the Gemini Program to a successful conclusion. Lovell and Aldrin rendezvoused with an Agena target vehicle, using backup onboard computations for the first time due to radar failure. Aldrin also performed EVA exercises and Gemini XII accomplished the first pictures from space of a solar eclipse.

Lovell also served as command module pilot for the epic six-day journey of Apollo 8 on man's maiden voyage to the moon, December 21–27, 1968, with former crewmate Frank Borman (spacecraft commander) and rookie William A. Anders (lunar module pilot, although Apollo 8 carried no lunar module and circled the moon without landing). Lovell then served as backup spacecraft commander for the Apollo 9 earth orbiting mission and became spacecraft commander for the unlucky Apollo 13 (April 11–17, 1970), which returned to the earth after an explosion crippled the service module. Lovell became the first person to journey twice to the moon (although he never landed on its surface).

In May 1971 he became Deputy Director of Science and Applications at the Johnson Space Center. Lovell retired from NASA and the Navy with the rank of Captain on March 1, 1973, to enter private business.

Gemini VII and VI: Gemini Goes the Limit

December 4–18, 1965 (VII)
December 15–16, 1965 (VI)

NASA had decided in November 1964 that Gemini VI would be a rendezvous mission. The veteran Wally Schirra would be spacecraft commander with rookie Thomas P. Stafford completing the crew as pilot.

For the seventh Gemini mission, NASA reached for the limits, scheduling the flight for 14 days. It would be the longest flight of the Gemini program. On July 1, 1965, NASA announced crew selections for Gemini VII. Rookies Frank Borman and James Lovell, who were the backup crew for Gemini IV, drew the assignment as commander and pilot respectively, with Edward White and Michael Collins chosen as alternates. Collins was the first member of the third group of astronauts (selected in October 1963) to be named to a flight.

The usually reliable Agena rocket, with its restartable engine, had been giving project officials problems when modified for use as a target vehicle for the planned Gemini orbital rendezvous tests. Now, however, the problems seemed well in hand as the launch team prepared for the October 1965 launch

date for Gemini VI. As the prelaunch checkout for this Gemini-Agena mission neared completion, the test operations group was confident that the Agena rocket would respond reliably to all spacecraft and ground-control commands.

Gemini VI was the last of the program's battery-powered spacecraft, a factor that limited the flight to two days. Schirra thought that even two days was stretching it a bit. Aware of the closeness of their planning for this mission, NASA would allow that the "mission may be cut to one day if all objectives are completed." As soon as the crew completed rendezvous and docking with the Agena, they could come home. Everything else was secondary, even the experiments.

Gemini-Agena Target Vehicle 5002 (GATV-5002) was readied for launch on October 25, 1965, and although this would be its first flight for Gemini, Agena in one configuration or another was a veteran of more than 140 flights since 1959. The countdowns for the Agena and Gemini VI proceeded simultaneously and without delay. Schirra and Stafford were placed

The Gemini VII spacecraft photographed through the hatch window of Gemini VI during the world's first space rendezvous.

aboard their spacecraft 15 minutes before the launch of the target vehicle, and if the Agena made it successfully into orbit, they would follow it a short time later.

Luck was not with Schirra and Stafford that day. The Atlas-Agena exploded shortly after launch, and for the time being Gemini VI was scrubbed. Their gloom was short-lived, however; an alternate plan that officials now proposed would still give Gemini VI its chance to make history: Gemini VII would be the *target* for Gemini VI. But could the tracking network handle two manned spacecraft at the same time?

The launch operations people felt they could handle the back-to-back manned launches, and the astronauts were enthusiastic. But for Flight Operations Director Christopher Kraft this plan was a big question mark. Kraft outlined the double launch proposal to his staff at Mission Control Center. Their response was, "It's a hell of a great challenge" and to a man, they wanted to press on as soon as possible. Then,

"Why don't we handle it as if one of the spacecraft were a Mercury-type and the other a Gemini-type spacecraft?" The passive Gemini VII target spacecraft could be monitored on the simpler Mercury tracking network, and Gemini VI, the active rendezvous partner, would be controlled on the more sophisticated Gemini tracking system.

The joint Gemini VII/VI mission was officially announced on Thursday, October 28, 1965. Gemini VII would be launched first, to be followed nine days later by Gemini VI. The crack launch preparations team girded itself to deliver a miracle. The usual interval between manned launches was two to three months.

Finally, on December 4, 1965, Gemini VII sat ready to begin its marathon flight. Four years earlier the chimpanzee Enos had barely completed "two" orbits of the earth, and now Borman and Lovell were reaching for more than 200 orbits during two weeks in space!

The countdown went like clockwork and lift-off

occurred promptly at 2:30 P.M. EST. With Cap Com Elliot See's countdown, the vibration of the Titan launch vehicle, and the roar of its engines, there was no doubt in Lovell's mind that they were under way. "We're on our way,' Frank!" he shouted. Shortly thereafter they entered the weightlessness of orbital space flight at their planned altitude of 99.2 statute miles.

After getting well into the flight with all life-support systems dutifully humming along, Borman and Lovell began conducting the more than 20 experiments assigned to Gemini VII—the most of any Gemini flight. Its eight medical experiments also were a record, among them a repeat of the cardiovascular conditioning carried out by Conrad earlier in Gemini V; now Jim Lovell wore the leg cuffs.

One of the innovations of this flight was the scheduling of two work shifts to coincide with the A.M. and P.M. routines the astronauts were used to and simultaneous sleep periods. An "Inflight Sleep Analysis Test" was to provide needed information on how to train astronauts to adjust to sleeping in this new environment. The Gemini VII astronauts also performed navigational tests, taking fixes on stars with a hand-held sextant. Their ability to determine their position without the aid of computers was a space first, opening up the possibility of other means of spatial navigation.

Spacecraft operations proceeded smoothly over the ensuing days with the most pressing concern being voiced by Borman in regard to the fuel needed to circularize his orbit for rendezvous with the soon-to-be launched Gemini VI spacecraft. After four orbital adjustment maneuvers Borman and Lovell were in a nearly circular 186-statute-mile-high orbit. With their "porch light" on, they waited for Schirra and Stafford to pay them a friendly visit.

After the launch of Gemini VII, the repair crew that had been standing in the wings quickly moved to ready Pad 19 for Gemini VI. Pad 19 had incurred minimal damage during the launch and spirits were high for making the next deadline. One official recalled, "Everybody was so excited you'd think they were going to launch the next day."

The preparations and countdowns were trouble-free and on Sunday, December 12, 1965, as the time for launch drew near, it appeared that the preparations team had beaten their schedule by one day. But luck again eluded Schirra and Stafford. The Titan II's engines had roared into life on schedule at 9:54 A.M. EST, only to shut down 1.2 seconds later when an electrical tail plug, loosened by the vibrations, dropped from the base of the rocket. The malfunction-detection system had sensed the problem and had stopped the engines. The dropped plug, however, had activated the mission clock directly in front of Schirra, signalling apparent lift-off.

In that split second, Schirra, with one hand on the D-ring for ejection, had to decide whether the clock was right and he had lift-off or whether the rocket actually was still sitting on the pad. His senses told him that the clock was wrong and that the rocket had not moved. Schirra elected to stay. The risk was enormous, for if the rocket had lifted only a few inches, it would come crashing down and the 150 tons of volatile fuel encased in the fragile metal shell would explode, engulfing astronauts and spacecraft in a holocaust.

At the moment of crisis, Schirra coolly reported, "Fuel pressure is lowering." Francis X. Carey, the Martin Company launch-vehicle test conductor, was just as matter-of-fact in acknowledging Schirra's transmission, knowing that any hint of crisis in his voice might prompt Schirra or Stafford to eject; he knew the Titan had not moved. After the exhaust had cleared and it was apparent that the rocket would not explode, the astronauts were safely removed from the craft and the launch crew immediately began preparations for the third launch attempt.

At 8:37 A.M. EST, on December 15, 1965, Gemini VI finally responded to the feverish effort of the last eleven days and the coaching of Schirra ("For the third time, Go!"). With a slight shimmying, Gemini VI climbed eagerly to meet her sister ship in orbital rendezvous.

At orbital insertion, Schirra and Stafford trailed their Gemini VII target by 1,244 statute miles; and after 94 minutes (a little over one orbit of maneuvering), they closed to 734 statute miles. Closing steadily on their target, Gemini VI got a flickering radar signal and then a solid lock-on (strong signal) on Gemini VII at 3 hours 47 minutes into their mission at a distance of 199 statute miles. By this time Schirra had maneuvered his craft into a nearly circular orbit of 167 by 170 statute miles and was in the same orbital plane as Gemini VII.

Schirra and Stafford placed Gemini VI in the computer (automatic) rendezvous mode at 3 hours 51 minutes into the flight, slowly gaining on their target. At 5 hours 4 minutes Stafford sighted Gemini VII, at first mistaking her for a star—"My gosh, there is a real bright star out there. That must be Sirius." The "star"—Gemini VII—was 62 statute miles distant.

Gemini VI demonstrates the feasibility of docking.

At 5 hours 50 minutes Schirra had Gemini VII in full view at 1,000 yards. Fittingly, both Schirra and Stafford saw the "twins," the stars Castor and Pollux in the Gemini constellation, aligned with their sister ship. At 2:33 P.M., December 15, 1965, Gemini VI pulled to within 130 feet of Borman and Lovell in Gemini VII, accomplishing the world's first manned rendezvous in space as they now were side by side and motionless relative to one another. The jubilant staff at Mission Control lit up cigars, waved small American flags, and cheered. Rendezvous had taken only four orbits to accomplish and Schirra still retained 62 percent of his fuel. Borman and Lovell on the other hand were not so lucky; they would have to carefully ration their remaining 11 percent supply of fuel.

The two spacecraft remained together for more than three orbits at distances ranging from 290 feet down to 1 foot, with first Schirra then Stafford taking turns at the controls. Both astronauts were impressed at their ability to control the spacecraft as they darted about the passive Gemini VII. Their ability to maintain a fine control down to speeds of one-tenth of a foot per second led them to conclude that nuzzling into and docking with a target vehicle would not be a problem.

As the sleep portion of their mission approached, Schirra pulled away to a distance of about 10 miles. After a hearty space supper the weary crew of Gemini VI bedded down for the night, drifting synchronously within sight of Borman, who radioed, "We have company tonight." Awakening the next morning, the Gemini VI crew elected to return to earth, having completed their mission objectives of rendezvous and station-keeping. Schirra played a few strains of "Jingle Bells" on a miniature harmonica accompanied by Stafford shaking some small bells, and bid Gemini VII farewell, "Really a good job, Frank and Jim. We'll see you on the beach." Gemini VI triumphantly returned to earth using a computer-controlled reentry system for the first time, landing a mere 8 statute miles from its target and the recovery aircraft carrier *Wasp* in the Atlantic Ocean, on December 16, 1965. After 16 revolutions of the earth in 25 hours 15 minutes 58 seconds, it was nice to be back home.

Gemini VII was left to begin its twelfth day in orbit, leaving the remainder of the mission as much a test of the astronauts' willpower as anything else. Both men survived the routine of their last two full days in space in good spirits, returning to earth a record 14 days and 206 orbits later. Also using a computer-controlled reentry system, Gemini VII splashed down 6 statute miles from the target and the recovery aircraft carrier *Wasp* in the Atlantic Ocean and Borman won the bet he had made earlier with Schirra as to who would land closer to target.

After logging an incredible 330 hours 35 minutes 01 seconds in the cramped confines of their spacecraft, it was remarkable to the astronauts' physician, Dr. Berry, that Borman and Lovell could walk across the carrier deck without stumbling. They were in better shape than the crew of Gemini V. "Amazingly they had maintained their total blood volume.... Apparently, there had been enough time for an adaptive phenomenon to take place," said the pleased physician.

Gemini VI and VII were quite a Christmas present for the U.S.A. Clearly, she had met the Soviet challenge and could look forward confidently to fulfilling the goals set by her late beloved President, John F. Kennedy. On December 18, 1965, it appeared that the United States might very well land a man on the moon and return him safely to earth before the decade was out.

Neil Alden Armstrong

Birthplace	Wapakoneta, Ohio
Date of Birth	August 5, 1930
Height	5′ 11″
Weight	165 lbs.
Eyes	Blue
Hair	Blond
Marital Status/Wife	Janet
Sons	Ricky, Mark
Recreational Interests	Sailplaning (glider flying), music, fishing, reading, swimming, tennis, golf
Service Affiliation	Civilian
Flight Record	More than 3,290 hours flying time (more than 2,500 in jet aircraft) as of April 1967. Flew 78 combat missions flying Navy Panther jets in Korea. During his flying career, Armstrong flew over 200 different models of aircraft including jets, rockets, helicopters, and gliders. In training for the lunar landing he flew helicopters and made several flights in the lunar landing research vehicle. He logged 206 hours in two space flights and was the first human to walk on the surface of the moon, spending 2 hours 48 minutes in EVA.
Education and Training	Bachelor of Science degree in Aeronautical Engineering from Purdue University in 1955 and a Master of Science in Aerospace Engineering from the University of Southern California. He holds honorary doctorates from several universities.

Armstrong had won a Navy scholarship during his senior year of high school and in 1947 went to Purdue to study aeronautical engineering for two years. Subsequently, he reported to Pensacola for Navy flight training. After earning his wings in 1949, he was assigned to the aircraft carrier *Essex* and saw combat duty in the Korean conflict, earning three air medals.

After the Navy, Armstrong returned to Purdue and went on to a degree in aeronautical engineering. In 1955 he joined the National Advisory Committee on Aeronautics (the forerunner of the National Aeronautics and Space Administration). He spent seven years at Edwards Air Force Base in California during which he gained a reputation as one of the world's best test pilots. He made seven flights in the experimental rocket research aircraft, the X-15, reaching altitudes as high as 207,500 feet and a maximum speed five times the speed of sound.

Astronaut Career He was chosen with the second group of astronauts on September 17, 1962, becoming the first civilian astronaut. He received the nation's highest civilian award, the Presidential Medal for Freedom, for his flight on Apollo 11 in 1969. He was also awarded the NASA Distinguished Service Medal, and the NASA Exceptional Service Medal and was decorated by 17 different countries. In 1978 he was awarded the Congressional Space Medal of Honor.

Armstrong developed a passion for flying early in life. He had his first airplane flight in a Ford Tri-Motor at the age of six and as a teenager worked at Wapakoneta's tiny airport to help pay for his $9-an-hour flying lessons. Armstrong lived for flying, reading everything he could about aeronautics and earning a pilot's license before he was old enough to drive a car. He even built a windtunnel in the basement of his parents' house to learn what he could about the aerodynamics of flight. While in high school he also got caught up in space science, becoming fascinated with the subject after he viewed the moon through a telescope.

Armstrong's first flight assignment as an astronaut was as backup command pilot to the Gemini V mission. He became command pilot for his first space flight in Gemini VIII with Dave Scott, pilot, who also was making his first space flight. Armstrong's quick reactions on that flight when the spacecraft began spinning wildly out of control, were instrumental in saving the lives of the crew.

Armstrong, Aldrin, and rookie astronaut Fred Haise served as backup commander, command module pilot, and lunar module pilot, respectively, for the Apollo 8 mission to orbit the moon.

As commander of Apollo 11, Armstrong won the distinction of becoming one of the first humans to land a craft, the *Eagle*, on the moon and the first to step on its surface. With him in the lunar module was Edwin Aldrin, the second human to walk on the moon. Mike Collins served as command module pilot and awaited the triumphant return of Armstrong and Aldrin in the command ship *Columbia*, circling high overhead in lunar orbit.

In July 1970, Armstrong became Deputy Associate Administrator for Aeronautics at NASA. In August 1971 he retired from NASA after 17 years of exceptional service as engineer, test pilot, astronaut, and administrator. He is currently Professor of Aeronautical Engineering at the University of Cincinnati.

David Randolph Scott

Birthplace	San Antonio, Texas
Date of Birth	June 6, 1932
Height	6'
Weight	175 lbs.
Eyes	Blue
Hair	Blond
Marital Status/Wife	Ann
Daughter	Tracy
Son	Douglas
Recreational Interests	Swimming, handball, skiing, photography
Service Affiliation	Captain, U.S. Air Force
Flight Record	More than 5,000 hours flying time (more than 4,136 in jet aircraft). Logged 546 hours 54 minutes in three space flights, of which 1 hour 1 minute were spent during a stand-up EVA, and 19 hours 8 minutes during three separate excursions on the lunar surface during a three-day stay on the moon. The lunar EVA's were noted for the first use of the car-like Lunar Rover. (The 16-minute spacewalk by Al Worden on the return flight of Apollo 15 required depressurization of the command module; thus, technically speaking, Scott and Irwin accomplished 16 minutes additional EVA time.)
Education and Training	Bachelor of Science degree from the United States Military Academy at West Point, graduating fifth in a class of 633, in 1954. He chose an Air Force career, completing pilot training at Webb Air Force Base in Texas in 1955. He was then assigned to Laughlin Air Force Base, Texas, for gunnery training and then to Luke Air Force Base, Arizona.

After an assignment at Soesterberg Air Base (Royal Netherlands Air Force), Netherlands, from April 1956 to July 1960, he returned to the U.S. for study at the Massachusetts Institute of Technology, where he received a Master of Science degree in Aeronautics and Astronautics and an Engineer of Aeronautics and Astronautics degree in June 1962. His thesis at MIT concerned interplanetary navigation. He next attended the Air Force Experimental Test Pilot School, then the Aerospace Research Pilot School, both at Edwards Air Force Base, California.

Astronaut Career   He was selected with the third group of astronauts on October 18, 1963. He was awarded two NASA Distinguished Service Medals, the NASA Exceptional Service Medal, and the Manned Spaceflight Center Superior Achievement Award (1970). His first assignment as an astronaut—also his first space flight as pilot— was Gemini VIII on March 16, 1966, with command pilot Neil Armstrong who also was making his first space flight. The crew performed the first successful docking of two vehicles in space but had to return their wildly gyrating spacecraft back to earth shortly after docking due to a thruster malfunction.

Scott next flew on Apollo 9, March 3–13, 1969. As command module pilot, he remained in the command ship *Gumdrop* as Apollo 9 commander James McDivitt (also a veteran of Gemini) and lunar module pilot Russell Schweickart (on his first space flight) flew the lunar module *Spider* for its first manned space flight. They qualified it for flight in lunar orbit on the next Apollo mission. After performing the critical rendezvous and docking of the lunar module with the mother ship, the crew also demonstrated and confirmed the feasibility of crew transfers outside the spacecraft as well as other extravehicular techniques. Schweickart performed a 46-minute EVA outside the lunar module and was joined by Scott who photographed him during his 1-hour 1-minute stand-up EVA in the opened hatch of the command module. Scott also retrieved thermal samples from the exterior of the command ship adjacent to the hatch area.

Scott was backup spacecraft commander for Apollo 12 and made his third space flight as commander of Apollo 15, July 26–August 7, 1971. With him on that mission were Alfred M. Worden (command module pilot) and James B. Irwin (lunar module pilot), both making their first space flights. Scott and Irwin descended to the moon's surface in the lunar module *Falcon,* landing in the Hadley Rille area of the Apennine Mountains. Their 66-hour 54-minute stay on the lunar surface set a new record, and the Rover-1 transporter was used for the first time. Scott was the seventh person to walk on the moon.

In July 1972, he became Special Assistant for Mission Operations for the Apollo-Soyuz Test Project, and in April 1975 was appointed Director, NASA Dryden Flight Research Center, Edwards, California.

Gemini VIII: A Not-So-Routine Flight

March 16, 1966

The crew for Gemini VIII was named on September 20, 1965. Neil Armstrong was chosen as commander and although it would be his first space flight, he was a seasoned civilian test pilot with long experience in the X-15 rocket research aircraft program. He had been backup commander for Gemini V. His fellow crewmate was David Scott, a candidate from the third group of astronauts and brand new to the Gemini program. The backup crew was Charles Conrad (pilot from Gemini V) and Richard Gordon, who was also from the third group of astronauts and newly assigned to Gemini.

1965 had been a phenomenal year for Gemini, with most of the goals achieved. A successful EVA (spacewalk), back-to-back manned launches within an 11-day interval, and an impressive *five* manned launches in one year would be a tough act to follow for the seasoned Gemini team. Both men and machines had performed magnificently during the longest, most grueling space flight (the 14 days of Gemini VII). Medically, the human body showed a durability and adaptability that could only have been hoped for a year ago. The moon was looking closer every day.

NASA appeared near its objective of space flight on a routine basis. The flight of Gemini VIII would be a mild warning, however, that this day had not yet arrived.

The spacewalk planned for pilot David Scott was in effect a leapfrogging of EVA equipment technology, from the simpler hand-held maneuvering unit with its accompanying oxygen lifeline and tether to a far more complex personal propulsion system, the Air Force's Astronaut Maneuvering Unit (AMU). The usual step-by-step development having been skipped, this new EVA gear loomed as a big question mark for administrators and pilots alike.

Likewise, the fitful performance of the Agena rocket as a Gemini target vehicle was causing some doubts about its continued use in the program. With the Apollo program nearing the operational stage, the successes of Gemini and the failures of Agena might seem to be the ironic combination of events that would prompt Administrator James Webb to concentrate entirely on Apollo.

In late December 1965, however, NASA made it abundantly clear that the remaining five manned Gemini flights were still necessary to perfect the EVA, rendezvous, and docking techniques required for a successful moon mission. As preparations for Gemini VIII went on with renewed spirit, the first successful test of an Apollo spacecraft, a suborbital flight, was made on February 26, 1966.

On March 16, 1966, at 10 A.M. EST, the Atlas-Agena target vehicle lifted from Pad 14, soaring into a circular 186-statute-mile orbit, positioning itself invitingly for the ensuing rendezvous attempt. Agena's countdown had gone smoothly with no trace of the difficulties that had marred its performance in the past.

Now it was Gemini VIII's turn on Pad 19, where Armstrong and Scott sat in their spacecraft awaiting the news of Agena. When the good news finally arrived, Armstrong gave out with, "Beautiful, we will take that one." The powerful Titan II's engines turned on exactly on schedule at 11:41:02 A.M., EST, carrying Armstrong and Scott along the planned trajectory that would culminate with the union of Gemini VIII and the Agena rocket. Their orbit was elliptical, 100 by 169 statute miles.

On their way to find Agena, both astronauts made a number of sightings of landmarks and even of ships. The next three days would be busy ones and, taking a cue from the experiences of Schirra and Stafford, both astronauts began preparing their meals during the second orbit, before rendezvous. As they entered the third orbital revolution, the rendezvous radar on Gemini VIII locked on to the Agena, which was now about 206 statute miles distant. At 5:43:09 hours, high over the tracking ship *Coastal Sentry Quebec* stationed near Antigua Island, Armstrong brought his craft to rest 50 yards away from the Agena, achieving the second manned rendezvous in space.

Armstrong kept station with the Agena for 36 min-

utes, delicately maneuvering his ship around the Agena as Scott performed a careful inspection of the target. He would have to wait until docking, however, before he could get a good look at the docking instruments on the Agena. At that time they would be right in front of his windshield.

Armstrong eased his Gemini craft carefully towards the docking area of the Agena at a barely perceptible 3 inches per second. "About 2 feet out," he radioed to the tracking ship *Rose Knot Victor*. In a matter of seconds, Armstrong gleefully reported, "Flight [Control], we are docked! It's ... really a smoothie—no noticeable oscillations at all." There was a momentary pause at Flight Control in Houston and when the message sank in—the world's first manned docking—a pandemonium of cheers, backslaps, and wide grins suddenly erupted. One more goal was chalked up for Gemini, and after EVA it would be on to the moon! But things were not going to be that easy.

Earlier there had been some suspicion from Ground Control that Agena's attitude-control system was not quite responding to ground signals and Lovell had passed this information along to the crew: "If you run into trouble and the attitude-control system in the Agena goes wild, just turn it off and take control with the spacecraft." Both Armstrong and Scott proceeded with their docking chores with Lovell's warning ringing in their ears.

Scott began dialing command signals to the Agena's attitude controls from his own spacecraft. The Agena responded by turning the linked vehicles 90 degrees to the right. When this movement took five seconds less than the expected minute, Scott looked over to Armstrong. At that moment, his eyes skimmed the control panel. Something was wrong! The instruments indicated Gemini was making an unplanned roll. "Neil, we're in a bank," exclaimed Scott, using aviator's terminology.

Armstrong and Scott were passing through the earth's shadow and also were out of communications range. Without the earth's horizon or ground communications for guidance the two astronauts would

The smooth lift-off of Gemini VIII Agena target vehicle.

50

have to rely on their instincts and training to save themselves.

Initially, Armstrong blamed the Agena for the unplanned gyrations, but they grew steadily stronger even after complete shutdown of the Agena thrusters. Scott transferred control of the target vehicle to the ground as Armstrong elected to undock, signaling Scott to hit the undocking button. Still struggling with the controls, Armstrong backed off his ship. "And then we really took off," he said of this incident in a later report. Gemini VIII was tumbling uncontrollably end over end at a dizzying rate of one revolution per second.

By this time, the tracking ship *Coastal Sentry Quebec* came into communications range, but any help from ground control would have to be quick as the astronauts were nearing their body limits—their vision was blurring.

The trouble had to be with the Gemini VIII spacecraft and both astronauts began quickly to throw the switches that shut down the spacecraft maneuvering system and turn on the reentry control system. Armstrong and Scott got no response from their hand controllers. Immediately, they ran through the same pattern of switches. Maybe one had been thrown incorrectly. The hand controllers responded.

Armstrong wrestled the craft into control once again. Once he had her steadied, he carefully reactivated each thruster of the maneuvering system until he found that Number 8 was stuck in the open position and had caused the wild spinning.

With part of the reentry fuel gone, there was no question but that Gemini VIII must return to earth as soon as possible. If too much fuel was lost from this vital system, there would be no way of getting the craft in position for the critical retrofire necessary for reentry and no way to control it on the way down.

The Hawaiian tracking station told the astronauts what they already knew; the mission was terminated and they must prepare for reentry. The intended landing area had been the Atlantic Ocean, but with the emergency retrofire Gemini VIII found itself heading for a point in the Pacific 620 miles south of Japan and east of Okinawa. "Oh, yes, there's water! It's water!" exclaimed Scott, who was obviously relieved to see that they were not going to crash on land. The spacecraft was designed for water landings only.

As the flight ended after 10 hours 41 minutes 26 seconds, Scott yelled "LANDING—SAFE" and began broadcasting his call sign, "Naha RESCUE 1, Naha SEARCH 1." No answer came. They were out of range of everyone.

Department of Defense recovery forces from Naha Air Base, Okinawa, and Tachikawa Air Base, Japan, were first to reach the scene and assisted the astronauts until the secondary recovery ship, the destroyer *Leonard B. Mason,* took them aboard. Due to careful planning and close cooperation with NASA, the Department of Defense recovery forces had reacted to the emergency landing as though it were normal. As for carrying out space flights on a routine basis, that goal would have to wait a while longer.

The Agena Target Docking Vehicle as seen from the approaching Gemini VIII spacecraft.

Thomas Patten Stafford

Birthplace	Weatherford, Oklahoma
Date of Birth	September 17, 1930
Height	6′
Weight	175 lbs.
Eyes	Blue
Hair	Black
Marital Status/Wife	Faye
Daughters	Dionne, Karin
Recreational Interests	Handball, weight lifting, swimming
Service Affiliation	Captain, U.S. Air Force
Flight Record	More than 6,350 hours flying time (more than 5,250 hours in jet aircraft). Logged 507 hours 43 minutes in four space flights, including six rendezvous (no EVA).
Education and Training	Bachelor of Science degree from the United States Naval Academy in 1952, electing to receive his commission in the U.S. Air Force. After flight training he later attended the Air Force Experimental Flight Test Pilot School at Edwards Air Force Base, California. As Chief of the Performance Branch at the Air Force Aerospace Research Pilot School at Edwards, he was responsible for the supervision and administration of the flying curriculum for student test pilots. He was also an instructor in flight test training and specialized academic subjects, and co-author of the *Pilot's Handbook for Performance Flight Testing* and the *Aerodynamics Handbook for Performance Flight Testing*.

Astronaut Career He was chosen with the second group of astronauts on his thirty-second birthday, September 17, 1962. He received two NASA Distinguished Service Medals and two NASA Exceptional Service Medals. Stafford served as backup pilot for Gemini III and pilot for his first space mission, the historic flight of Gemini VI during which he and command pilot Walter Schirra performed the first manned rendezvous in space with the Gemini VII crew of Frank Borman (commander) and James Lovell (pilot), who were already in orbit, on December 15, 1965. Gemini VI returned to earth the next day, December 16, after 25 hours 51 minutes 24 seconds of space flight.

Stafford became command pilot of Gemini IX after the death of its prime crew members, Elliot See (commander) and Charles Bassett (pilot), in the crash of a T-38 jet near St. Louis. He later served as backup commander for his old crewmate Schirra on Apollo 7 and as commander of Apollo 10 (May 18–26, 1969), circling the moon in the first lunar flight of the lunar lander (LM). Flying the "Lem," he and lunar module pilot Eugene Cernan performed the first rendezvous and docking in lunar orbit with John Young in the Apollo 10 spacecraft. Stafford was Chief of the Astronaut Office from August 1969 through May 1971, with responsibility for coordination, scheduling, and control of all activities involving NASA astronauts. In June 1971 he was named Deputy Director of Flight Crew Operations until February 1974, when he was assigned as commander of the Apollo-Soyuz Test Project, July 15–24, 1975. Stafford resigned from NASA on November 1, 1975, to assume command of the Air Force Flight Test Center at Edwards Air Force Base, California, with the rank of Major General.

Gemini IX Astronauts Cernan and Stafford aboard their spacecraft awaiting recovery.

Elliot McKay See, Jr.

Birthplace	Dallas, Texas
Date of Birth	July 23, 1927
Height	5' 8"
Weight	150 lbs.
Eyes	Blue
Hair	Brown
Marital Status/Wife	Marilyn
Daughters	Sally, Carolyn
Son	David
Recreational Interests	Swimming
Service Affiliation	Civilian
Flight Record	More than 3,900 hours flying time (more than 3,300 in jet aircraft).
Education and Training	Bachelor of Science degree, U.S. Merchant Marine Academy in 1949. He later received a Master of Science degree in Engineering from UCLA in 1962. He served as an aviator in the U.S. Navy from 1953 to 1956. From 1949 to 1953 and 1956 to 1962 he was employed as a flight test engineer, group leader, and experimental test pilot for the General Electric Company. He served as project pilot of the J79-8 engine development program in connection with F4H aircraft. He conducted powerplant flight tests on the J-47, J-73, J-79, CJ805, and CJ805 aft-fan aircraft engines, flying in F-86, XF4D, F-104, F11F-1F, RB-66, F4H, and T-38 aircraft during their developmental stages.
Astronaut Career	He was selected with the second group of astronauts on September 17, 1962. He participated in all phases of the astronaut training program and was selected as the pilot of the backup crew for the Gemini V flight. He was selected as command pilot for the Gemini IX flight. He and Major Charles A. Bassett, the pilot for the Gemini IX flight, were killed on February 28, 1966, during an instrument-landing approach at the McDonnell Aircraft Corporation's St. Louis plant.

Eugene Andrew Cernan

Birthplace	Chicago, Illinois
Date of Birth	March 14, 1934
Height	6′
Weight	175 lbs.
Eyes	Blue
Hair	Brown
Marital Status/Wife	Barbara
Daughter	Teresa Dawn
Recreational Interests	Hunting, fishing, competitive sports, horses
Service Affiliation	Lieutenant, U.S. Navy
Flight Record	More than 4,500 hours flying time (more than 4,300 hours in jet aircraft). Logged 566 hours 16 minutes in three space flights. A total EVA time of 24 hours 11 minutes, of which 22 hours were spent walking on the lunar surface.
Education and Training	Bachelor of Science in Electrical Engineering from Purdue University in 1956. Received a commission through the Navy Reserve Officers' Training Corps program at Purdue. He entered flight training upon graduation. Received a Master of Science degree in Aeronautical Engineering from Naval Postgraduate School and Purdue University in 1961.
Astronaut Career	He was chosen with the third group of astronauts on October 18, 1963. He received two NASA Distinguished Service Medals and the NASA Exceptional Service Medal and the Johnson Space Center Superior Achievement Award. As backup pilot, he assumed the role of pilot of Gemini IX upon the deaths of the prime crew and made his first space flight, June 3–6, 1966. During Gemini IX he

became the second American to walk in space (2 hours 7 minutes EVA). Cernan later served as backup pilot for Gemini XII and backup lunar module pilot for Apollo 7.

On his second space flight, he was lunar module pilot of Apollo 10, May 18–26, 1969, serving with Thomas P. Stafford, spacecraft commander, and John W. Young, command module pilot. While orbiting the moon, Stafford and Cernan entered the lunar module (LM) and flew within 38,000 feet of its surface to qualify it for the first lunar landing by Apollo 11.

Cernan later served as backup commander for Apollo 14 and made his third space flight on the final lunar landing mission, Apollo 17, December 7–19, 1972. His crew on Apollo 17 consisted of Ronald Evans, command module pilot, and Harrison H. Schmitt, who served as lunar module pilot and descended with Cernan to the moon's surface aboard the LM. From their lunar base in the mountainous Taurus-Littrow region, Cernan and Schmitt, a geologist, completed three highly successful excursions to the nearby craters of the Taurus mountains of the moon. Their extravehicular activities on the lunar surface lasted a record 22 hours and 4 minutes. The Apollo 17 mission was also the longest manned lunar landing flight, 301 hours 52 minutes, and returned the largest collection of lunar samples, 249 pounds. Cernan was the eleventh person to walk on the moon and the last to leave his footprints on its surface.

In September of 1973, Cernan assumed additional duties as Special Assistant to the Program Manager of the Apollo Spacecraft Program at Johnson Space Center. In this capacity, he assisted in the planning, development, and evaluation of the joint United States–Soviet Union Apollo-Soyuz Mission. He acted as the senior United States negotiator in direct discussions with the USSR on this joint space project.

He resigned from NASA and the Navy with the rank of Captain on July 1, 1976, to enter private industry.

Navy frogmen stabilize the Gemini IX spacecraft during the approach of the recovery ship USS *Wasp*.

Charles Arthur Bassett II

Birthplace Dayton, Ohio

Date of Birth December 30, 1931

Height 5′ 9½″

Weight 160 lbs.

Eyes Brown

Hair Brown

Marital Status/Wife Jean

Daughter Karen

Son Peter

Service Affiliation Captain, U.S. Air Force

Flight Record More than 3,200 hours flying time (more than 2,600 in jet aircraft). No space flight.

Education and Training Bachelor of Science in Electrical Engineering from Texas Technological College. He did graduate work at the University of Southern California and subsequently entered the Air Force.

Astronaut Career He was chosen with the third group of astronauts on October 18, 1963. His abilities were highly regarded and he was assigned as the representative from the Astronaut Office to oversee the design and development of the flight simulators that would be used to train the astronauts to fly the spacecraft. The multimillion-dollar simulators were supposed to duplicate as much as possible the moves and views from the actual spacecraft. Bassett's judgment was considered during the construction of these machines, and he became instrumental in organizing the tremendous library of training documents, making them readable for the astronaut crews as they prepared for their flights.

Bassett was assigned as pilot for the Gemini IX flight with Elliott See as commander. Bassett and See perished in the crash of their T-38 jet in bad weather on February 28, 1966, near the McDonnell Assembly Plant at St. Louis, Missouri. His rank at the time of his death was Major, U.S. Air Force.

Gemini IX: The Angry Alligator

June 3–6, 1966

Elliot See and Charles A. Bassett II learned that they would fly Gemini IX as commander and pilot, respectively, in October 1965. Chief astronaut Donald Slayton also informed them that their backups would be Thomas Stafford and Eugene Cernan. At that time, Stafford was copilot for Gemini VI. This was to be the first space flight for See, a civilian test pilot with ten years' experience and a second-generation astronaut. Bassett was selected with the third group of astronauts and this also was to be his first space flight.

As had been the custom, the astronauts followed the development of their spacecraft through its building and testing stages and familiarized themselves with the Gemini systems. Bassett and Cernan gave particular attention to EVA aspects of the planning because one of them as pilot would leave the spacecraft to test the untried Astronaut Maneuvering Unit (AMU).

See and Bassett were on a routine flight out to St. Louis to check on their spacecraft at the McDonnell Assembly Plant when their T-38 jet aircraft crashed during poor weather conditions, killing both astronauts.

Stafford and Cernan became the first astronaut backup crew to assume primary status, and James Lovell and Edwin Aldrin (a third-generation astronaut on his first assignment) became backup commander and copilot respectively.

On May 17, 1966, Gemini IX stood ready on Pad 19 to join the Agena that had just departed for orbit at 10:12 A.M. EST. The smooth countdown preceding the Agena lift-off gave no indication that the old problems would come back to haunt the hapless target vehicle. However, at 7 minutes 36 seconds after launch, telemetry indications announced the second loss of an Agena rocket.

The launch scene was repeated on June 1, 1966. This time the Atlas booster performed perfectly, lifting off at exactly 10:00 A.M. EST. The payload, an alternate docking target, entered a planned 186-mile orbit. Problems arose when it came time to jettison the covering (shroud) protecting the docking collar; the shroud opened only partially. Stafford would

later report when he came upon the Atlas in orbit with its clamshell doors ajar, "It looks like an angry alligator out here."

A hitch in the countdown of Gemini IX delayed its flight two days, and on June 3, at precisely 8:39 A.M. EST, Stafford and Cernan were at last under way. Including Gemini VI launch delays, Stafford had made the trip to Pad 19 in his flight suit a record six times in two launches!

Seventeen minutes into the flight and high over the Canary Islands, the astronauts began receiving ground-fed computer data needed for a successful rendezvous. They circularized their orbital flight path and went after their target. Unlike the Agena, the modified Atlas target vehicle wobbled in orbit, continually changing attitude.

In less than two orbits, Stafford succeeded in catching his target, pulling to within 100 feet of it after a little more than 4 hours into the mission. He exclaimed, "Look at that moose!" His graphic description of the jaw-like doors of the shroud surrounding the docking equipment prompted Mission Control to order Stafford to keep his distance and call off the docking test.

Stafford, however, was able to maneuver remarkably close to the target vehicle, at times approaching to within inches during his inspection of it. The delicate maneuvers performed by Gemini IX in such close proximity to its target were some consolation to the Gemini team. Mastery of the intricacies of docking was close at hand.

Gemini IX performed three types of rendezvous with the target vehicle in less than 24 hours of space flight. Shortly after the third rendezvous, Stafford backed off from the angry alligator, leaving it to drift alone in space.

On the third day, June 5, 1966, nearly 45 hours and 30 minutes into the mission, Stafford and Cernan began preparations for the EVA. Cernan cracked open his hatch near sunrise. Feeling no disorientation, and rather comfortable, he began a 128-minute spacewalk that would carry him standing, walking, and floating nearly twice around the world.

Cernan was startled at finding movements slower

and more difficult than he had practiced. The slightest movement upset his equilibrium. The spacewalk was a taxing wrestling match from beginning to end, complicated by fogging of the faceplate of his helmet approximately 63 minutes after hatch opening.

He kept floating out of control as he moved aft to the adapter section of the spacecraft. Nothing helped in maintaining body control, neither the few footbars or stirrups, nor the handbars installed on the craft's exterior. In preparing the maneuvering unit for flight—the nitrogen and oxygen shut-off valves, the sidearm controllers, umbilicals, restraint harness, and tether—everything took much longer than expected and sapped his strength. Finally, 39 minutes short of the planned 167-minute spacewalk, blinded (by a fogged faceplate) and weary, Cernan returned to his seat in the spacecraft. In his condition, testing

the AMU (Astronaut Maneuvering Unit) was too risky to attempt.

Safely inside with the hatch sealed, the two astronauts rested and then settled into the remaining on-board experiments.

On the morning of June 6, after three days of space flight, Gemini IX came home. Splashdown occurred in the Atlantic, with a remarkable precision landing less than one-half mile (0.42 statute miles) from the recovery carrier *Wasp*.

In terms of flying a spacecraft accurately through space, man was finally coming of age. But as Gemini IX and succeeding flights would show, the time when man would be able to easily perform useful tasks in the weightlessness outside his spacecraft was still a long way off.

Astronaut Stafford's "Angry Alligator," with clamshell doors hanging ajar.

Michael Collins

Birthplace	Rome, Italy
Date of Birth	October 31, 1930
Height	5′ 10½″
Weight	168 lbs.
Eyes	Brown
Hair	Brown
Marital Status/Wife	Pat
Daughters	Ann, Kathleen
Son	Michael
Recreational Interests	Handball, music, fishing
Service Affiliation	Captain, U.S. Air Force
Flight Record	More than 5,000 hours flying time in a wide variety of aircraft (more than 3,200 hours in jet aircraft). Logged 266 hours 6 minutes in two space flights, of which 1 hour 27 minutes were spent walking in space (EVA).
Education and Training	Bachelor of Science from the United States Military Academy, West Point, in 1952. Following graduation he chose an Air Force career. After earning his wings in 1953 he was subsequently assigned to Nellis Air Force Base, Las Vegas, Nevada, for advanced day fighter training. Upon graduation he was assigned to the 21st Fighter Bomber Wing at Victorville, California. In mid-December 1954, the Wing transferred to Chaumont, France. From there he was assigned to Chanute Air Force Base, Illinois, where he became commander of a mobile training detachment. He shortly was reassigned to command a field training detachment at Nellis Air Force Base. After achieving the 1,500 hours flying time required for

consideration as a test pilot, Collins applied to the U.S. Air Force Experimental Flight Test Pilot School at Edwards Air Force Base, California.

Astronaut Career   He was accepted into training in August 1960. Future astronauts Frank Borman and Jim Irwin were classmates, and astronaut-to-be Tom Stafford was one of his instructors. Upon completion of the 32-week course, Collins was assigned to Edwards to test new fighter aircraft. In October 1962, he gained admission to the newly established U.S. Air Force Aerospace Research Pilot Program at Edwards. He was chosen with the third group of astronauts on October 18, 1963. He received the Presidential Medal for Freedom, the nation's highest civilian award, for his flight on Apollo 11 in 1969. He also was awarded the NASA Distinguished Service Medal and the NASA Exceptional Service Medal, and decorations from 11 different countries.

Collins had his first taste of flying at the age of ten in an amphibious aircraft, the Grumman *Widgeon*. Although the pilot allowed him to handle the controls, Collins was more wide-eyed about flight when listening to his dad telling of *his* first plane ride in 1911 in the Philippines. The aircraft was an early Wright military plane in which the crew sat on the wing. The pilot was Frank Lahm, only the second military pilot to be trained to fly by the Wrights. It appears that the romance of the heroic age of flight kindled Collins' interest. This interest waxed and waned through his early years, including his years at West Point. His choice of an Air Force career was more a matter of circumstance than of desire. One of Collins' uncles, J. Lawton Collins, was a World War II hero and later was Army Chief of Staff. Another had been a brigadier general. Collins' brother was a colonel and a cousin, a major. Collins' father, Major General James L. Collins, was Aide to General John J. Pershing in the Philippines and had served in the Mexican campaign against Pancho Villa and with the Allied Expeditionary Force during World War I.

Lacking the drive and direction that would characterize his later years, Collins settled for the Air Force, according to his autobiography, as a simple way to build his own career. It was his brother-in-law's budding career as a Navy test pilot that eventually caught Collins' interest and whetted his appetite to fly the best aircraft the U.S. had to offer.

Once accepted into Edwards Air Force Base, Collins was stimulated by the competitiveness of the training and soon space flight became his ultimate goal.

Collins' first flight assignment as an astronaut was as backup pilot for Gemini VII. He realized his goal as pilot for Gemini X, July 18–21, 1966, with command pilot John Young. It was Collins' first space flight. Young had flown previously with Grissom in Gemini III, the first manned flight of the Gemini spacecraft. Collins and Young docked with a target Agena and later in the mission he performed a spacewalk, retrieving a meteorite experiment package from an Agena target vehicle from the Gemini VIII mission. Collins made two separate spacewalks, becoming the third American astronaut to walk in space.

Collins was assigned as command module pilot for the Apollo 8 mission to orbit the moon but was removed from flight status to undergo surgery on a disk in his neck. After successful surgery and a perfect recovery, Collins was assigned to make his second and most memorable space flight as command module pilot for the first mission to land on the moon. By various accounts, Collins was described as the most solitary of human beings as he circled alone in the command ship *Columbia* while Apollo 11 commander Neil Armstrong and lunar module pilot Edwin Aldrin became the first and second humans, respectively, to set foot on the moon.

Collins resigned from NASA in November of 1969 and retired from active duty with the Air Force. He continues to remain Major General, U.S. Air Force Reserve. He was appointed Assistant Secretary of State for Public Affairs upon his resignation from NASA and in April 1971 became Director of the National Air and Space Museum at the Smithsonian Institution. He oversaw the construction of this national monument to flight, which opened in July 1976 during the Bicentennial celebrations. Collins is currently Undersecretary of the Smithsonian Institution. His autobiography, *Carrying the Fire*, was described by *Time* magazine as "the best-written book yet by any of the astronauts."

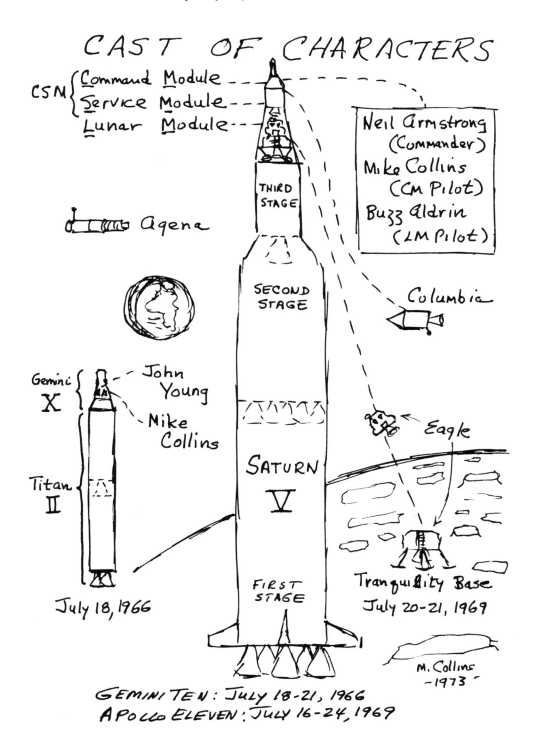

CAST OF CHARACTERS

CSM { Command Module
Service Module
Lunar Module

Neil Armstrong
(Commander)
Mike Collins
(CM Pilot)
Buzz Aldrin
(LM Pilot)

THIRD STAGE

Agena

SECOND STAGE

Columbia

Gemini X { — John Young
— Mike Collins

Eagle

Titan II

SATURN V

Tranquility Base
July 20-21, 1969

FIRST STAGE

July 18, 1966

M. Collins
-1973-

GEMINI TEN: JULY 18-21, 1966
APOLLO ELEVEN: JULY 16-24, 1969

62

Clifton Curtis Williams, Jr.

Birthplace	Mobile, Alabama
Date of Birth	September 26, 1932
Height	6'
Weight	178 lbs.
Eyes	Brown
Hair	Brown
Marital Status/Wife	Jane
Daughter	Catherine
Recreational Interests	Hunting, golf, water sports
Service Affiliation	Captain, U.S. Marine Corps
Flight Record	More than 2,600 hours flying time (more than 2,200 hours in jet aircraft).
Education and Training	Bachelor of Science in Mechanical Engineering from Auburn University, Alabama. He served as a Marine Corps aviator, later graduating from Navy Test Pilot School at Patuxent River, Maryland. He served for three years in the Carrier Suitability Branch of the Flight Test Division at Patuxent. His work there included land-based and shipboard tests of the F8E, TF8A, F8E (attack), and the A4E jet aircraft and automatic carrier landing systems. He was attending the Marine Corps Intermediate Staff and Command School at Quantico, Virginia, when he was selected as an astronaut.

He was chosen with the third group of astronauts on October 18, 1963. His first and only flight assignment as an astronaut was as backup pilot for Gemini X with astronaut Alan L. Bean as command pilot.

Aside from his backup assignment, his specific area of responsibility as a representative of the Astronaut Office was range operations and crew safety. He was the astronauts' representative during the planning of emergency evacuation procedure for the crews during a crisis at the launch area and the planning of the ground rules for the crew abort and abandoning of an out-of-control booster vehicle already in flight.

Williams died in a T-38 jet crash near Tallahassee, Florida, on October 5, 1967. His last attained rank was Major, U.S. Marine Corps.

Gemini X: Getting It All Together

July 18–21, 1966

On January 24, 1966, veteran John Young and rookie astronaut Mike Collins were named as commander and copilot, respectively, of Gemini X. Collins had been chosen with the third group of astronauts on October 18, 1963, and would be only the third (first Scott in Gemini VIII, then Cernan in Gemini IX) astronaut from that group to make a space flight.

The Agena had yet to be fully utilized in docking configuration and with only three manned flights remaining in Project Gemini, mission planners boldly outlined a double rendezvous test involving the active Agena X and the inert Agena left behind during the Gemini VIII mission. The planners were that high on the flying ability of their astronauts and the reliability of the Gemini spacecraft, and time was running out.

EVA, however, was another question. Although the planned activity was likewise bold—a walk to another satellite—the equipment to be used by the pilot, astronaut Collins, was not as complex as the Astronaut Maneuvering Unit (AMU) that had challenged Cernan to the limits.

Launch day, July 18, 1966, saw the second perfect sequential launch of an Agena target vehicle (lifting off 2 seconds behind schedule at 3:39:46 P.M. EST) followed by a Gemini spacecraft. Gemini X was on the money all the way, lifting off at exactly 5:20:26 P.M. EST, and establishing its orbit at just the right point to enable the planned double rendezvous and docking maneuvers. They began their chase of Agena X, 1,125 statute miles ahead of them.

Initially, Collins attempted to provide Young with navigational readings by star sightings with a sextant. Although his attempts were admirable, his measurements failed to match up with the figures from Ground Control. With the sextant now stowed, Young and Collins continued to stalk their quarry with guidance from the ground controllers.

Gemini X's erratic approach to Agena X proved too costly for the astronauts' liking, consuming three times the fuel expended by any earlier rendezvous mission (398 pounds of fuel). Docking was achieved 5 hours and 52 minutes after launch, and any repeat docking practice had to be cancelled due to the existing low fuel levels.

At 6 hours 30 minutes into the mission, Ground Control began providing the Gemini X crew with the data needed to boost their altitude via a burn of the Agena X's engine.

The Agena X main engine roared into life right on time, burning for 80 seconds and boosting the linked vehicles upwards, adding 419 feet per second to their speed.

There was no way to prepare for the Agena's wild ride once the astronauts had adjusted to weightlessness. They were suddenly thrown forward against their body straps, causing Young, after the flight, to describe the ride as "just unbelievable. It was a quick jolt. . . . And the tail-off. . . . I never saw anything like that before, sparks and fire and smoke and lights!"

Young and Collins were pushed to a record altitude into an orbit reaching 477 statute miles out into

Gemini X astronaut Young's recovery after splashdown.

space at its highest point and 184 statute miles at its lowest altitude. At this height, both astronauts kept a close eye on the radiation dosage instruments (which gave them readings of tolerable limits). This territory was still unknown to man and nothing was being left to chance.

Nine hours into the flight the crew bedded down into fitful sleep with Mission Control keeping an eagle eye on all the instrument dials.

When Young and Collins were awakened to begin the eighteenth hour of the mission, they were happy to find that they were Go for the next Agena firing. Young completed the 78-second burn of the Agena main engine. "It may be only 1 G, but it's the biggest 1 G we ever saw! That thing really lights into you," he said, speaking of the mule-like kick that pushed him against his body straps for the second time.

Before the third burn of the Agena engine, Collins performed his first EVA (by standing with the hatch open) as the sun set on earth's horizon. This entire night pass was devoted to photographing the southern Milky Way and another attempt at developing a navigation technique using visual star sightings.

After being docked with the Agena X for 39 hours, Gemini X achieved separation and took off after the lifeless Agena VIII vehicle, which was now coming into range. Young would draw as close as possible to the target in preparation for the most spectacular EVA of the program—Collins' walk to the lifeless Agena rocket.

As they closed on Agena VIII, Young reported that it looked like "a dim, star-like dot until the sun rose above the spacecraft nose." The North American Defense Network (NORAD) of the Department of Defense had been babysitting with the Agena since the Gemini VIII mission, and Mission Control was pleased to see she was right where they said she would be.

At less than 48 hours into the mission, Gemini X was station-keeping with her new quarry. Mission Control determined that fuel supplies were sufficient for Collins' EVA and radioed a go-ahead to Young. "Glad you said that, because Mike's going outside right now," was Young's reply.

Emerging from the spacecraft at dawn, Collins went about his tasks with the same difficulties experienced earlier by Cernan—extreme effort resulting in slow-motion movements. With the laborious EVA preparations now completed and his nitrogen-fueled space gun in hand, Collins pushed off in the direction of the Agena floating 6 feet from his spacecraft. He floated up to the outer lip of the docking cone of the Agena and, grasping it, he became the only human, to this day, to visit and make physical contact with another free-floating satellite!

Collins made his way to the micrometeorite package (S-10 experiment) attached to the Agena, taking care not to foul his lifeline on the sharp metal edges on the Agena's components. On his return "walk" to his Gemini spacecraft, Collins was informed by Young that Hawaii Ground Control had decided to scrub the planned test of the space gun due to low fuel levels. As Collins later described in *Carrying the Fire*, he returned to his spacecraft with deep regrets.

Safely inside and with the hatch secured, the two astronauts performed a short round of experiments and then settled into a well-earned sleep period.

The remaining flight time was spent attending to the 14 experiments carried aboard Gemini X. Of significance were the three radiation experiments which would help Apollo planners map a safe lunar route through earth's radiation belts.

Gemini X came home on July 21, 1966, landing in the Atlantic at 4:07 P.M. EST, less than 3.5 statute miles from the target and the recovery aircraft carrier *Guadalcanal*. With the completion of rendezvous, docking, and EVA's all in one mission, Gemini had finally gotten it all together.

Richard Francis Gordon, Jr.

Birthplace	Seattle, Washington
Date of Birth	October 5, 1929
Height	5′ 7″
Weight	150 lbs.
Eyes	Hazel
Hair	Brown
Marital Status/Wife	Barbara
Daughters	Carleen, Diane
Sons	Richard, Lawrence, Thomas, James
Recreational Interests	Waterskiing, sailing, golf
Service Affiliation	Lt. Commander, U.S. Navy
Flight Record	More than 4,500 hours flying time (more than 3,500 hours in jet aircraft). Logged 315 hours 53 minutes in two space flights, of which 2 hours 4 minutes were spent on one spacewalk and a stand-up EVA.
Education and Training	Bachelor of Science degree in Chemistry from the University of Washington in 1951. He then entered the Navy and after flight training earned his wings as a naval aviator in 1953. In 1957, he attended the Navy Test Pilot School at Patuxent River, Maryland, and served as a flight test pilot until 1960. During this tour of duty, he did flight test work on the F-8U Crusader, F-11F Tigercat, FJ Fury, and A4D Skyhawk jet aircraft and was the first project test pilot for the F-4H Phantom II jet.

In May 1961, he won the Bendix Air Trophy Race from Los Angeles to New York, setting a new speed record of 869.74 mph and a transcontinental speed record of 2 hours 47 minutes.

He was also a student at the U.S. Naval Postgraduate School at Monterey, California.

Astronaut Career He was chosen with the third group of astronauts on October 18, 1963. He received the NASA Distinguished Service Medal and the NASA Exceptional Service Medal.

Gordon was backup pilot for Gemini VIII and flew in space for the first time as pilot for Gemini XI, September 12–15, 1966. The command pilot on that flight was Charles Conrad, a veteran of Gemini V. Gordon performed a spacewalk and a stand-up EVA exercise. Firsts on Gemini XI included: the first tethered station-keeping (between Gemini XI and an Agena target vehicle), establishment of a new altitude record for that time of 850 miles, and the first fully automatic controlled reentry.

Gordon was subsequently assigned as backup command module pilot for Apollo 9 and made his second space flight as command module pilot for Apollo 12, November 14–24, 1969. Other crewmen on man's second lunar landing mission were Charles Conrad, spacecraft commander, and Alan L. Bean, lunar module pilot. Throughout the 31-hour stay on the lunar surface by Conrad and Bean, Gordon remained in the command ship *Yankee Clipper,* circling high overhead in lunar orbit. The Apollo 12 mission accomplished the first precision lunar landing when the lunar module *Intrepid* touched down in the moon's Ocean of Storms within 600 feet of the U.S. Surveyor III spacecraft, which had landed at that spot 31 months earlier.

Gordon served as backup spacecraft commander for Apollo 15.

He retired from NASA and the Navy with the rank of Captain on January 1, 1972, to go into private business.

Gemini XI: The First-Orbit Horse Race

September 12–15, 1966

On March 21, 1966, Charles Conrad and Richard Gordon were named as command pilot and pilot of Gemini XI. Gordon was the fourth man from the third class of astronauts to make a Gemini flight, and Conrad had earned this assignment after his fine performance on the Gemini V flight. Neil Armstrong and rookie William A. Anders were picked as the backup crew.

By now, NASA had firmly fixed Gemini's final deadline, the end of January 1967. Apollo was just around the corner, and to many of the people involved, the XI and XII missions seemed anticlimactic. For Gemini officials, the hurdles they had overcome in the beginning were as equally challenging as the distractions at the end. Nevertheless, the

"orphan" Gemini team pressed doggedly on to complete the bridge between Mercury and Apollo.

On September 12, 1966, at 8:05:01 A.M. EST, after two launch delays, Agena XI lifted obediently into orbit to await its meeting with Gemini XI. With the smallest allowable margin of error tolerated in any Gemini launch, the XI mission had to rise off the pad with perfect velocity and direction within *two seconds* of the scheduled launch time or it would miss the opportunity for the intended first-orbit rendezvous. Gemini XI proved equal to this challenge of split-second timing and marksmanship, lifting off just a half-second off the mark at 9:42:26.5 A.M. EST, with a near-perfect entry into orbit.

With the help of accurate computer data from

Ground Control, the astronauts began to close on their 267-mile-distant target. During the chase, Conrad and Gordon obtained surprisingly accurate measurements with their own spacecraft's computers and used their own figures for the final run at the target. The horse race ended only 85 minutes after launch high over the coast of California, as Conrad brought Gemini XI to a halt within 50 feet of the target vehicle. An exhilarated crew radioed, "Mr. Kraft, would [you] believe M equals 1?" referring to the radio code Mission Control had used soon after their orbit insertion to indicate they were Go for first-orbit rendezvous.

The crew still had 56 percent of their maneuvering fuel remaining after docking. The first-orbit docking was a simulation of an emergency lunar lift-off, a technique Apollo program would have to master in order to reach the moon within the decade.

Having been given appropriate congratulations, Conrad and Gordon were rewarded with a Go for docking *and* undocking maneuvers, another Gemini first. Each pilot tried his hand at the controls, practicing both in daylight and darkness with more apparent ease than they'd had with their docking trainer on the ground. For the first time, a copilot performed the docking maneuver.

After completing the last docking, the crew tested the main Agena engine before shooting to high altitude.

Six hours into the mission, the astronauts were ordered into their planned eight-hour sleep period. Upon awakening, the crew prepared for Gordon's EVA. Gordon began his spacewalk right on schedule, at 24:02 hours into the flight. His initial experience was no different from that of his predecessors, Cernan and Collins; it began as a wrestling match in slow motion. Gordon's movements were ineffective and taxing and after 33 minutes of a planned 107-minute spacewalk, Conrad radioed to Ground Control that he had "brought Dick [Gordon] back in. He got so hot and sweaty he couldn't see." Each spacewalker had warned his successor of the problems but the solution remained elusive. As Gordon related later, "Gene Cernan warned me about this and I took it to heart. I knew it was going to be harder [than expected], but I had no idea of the magnitude."

Conrad and Gordon soon restored order in their spacecraft cabin and dutifully continued the mission.

The next day the crew fired their Gemini-Agena combination for 26 seconds, utilizing the main Agena engine to push them to a new record altitude of 850 statute miles, deeper in space than any human had thus far traveled. From this height the earth began to take on the appearance of a great round ball, prompting Conrad to say, "You can't believe it. . . . I can see all the way from the end, around the top. . . . That water really stands out and everything looks blue . . . The curvature of the earth stands out a lot. [There are] a lot of clouds . . . over the ocean . . . [but] Africa, India, and Australia [are] clear. Looking straight down, you can see just as clearly. . . . There's no loss of color and details are extremely good."

After a few more orbits and a relaxing stand-up EVA performed by Gordon, the crew practiced maneuvers with the two vehicles, Gemini and Agena, united by a tether. Conrad effected a cartwheeling of the tethered vehicles in an attempt to produce artificial gravity via the centrifugal forces created. Only the hand-held camera responded to this artificially produced gravity as it floated in a line to the rear of the cabin away from the center of rotation of the linked vehicles. Neither Conrad nor Gordon felt any effect from their spinning ride.

The crew backed off the Agena upon completion of the artificial gravity tests, performed a few docking maneuvers, and finished what was left of the remaining experiments. Of significance were the results of the radiation experiments, which showed that increased altitude did not necessarily mean increased radiation. Radioactivity appeared in definite zones, and it looked like Apollo could chart a safe path through them all the way to the moon.

The Gemini XI flight ended on September 15, 1966, after 70:41 hours of flight, with an accurate splashdown in the Atlantic just 2.9 statute miles from the recovery aircraft carrier *Guam*. It was the first fully automatic reentry, and close enough to the mark to prompt Cap Com (Mission Control Capsule Communicator) John Young to radio the crew, "You're on TV now."

NASA officials now turned to Gemini XII which, according to the feelings of its commander, James Lovell, "didn't have a mission. It was, I guess, by default . . . supposed to wind up the Gemini program and catch all those items that were not caught on previous flights."

Edwin Eugene Aldrin, Jr.

Birthplace	Montclair, New Jersey
Date of Birth	January 20, 1930
Height	5′ 10″
Weight	165 lbs.
Eyes	Blue
Hair	Blond
Marital Status	Divorced, subsequently remarried
Daughter	Janice
Sons	J. Michael, Andrew
Recreational Interests	Jogging, scuba diving, high-bar exercises
Service Affiliation	Major, U.S. Air Force
Flight Record	More than 3,500 hours flying time (more than 2,860 hours in jet aircraft). Flew 66 combat missions in Korea (F-86 jet fighters) and was credited with downing two enemy MIG aircraft. He received many awards including the Distinguished Flying Cross. In training for the lunar landing, he logged 139 hours in helicopters and made several flights in the lunar landing research vehicle. He logged 289 hours 54 minutes in two space flights, of which 8 hours 18 minutes were spent in extravehicular activities (EVA). Aldrin spent 5 hours 30 minutes during a spacewalk on Gemini XII and 1 hour 50 minutes walking on the lunar surface (lunar EVA: 2 hours 48 minutes).

EVA was measured in different ways for different U.S. space programs. During Gemini, the time was computed from hatch opening to hatch closing. For Apollo and Skylab, both space and lunar EVA's were computed from the time cabin pressure reached 3.0 pounds per square inch during depressurization and repressurization. The depressurization of the lander and the departure of Armstrong occurred approximately 42 minutes earlier than Aldrin's walk on the moon. Aldrin returned to the lander approximately 16 minutes ahead of Armstrong.

Education and Training Bachelor of Science degree from the United States Military Academy at West Point, graduating third in his class in 1951. After graduating West Point, he chose a commission in the Air Force and went into flight training at Bryan, Texas, receiving his wings in 1952. He was assigned to the 51st Fighter Interception Wing during the Korean War. Subsequently, he was assigned as an aerial gunnery instructor at Nellis Air Force Base, Nevada. Later, he attended the Squadron Officers' School at the Air University, Maxwell Air Force Base, Alabama. He later was assigned as Aide to the Dean of Faculty at the United States Air Force Academy. He subsequently attended the Massachusetts Institute of Technology and in 1963 received a Doctor of Science degree in Astronautics. His doctoral thesis was on guidance for manned orbital rendezvous. He was then assigned to the Gemini Target Office of the Air Force Space Systems Division, Los Angeles. Later he was transferred to the U.S. Air Force Field Office at the Manned Spacecraft Center, which was responsible for integrating Department of Defense experiments into the NASA Gemini flights.

Astronaut Career Aldrin was chosen with the third group of astronauts on October 18, 1963. He received the nation's highest civilian award, the Presidential Medal for Freedom, for his flight on Apollo 11 in 1969. He was also awarded the NASA Exceptional Service Medal and the NASA Distinguished Service Medal, and was decorated by 11 different countries.

Aldrin's career as an astronaut was almost inevitable. His father, Air Force Colonel Edwin Aldrin, had been a close associate of Orville Wright (of the Wright brothers, who in 1903 made the first powered flight of a heavier-than-air flyer, with Orville as the pilot) and a student and friend of Robert H. Goddard, the father of modern rocketry. It was he who introduced Charles A. Lindbergh to Dr. Goddard in 1929. Lindbergh subsequently became instrumental in getting the backing which enabled Goddard to continue his experiments. The elder Aldrin also was founder of what is now the Air Force Institute of Technology in Dayton, Ohio; for a time he served as Aide to General Billy Mitchell.

Aldrin was the first astronaut with a doctoral degree to join the corps, and was not a test pilot (NASA had waived that requirement for the third group of astronaut candidates). His first flight assignment was that of backup pilot for Gemini IX. His first space flight was with Gemini VII veteran James Lovell in the Gemini XII mission, November 11–15, 1966. While Lovell, as command pilot, flew Gemini XII, Aldrin became the fifth American astronaut to walk in space, setting a new record of 5 hours 30 minutes. His performance was flawless, as he put into practice many of his theories during his activities outside the spacecraft.

Nicknamed "Dr. Rendezvous" by his peers, Aldrin was recognized as a master at the techniques of orbital rendezvous, and he played a large part in salvaging the Gemini XII mission when the craft's rendezvous radar failed and he had to compute trajectories for catching the Agena target vehicle using backup onboard computations.

He was assigned as the backup command module pilot for Apollo 8 and became lunar module pilot on Apollo 11 during the first manned lunar landing mission, July 16–24, 1969. His crewmates were Neil Armstrong, Apollo 11 commander, and command module pilot Michael Collins. Descending to the surface in the lunar module *Eagle,* Armstrong and Aldrin (in that order) became the first and second humans to walk on the moon, on July 20, 1969.

Aldrin spent 1 hour 50 minutes walking on the lunar surface, assisting in the collections of samples and the deployment of scientific experiments. After completing man's first ascent from the lunar surface, Aldrin and Armstrong maneuvered their lunar module to a rendezvous with command module pilot Michael Collins, who had remained behind in lunar orbit in the command module, *Columbia.*

Aldrin retired from NASA in July 1971 to become Commandant of the Aerospace Research Pilot School at Edwards Air Force Base, California. On March 1, 1972, he retired from the Air Force with the rank of Colonel to enter private business. He has written a book, *Return to Earth,* describing some of the postflight experiences and problems he encountered as an astronaut.

Gemini XII: The Last Curtain Call

November 11–15, 1966

Veteran astronaut James Lovell and rookie Edwin Aldrin were officially announced as commander and pilot of Gemini XII on June 17, 1966, with Gordon Cooper and Eugene Cernan as their backup crew. Previously Aldrin had been assigned along with Lovell to Gemini IX as a backup, but this would be his first space flight. The selection of Aldrin for this particular Gemini flight was fortunate. He had received a Ph.D. from MIT, with a doctoral thesis on the mechanics of orbital rendezvous.

It would be Lovell's experience (backup for Gemini IV and IX and flight on Gemini VII) and Aldrin's ability to put scientific theory into practice that would make the difference on Mission XII between a flight that was a dismal failure and one that ended the Gemini program with a flourish.

On November 11, 1966, the Gemini XII astronauts entered the Pad 19 area with signs on the backs of their pressure suits containing the words THE and END. This little gesture was to hold a deeper meaning than the simple attempt at humor intended. As Gemini-Titan XII climbed heavenward for the last time at 3:46:33 P.M. EST, the Gemini Preparations Team faded into history. They had answered every challenge, 12 for 12, and now, almost as the twelfth flight disappeared from view, the wrecking crew moved into the Pad 19 area to reduce the launch stand to scrap iron.

Things proceeded smoothly after launch, and a little over an hour into the flight Gemini XII had a solid signal (lock-on) from the Agena target launched earlier in the day at 2:08 P.M. EST. A short time later, however, the rendezvous radar on board the spacecraft broke down, forcing the astronauts to go to the backup charts they carried to obtain the readings they would need to complete rendezvous. Using a sextant to check the target, Aldrin began to feed his figures into the computers, which were now out of the customary automatic rendezvous mode. As Aldrin fed in the numbers, Lovell began closing in on the target, arriving in a parking position alongside the Agena at 3 hours and 45 minutes into the space flight. At 4:13 hours elapsed time, Lovell radioed the tracking ship below, the *Coastal Sentry Quebec,* "We are docked."

The ability of Lovell and Aldrin to overcome the radar malfunction as matter-of-factly and effectively as they did vividly pointed out the need for backup techniques using onboard charts and computations.

For only the second time in the program, a Gemini crew could practice docking *and* undocking. The crew alternated as they practiced this procedure a number of times with the Agena, and then they bedded down for the night.

The next morning, Canary Islands Ground Control greeted the crew with a Go for Aldrin's EVA. This was the heart of the mission, and at the appointed time, 20 minutes before sunset, Aldrin, awed at the spectacle of earth and universe that lay before him, was heard to say "Man! Look at that!" Overcoming

The curvature of the earth is clearly visible in this Gemini XI photograph taken 540 nautical miles above India and Ceylon. The view is looking north with the Bay of Bengal to the right and the Arabian Sea to the left.

the impact of this sight on his senses, Aldrin, still standing on the seat of his Gemini spacecraft, went about his chores with slow, deliberate movements. From experiences in past spacewalks, it was found that the astronaut performed better if he were first allowed merely to stand up with the hatch open and get the feel of working outside the spacecraft rather than plunging bodily into this new environment.

After a 2-hour and 20-minute stand-up exercise, the hatch was closed and the crew tended to other aspects of the mission.

The next day, at nearly 43 hours into the flight, Aldrin again opened his hatch in preparation for the main event of the mission—to see if a man could perform useful tasks in space while outside the spacecraft. Soon Aldrin was moving hand over hand along the rail to the nose of the Agena docking adapter. Using his waist tether for restraint and without any of the difficulties experienced by Gordon's earlier spacewalk, Aldrin tied the two vehicles, Agena and Gemini, together with a tether in preparation for the artificial gravity experiment performed by rotating the tethered craft.

Then Aldrin moved along the handrail to the back of the Gemini spacecraft where he placed both feet into the overshoe-type foot restraints that were installed there. He was able to stand up comfortably and control side-to-side movements of his body as he carefully performed the planned exercises. Aldrin also performed a number of mechanical tasks involving turning bolts with wrenches, cutting metal with a pair of clippers, and separating and rejoining electrical connectors. In these maneuvers, Aldrin demonstrated the future possibility of assembling and repairing structures in space.

On returning to the spacecraft at the end of his second EVA, Aldrin paused to wipe Lovell's window, prompting him to ask, "Hey, would you change the oil too?" Aldrin reentered the spacecraft and then closed the hatch with the same ease with which he had performed the two-hour spacewalk. Before they left orbit, Aldrin was to perform a third hatch opening, standing up for one hour on his seat for the last EVA.

The crew also completed four hours of tether exercises during the link-up with Agena. Along with this artificial gravity experiment, they managed to complete 12 of the 15 experiments they carried.

Employing the automatic reentry system, Gemini XII left orbit during the fifty-ninth revolution. It landed 3 statute miles from its Atlantic target area and was recovered by the aircraft carrier *Wasp*. There, on November 15, 1966, at 2:21 P.M. EST, Gemini completed its final curtain call.

The determination of the crew to complete the mission despite the failure of the critical rendezvous radar, together with Aldrin's well-planned and flawless spacewalk, reflected the resolve of the space program itself. By whatever means of skill, ingenuity, and determination, man was in space to stay.

Theodore Cordy Freeman

Birthplace Haverford, Pennsylvania

Date of Birth February 18, 1930

Height 5′ 10½″

Weight 139 lbs.

Eyes Brown

Hair Brown

Marital Status/Wife Faith

Daughter Faith

Service Affiliation Captain, U.S. Air Force

Flight Record More than 3,000 hours flying time (more than 2,000 hours in jet aircraft).

Education and Training Bachelor of Science degree from the U.S. Naval Academy, Annapolis, Maryland, in 1953, after first attending the University of Delaware for one year. He elected to serve in the Air Force. In 1960, he received his Master of Science degree in Aeronautical Engineering from the University of Michigan. His last Air Force assignment just prior to entering the astronaut corps was as a flight test aeronautical engineer and experimental flight test instructor at the Air Force Aerospace Research Pilot School, Edwards Air Force Base, California, where he served primarily in performance flight testing and stability testing.

Astronaut Career He was chosen with the third group of astronauts on October 18, 1963. Aside from his regular astronaut training duties, Freeman's specific responsibility was to be the astronaut corps' representative in work to determine criteria for when an astronaut should abandon a launch rocket that had deviated from its planned course. Two sets of limits had to be established: (1) the maximum allowable deviation change, and (2) the speed at which a rocket's directional change becomes too fast for the safety of the crew.

Freeman had never been assigned a space flight. He died in a T-38 jet crash at Ellington Air Force Base, Texas, on October 31, 1964. The T-38 was an advanced jet-training aircraft used by the astronauts to hone their flying skills and for travel when on official assignments.

Project Apollo

MERCURY HAD been the beginning of America's manned venture into space, and in a way it was an answer to the challenge put forth by the Soviet Union. In bridging the years between Mercury and Apollo, Gemini not only met that challenge in highly successful fashion—ten regularly scheduled manned launches in less than twenty months, plus the stunning achievements of rendezvous and docking—it also carried America to the forefront of space exploration. More importantly, man had gained a victory over his own physiologic limitations. With skill and determination born out of a spirit to explore, he had thrust his fragile being into an environment hostile to his very existence. He not only prevailed over its hazards, but taught himself to respond to its physical laws. Men now flew through the void as birds flew through the air. Man had become a creature of space and for the first time felt capable of leaving earth to venture to another heavenly body. Apollo was going to take him there.

Up to this point, all the instrumentation, tracking, and flight equipment had been designed to handle the requirements of orbital flight around the earth. Developing a means of navigation between the earth, which revolves around the sun at a speed of 66,000 mph, and the moon (239,000 miles away), which speeds around the earth at 21,600 mph, was considered the most formidable task for Apollo and was given priority status at the very start of the program.

A traveler on the earth deals essentially in two dimensions as he moves from point to point on its surface. He is also supplied with a multitude of references as he travels distances that are relatively small in comparison with space distances.

During the earth-orbiting operations of Mercury and Gemini, there was no up or down in the condition of weightlessness, and the customary references such as earth's horizon, were far removed. An astronaut was operating in "three dimensions" when charting his route. If he remained in sight of the earth, he still had a strong reference point with which to correlate his instrument readings, but it was nothing like the orientation he obtained when flying an aircraft.

The problems of an Apollo astronaut would go one step further. The earth reference point completely disappeared once the course was set for the quarter-million-mile journey to the moon. On that astronomical scale an error of a few degrees at the outset would result in missing the planned destination by thousands of miles if left uncorrected. Also, the only reference points in the emptiness of space were the distant stars.

With that challenge ahead of them, the Apollo planners had to chart a fail-safe course from earth to moon which would bring the Apollo spacecraft to an imaginary point in space where two and a half days later it would miss the leading edge of the on-rushing moon by a scant 115 miles and then be pulled by lunar gravity into a path around the moon and enter lunar orbit only if its main engine fired properly and slowed it down as planned.

If by some terrible circumstance the engine failed to work, a crippled spacecraft could still be saved, because on this particular path the lunar gravity would merely swing the Apollo spacecraft around, heading it back to earth like a boomerang with no need to fire the main engine. If all went well and the Apollo craft established lunar orbit, then the complexities of navigation would really begin. The attached lunar module (LM) would have to ferry two of the crewmen to the moon's surface and back, and the lone crewman of the Apollo spacecraft would have to find his partners in lunar orbit and successfully dock with them—an accomplishment that was cause for celebration when performed in earth orbit only a few years earlier.

The seemingly impossible task of developing the

Guidance and Navigation System (G&N) to be carried on board Apollo fell to the wizards of the Massachusetts Institute of Technology's Instrumentation Laboratory under the leadership of Dr. Charles Stark Draper. They would develop a "black box," the size of a normal suitcase, that could take man into space.

The G&N System contained a miniature computer, three gyroscopes that would initiate course corrections if an Apollo strayed from its planned flight path, and a speedometer—the inertial-measurement unit. The miniature computer had a 38,000-word memory bank and contained the spatial coordinates of 37 specific reference stars along with information about the position and gravitational fields of the sun and moon. It was the brain that helped Apollo fly.

Project Apollo was unique in respect to Mercury and Gemini in another way. It required the development of two separate spacecraft: the conical command module (CM) with attached service module (SM) at the rear, and the bug-like lunar module (LM) which would carry two of the three crewmen to the lunar surface.

The CM had five windows as compared to Gemini's two windows and the single porthole of Mercury. Two of the windows were located at the sides of the left and right couches (seats) and were intended for visual observations and photography. Two rendezvous windows were placed directly in front of the right and left couches and permitted a view of the conical nose of Apollo that housed the docking mechanisms. This area became active during rendezvous and docking. The remaining hatch window was situated directly over the center couch.

The 12,500-pound command module (CM) carried its own life-support system along with the G&N System, had small rocket thrusters for orienting the spacecraft, and was designed to allow its three crewmen to work, eat, and sleep without wearing pressure suits. The crew compartment was 210 cubic feet as compared to 50 cubic feet for Gemini and 36 cubic feet for Mercury. A heat shield at its 12-foot 10-inch base would protect the astronauts from the searing 5,000-degree F. heat of reentry as the craft plunged into the earth's atmosphere at 25,000 miles per hour. The 10-foot 7-inch-high cone-shaped CM would be the only component of the three modules to return to earth.

In terms of complexity, Mercury contained 750,000 separate parts and 7 miles of wiring as compared to Gemini's 1,230,000 items and 10.5 miles of wiring. On the other hand, the Apollo CM contained an incredible 2,000,000 items, not including electrical circuits and components, and an astronomical 15 miles of wiring.

The first command module to fly around the moon, Apollo 8, had 5,600,000 parts including electrical circuitry and components and 1.5 million systems, subsystems, and assemblies. If the spacecraft functioned with 99.9 percent reliability, 5,600 defects could be expected. The Apollo team would have to strive for perfection and build as many backup systems as possible to insure the safety of the vital human element of this magnificent flying machine.

The service module (SM) was the cylindrical attachment directly behind the heat shield of the CM. It housed the propellants and the main spacecraft engine. It was as wide (12 feet 10 inches) as the CM and nearly twice as long (24 feet 2 inches). With its full complement of fuel and oxidizer, it weighed approximately 53,000 pounds.

The SM's restartable Service Propulsion System engine (the SPS, or main spacecraft engine), with its large bell-shaped nozzle protruding from the rear, had no backup; it had to work perfectly to rocket the spacecraft into and, more importantly, out of lunar orbit.

Besides the propellants for the SPS engine, the SM carried three fuel cells for producing electricity and water, as well as part of the crew's oxygen supply. Like the CM, it also had rocket thrusters to effect control of the orientation of the spacecraft. It had no heat shield and would be cast off just prior to reentry into the earth's atmosphere. During the final minutes between reentry and splashdown, the CM would have to depend on its own batteries for electricity and its reserve supply of oxygen.

The bug-like lunar module (LM) almost defied description. Designed to carry the maximum amount of navigational and life-support equipment with the least amount of weight, it was essentially a platform with four legs, a large central rocket engine, and a series of cubes piled on top of each other in apparently haphazard fashion. Since the LM would fly only in the vacuum of space, no effort was made to streamline its eggshell-thin aluminum frame or to provide a heat shield.

It was 22 feet 11 inches tall and, including the legs, had a 31-foot diameter. The total weight of the LM was 33,000 pounds, 24,000 pounds of which was propellants. The LM consisted of two modules, the ascent stage and the descent stage.

The lower, descent, stage was 10 feet 7 inches high and its four legs provided the landing gear for the LM and later the launch platform for the ascent stage.

Engineers at Houston Control Center monitor EVA inflight exercise by Apollo astronaut.

Most of its weight was attributable to the four propellant tanks and the (throttleable) 10,000-pound-thrust rocket engine fired during its descent to the lunar surface. It also served as a shed to house the scientific equipment and the Lunar Rover that would be used by the astronauts. This lower stage would be left on the moon's surface after the astronauts departed.

The ascent stage was essentially the crew's cabin as well as the spacecraft that would rocket the astronauts back into lunar orbit. The crew had 157 cubic feet within which to work and they also were provided with an equipment bay. There were no seats; both astronauts would fit into harnesses as they stood in front of their control panels during flight.

This upper stage carried the heart of the "Lem's" navigational and communication system as well as its own life-support system, and the 3,500-pound-thrust ascent engine. It also carried 16 small rocket thrusters and radar for the critical rendezvous and docking maneuvers. As previously stated, its function was to get the astronauts back to the CM orbiting high overhead.

A massive stream of information from the earlier manned flights and unmanned probes had been flowing into Project Apollo since its inception in July 1960. Since the launch of America's first satellite, Explorer I in 1958, unmanned space probes had been charting the path between earth and moon and testing for hazards such as radiation and micrometeorites. Robot spacecraft began sending back photographs of the lunar surface as early as 1964, when Ranger VII provided an impressive series of pictures of the moon before it crash-landed on its surface. The Ranger program continued with successful Ranger VIII, and IX flights in 1965. Next, Surveyor I, which achieved its first soft landing on the moon on June 2, 1966, began an unmanned lunar venture on the moon's surface, which saw four more successful Surveyor landings before the program concluded in 1968, after 17 months of on-site chemical and mechanical inspection of the lunar surface and the transmission of 87,000 photographs. Finally, five Lunar Orbiter flights between 1966 and 1967 photographed more than 99 percent of the lunar surface during more than 6,000 orbits, providing valuable data (including 1,950 black-and-white pictures of the lunar surface) for use in Apollo landing-site selections. All five Lunar Orbiters were successful. All three series of unmanned lunar probes—Ranger, Surveyor, and Lunar Orbiter—also collected data on meteoroids and radiation in the moon's vicinity in preparation for the arrival of man.

Six of the Group III astronauts selected on October 18, 1963, did not fly in Project Gemini and went on to assignments in the Apollo program. Two were from the Air Force: Captains William Anders and Donn Eisele. Two were Navy men: Lieutenants Alan Bean and Roger Chaffee. Walter Cunningham and Russell Schweickart were civilians with jet pilot experience.

To ensure an adequate supply of astronauts for the expanding Apollo program two more groups of candidates were selected in 1965 and 1966.

On June 28, 1965, NASA announced the selection of the first group of "scientist astronauts." Six applicants selected had the required degrees in the natural sciences, medicine, and engineering.

Of the six chosen, only four would remain with NASA and make a space flight. Dr. Harrison H. Schmitt (Ph.D. in Geology) made his first space flight as the lunar module (LM) pilot on Apollo 17 and became the only scientist to walk on the moon. Navy Lt. Commander Joseph P. Kerwin (M.D.) became the science pilot for Skylab 2. Dr. Owen K. Garriott (civilian, Ph.D., Engineering) and Dr. Edward G. Gibson (civilian, Ph.D., Engineering) were science pilots for Skylab 3 and 4, respectively. The men were not required to have flight experience (although Kerwin was a jet pilot); they received one year of flight training after joining the astronaut corps.

The fifth group of astronauts, chosen on April 4, 1966, formed the largest group (19) of astronaut candidates up to that time. Nine of the Group V candidates would fly Apollo before it concluded: Air Force Major James B. Irwin and Captains Charles M. Duke, Jr., Stuart A. Roosa, and Alfred M. Worden. The Navy contributed Commander Edgar D. Mitchell, Lt. Commander Ronald E. Evans, and Lt. Thomas K. Mattingly II. Fred W. Haise, Jr., and John L. Swigert, Jr., were civilians.

Four of the Group V astronauts would fly in the post-Apollo Skylab program: Navy Lt. Commander Paul J. Weitz (Skylab 2), Captain Jack R. Lousma (Skylab 3), and Major Gerald P. Carr (Skylab 4), from the Marine Corps, and Air Force Major William R. Pogue (Skylab 4). Civilian Vance Brand would fly on the last Apollo sent into space, the Apollo-Soyuz Mission launched July 15, 1975. Five of the Group V astronauts did not make a space flight.

The qualifications were the same as for the Group III astronauts, and 11 of the 19 candidates had advanced degrees. Evans and Lousma were not jet test pilots.

The enterprise of putting a man on the moon had enlisted the heart of America's technological power, and before it was over, it would keep a task force numbering from 50,000 to a peak of 409,900 busy for more than ten years. Everything that was humanly possible was done to assure the safe completion of its goal, but for a few dark months in 1967, it seemed as if that wouldn't be enough.

Roger Bruce Chaffee

Birthplace	Grand Rapids, Michigan
Date of Birth	February 15, 1935
Height	5' 9½"
Weight	152 lbs.
Eyes	Brown
Hair	Brown
Marital Status/Wife	Martha
Daughter	Sheryl
Son	Stephen
Recreational Interests	Woodcrafts, hunting, fishing, boating
Service Affiliation	Lieutenant, U.S. Navy
Flight Record	More than 2,300 hours flying time (more than 2,000 in jet aircraft).
Education and Training	Bachelor of Science degree in Aeronautical Engineering from Purdue University in 1957. He took his first pilot training at the Purdue University Airport as a cadet in the Naval Reserve Officers' Training Corps during his last semester at the university. He began training as a Navy fighter pilot at Pensacola, Florida, in the summer of 1957. He was transferred in 1958 to Kingsville, Texas, for more advanced training in the F9F Cougar jet fighter, completing his training in 1959. Subsequently he was assigned as safety and quality-control officer for Heavy Photographic Squadron 62 at the Naval Air Station in Jacksonville, Florida. While

here, he was assigned to fly over the coast of Florida and make aerial photographs of Cape Canaveral for mapping purposes. In January 1963, he entered the Air Force Institute of Technology at Wright-Patterson Air Force Base, Ohio, to work on a Master of Science degree in Reliability Engineering.

Astronaut Career He was chosen with the third group of astronauts on October 18, 1963. Chaffee had participated in all phases of the astronautic training program and was selected as lunar module pilot for the first manned Apollo flight.

He died on January 27, 1967, at the launch pad at Cape Kennedy when the Apollo spacecraft in which he and crewmates Grissom and White were training burst into flame, killing all three astronauts.

On October 23, 1967, he was posthumously awarded the NASA Exceptional Service Medal.

Apollo 1: A Time for Reappraisal

January 27, 1967

Throughout the operational period of Gemini, program managers for Apollo struggled with the task of knitting the sprawling network of contractors (20,000 companies) with a work force from industry, government and the universities (it at one time numbered 409,900 persons) into a cohesive team, with each element aware of and responsive to the needs of the other.

In a venture such as Apollo, new ground was broken every day. Volumes of information poured into the program faster than it could be assimilated. Solutions as to what must be done to place a man on the moon began coming in, but the solutions often required changes in the spacecraft, and that is where problems began creeping into the Apollo program. Too many changes were occurring too rapidly and the tight control that was NASA's trademark during Mercury and Gemini began to loosen. The mammoth moon project was becoming an untamed giant.

The pressure of maintaining the schedule and budget was felt, too, in other areas. In developing the huge boosters that would launch Apollo, NASA decided to forego the usual stage-by-stage flight testing of the launch vehicles, feeling confident that intensive ground testing of components would allow the entire stack of stages to be flight-tested right from the beginning.

The first attempt at the new "all-up" testing occurred on February 26, 1966, when a complete Saturn IB rocket carrying an unmanned Apollo command module (AS-201) flew a perfect suborbital flight. The Apollo heat shield passed its first test, as the undamaged spacecraft landed in the Atlantic Ocean near its recovery ship, the aircraft carrier USS *Boxer*. Two more successful unmanned Apollo-Saturn IB flights, AS-203 on July 5 and AS-202 on August 25, qualified the launch vehicle and Apollo command module for manned space flight. In the face of these successes the new system for testing launch vehicles seemed justified. However, during the final testing of the Apollo spacecraft, luck would run out. Conquering new frontiers is not without its risks. Early in 1967, three American astronauts would pay the ultimate price.

The crew for the first manned Apollo space flight (AS-204) was announced on October 28, 1966. Two veteran astronauts, Virgil Grissom, command pilot, and Ed White, senior pilot, would be accompanied by Roger Chaffee, who would be making his first space flight. Their backup crew would be James McDivitt and David Scott, both veterans, and rookie Russell Schweickart. Both Chaffee and Schweickart were Group III astronauts chosen in 1963.

On Friday, January 27, 1967, at 1:19 P.M., Grissom, White, and Chaffee, the prime crew of AS-204, entered their spacecraft which sat atop its Saturn IB booster 218 feet above Launch Pad 34 to begin a simulated launch countdown.

When the hatch was sealed, the cabin of the Apollo command module was filled with pure oxygen up to a pressure 2 pounds higher than that found at normal sea level (16.7 pounds per square inch), just as it would be filled during the actual launch. A few moments later Grissom summoned the ground crew to check an odd odor he detected in the spacecraft. A careful check revealed nothing abnormal and the countdown resumed.

A short time later, the countdown again was halted due to trouble that developed with radio communication, prompting the now irritated Grissom to ask the controllers how they expected to talk with him in space if they couldn't hear him 5 miles away.

Another interruption occurred at T–10 minutes and holding, and then suddenly, it happened! At exactly 6:31:03 P.M. one of the crewmen inside Apollo sounded the alarm—"Fire in the spacecraft!" Instantly, the ground crew saw a flash fire break through the shell of the spacecraft and envelop it in smoke. They rushed to open the cumbersome spacecraft hatch, but it was too late. The three astronauts had expired long before it was opened, having died from asphyxiation.

The tragic news spread like a shockwave across the nation and around the world. Administrator James Webb expressed the shock within NASA: "We've always known that something like this would happen sooner or later. . . . Who would have thought the first tragedy would be on the ground?"

On April 24, 1967, fate once again reminded us all of the dangers that threaten when crossing new boundaries. The Soviet press agency Tass reported the tragic news of the loss of one of their cosmonauts, Vladimir M. Komarov, killed during the landing of a new spacecraft, Soyuz I.

In the months ahead, both American and Soviet space programs would go through an agonizing self-appraisal. The accident had pointed out weaknesses from the management level right down to the design of the spacecraft, and it would be almost two years before an astronaut would fly Apollo. The lessons learned would be hard ones, but the sacrifice of the Apollo 1 fire would not be in vain. NASA never again lost an astronaut during an Apollo space flight.

Roger Chaffee had discussed the hazards of his profession with his father, Don Chaffee, about six months before he died. Walking along a Florida beach one evening, he said to his father, "Dad, if I buy the farm [a pilots' expression for dying], I don't want you to be bitter about the space program. I know I'm in a dangerous profession, but I believe our work will mean a great deal to mankind. I want you to do all you can to promote the space program. And Dad, I want your promise on that."

As Don Chaffee later recalled the moment, "I patted him on the shoulder and assured him the mission would do fine, but he insisted. I then gave him my promise that I would do as he asked." After Roger's death, Don Chaffee kept that promise to his son.

The Apollo 1 crew—Grissom, Chaffee and White.

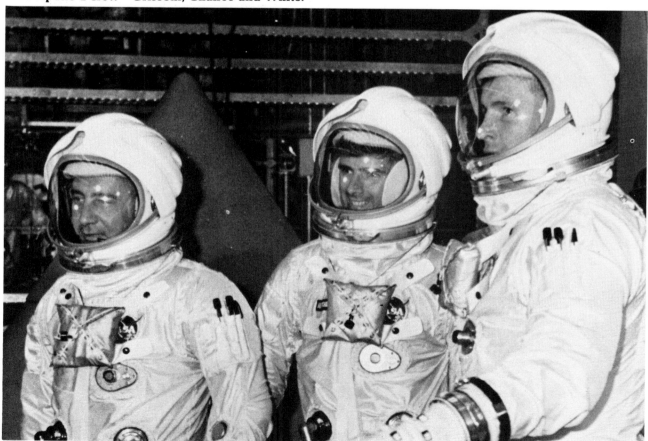

Donn Fulton Eisele

Birthplace	Columbus, Ohio
Date of Birth	June 23, 1930
Height	5' 9"
Weight	160 lbs.
Eyes	Blue
Hair	Brown
Marital Status	Divorced, subsequently remarried
Daughters	Melinda, Kristin
Sons	Donn, Jon
Service Affiliation	Captain, U.S. Air Force
Flight Record	More than 4,200 hours flying time (more than 3,600 hours in jet aircraft). Logged 260 hours 9 minutes in one space flight (no EVA).
Education and Training	Bachelor of Science degree from the U.S. Naval Academy, Annapolis, in 1952. He chose a career in the Air Force and received a Master of Science degree in Astronautics in 1960 from the Air Force Institute of Technology, Wright-Patterson Air Force Base, Ohio. He also attended and graduated from the Air Force Aerospace Research Pilot School at Edwards Air Force Base, California. He was a project engineer and experimental test pilot at the Air Force Special Weapons Center at Kirtland Air Force Base, New Mexico. In this capacity, he flew experimental test flights in support of special-weapons development programs.
Astronaut Career	He was chosen with the third group of astronauts on October 18, 1963, and received the NASA Exceptional Service Medal. His only space flight was the first manned Apollo mission, Apollo 7, October 11–22, 1968. He served as command

module pilot with spacecraft commander Wally Schirra, a veteran of Mercury and Gemini, and Walter Cunningham (lunar module pilot), also making his only space flight. Eisele performed station-keeping and rendezvous exercises with the S-IVB second stage of their Saturn IB launch vehicle.

Eisele served as backup command module pilot for the Apollo 10 mission.

He resigned from the astronaut corps in June 1970 to become a technical assistant (manned flight) assigned to the Space Systems Division at NASA's Langley Research Center in Hampton, Virginia. He acted as consultant and advisor on experiments and life-support research for the manned Skylab, Space Shuttle, and Space Station programs. He retired from NASA and the Air Force with the rank of Colonel in July 1972 to become Peace Corps Director in Thailand. He subsequently left that post to enter private industry.

Apollo 7 astronauts Eisele and Schirra during their first TV transmission.

Ronnie Walter Cunningham

Birthplace	Creston, Iowa
Date of Birth	March 16, 1932
Height	5′ 10″
Weight	155 lbs.
Eyes	Hazel
Hair	Blond
Marital Status/Wife	Lo
Daughter	Kimberly
Son	Brian
Recreational Interests	An avid sports enthusiast, particularly gymnastics, handball, and hunting
Service Affiliation	Civilian
Flight Record	More than 4,400 hours flying time (more than 3,500 hours in jet aircraft). Logged 260 hours 9 minutes on one space flight.
Education and Training	Bachelor of Arts degree with honors in Physics in 1960. Joined the Navy in 1951 and began his flight training in 1952. In 1953 he joined a Marine squadron and served on active duty with the U.S. Marine Corps until August 1956, after which he entered UCLA, majoring in physics. After graduating in 1960, Cunningham went on to receive a Master of Arts degree in Physics from UCLA in 1961 and presently has completed work (with the exception of a thesis) at UCLA for a Ph.D in Physics. His doctoral thesis problem involved work on the development, analysis and testing of a triaxial search coil magnetometer of the same type that was later flown aboard the first NASA Orbiting Geophysical Observatory Satellite.

At the time he applied for astronaut duty, Cunningham was employed by the Rand Corporation as a research scientist working on error analysis and feasibility studies of defenses against ballistic missiles launched from submarines and on research concerning the earth's magnetosphere.

Astronaut Career He was chosen with the third group of astronauts on October 18, 1963. He was awarded the NASA Exceptional Service Medal for his flight on Apollo 7, October 11–22, 1968. He was designated the lunar module pilot (although the mission carried no lunar module) on this, his only space flight.

Apollo 7 was commanded by veteran Mercury and Gemini astronaut Wally Schirra, with Donn Eisele as command module pilot, also making his only space flight.

The 260-hour, 4.5-million-mile earth orbital shakedown flight of Apollo 7 was the first Apollo flight to carry men aboard and was so successful in qualifying the spacecraft for manned flight that a second qualifying flight was cancelled, resulting in the planning of the lunar orbital flight of Apollo 8 on only the second manned Apollo mission.

Cunningham was assigned to head the Orbital Workshop (later known as Project Skylab) Branch of the Astronaut Office in the latter part of 1968. He resigned from NASA on August 1, 1971, to enter private industry.

Apollo 7: Back on Course

October 11–22, 1968

The investigation of the Apollo 1 fire was nearing completion when the announcement was made, on May 9, 1967, that Walter M. Schirra, veteran of Mercury and Gemini space flights, would command the first crew to fly Apollo. Flying with him on their first space flights would be Donn Eisele, senior pilot, and Walter Cunningham, pilot. The backup crew would be Thomas Stafford, John Young, and Eugene Cernan—veteran astronauts from Project Gemini.

At a press conference held the next day (May 10, 1967) at North American Aviation's Apollo assembly plant in Downey, California, the prime and backup crews for Apollo 7 had expressed complete satisfaction with the design changes that were being made as a result of the spacecraft fire. Nearly 5,000 engineering changes had been made to the spacecraft, including a new hinged hatch that could be opened outward in about two seconds by activating a springed lever, and the replacement of many highly flammable materials such as nylon netting. A further precaution against fire was taken by sheathing all open wires with hard paneling and by clothing the astronauts in flame-resistant space suits.

After the fire, ingenious tests were devised in an effort to find materials that would not burn violently in a pure oxygen atmosphere. If a test fire did not put itself out, the material or wire routing was redesigned and then retested.

On November 9, 1967, the launch of the unmanned Apollo 4 spacecraft marked the first time the giant Saturn V moon rocket was used to carry an Apollo spacecraft. The unmanned CM was rocketed back to earth from a height never before achieved at a speed of 25,000 miles per hour. The heat shield was subjected to a temperature over 5,000 degrees Fahrenheit during a test that simulated reentry from lunar flight. It also marked the first test flight of the liquid-hydrogen second stage.

Standing 363 feet tall with the command module in place, the 7.5-million-pound-thrust Saturn V towered over its Saturn IB predecessor, which stood at 225 feet and developed only enough thrust (1,300,000 pounds) to lift Apollo into earth orbit.

Apollo 5 flew unmanned on January 22, 1968. Originally planned as manned orbital flight AS-204, the mission had been drastically revised after the fatal Apollo 1 fire twelve months earlier. On this flight, a Saturn IB carried the first lunar module (LM) into earth orbit, where its descent engines were successfully tested. The LM had no heat shield and later burned up on reentry into the atmosphere.

The huge Saturn V was finally put through its paces on April 4, 1968, during the unmanned launch of Apollo 6. Most of the mission objectives were met and Apollo was ready for its final exam—a manned space flight.

Launch preparations for Apollo 7's Saturn IB continued around-the-clock at Pad 34.

As launch preparations neared completion at Pad 34, there was more than the usual tension in the air. It was October 11, 1968, nearly two years since the last manned launch, Gemini XII. A faltering step, any miscue today and America's hopes in space could be dealt a serious blow.

Apollo, as well as NASA, was on trial this day. When the Saturn IB booster lifted from the pad at exactly 10:02:45 A.M. EST, she not only carried men for the first time but the hopes of the nation as well. The launch went perfectly, and when Apollo 7 received a Go for orbiting, the United States was back into the manned space flight business.

Riding high atop the Saturn, the crew had no sensation of lift-off. As the first stage of the Saturn IB shut down at 2 minutes and 25 seconds, the S-IVB second stage kicked in, right on schedule, giving the astronauts their first ride atop a liquid-hydrogen-propelled vehicle. At 5 minutes 54 seconds into the mission, Schirra reported, "She is riding like a dream."

The first ten minutes of an Apollo flight were automatically controlled by an onboard computer, and all Mission Control or the crew could do was watch the dials. If something went wrong, however, the crew could resort to manual controls or blast their command module clear, using the powerful escape tower rocket (33 feet high with a 147,000-pound thrust), and float back to earth using its three huge parachutes. On this flight, all was going according to plan and the escape tower was jettisoned. The S-IVB stage stayed with the command and service modules for one and a half orbits. After firing small rockets to achieve separation, Schirra pulled Apollo 7 about 50 feet ahead of the S-IVB, turned the spacecraft around, and simulated the docking procedure, coming to within 4 or 5 feet of the rocket. This procedure would have been necessary to pull a lunar module from its housing in the second stage if they had been carrying one and were on their way to the moon.

The importance of the Apollo 7 flight was underscored with this message sent by President Johnson to the crew: "Everything in the Presidential office came to a halt as Foreign Minister Debré of France and I watched with mounting excitement the magnificent launch of the Saturn." Thousands of spectators had watched the launch from beaches around the Cape, and Europeans were able to view the launch along with the American TV audience via a television relay with NASA's ATS III (Applications Technology Satellite).

The scheduled first live TV broadcast from on board the spacecraft was cancelled on Apollo 7's second day in space due to a busy schedule which included a rendezvous with the lifeless S-IVB stage 80 miles away. The crew fired the Service Propulsion System engine for ten seconds and eight seconds to set up for rendezvous. Eventually, they maneuvered their spacecraft to within 70 feet of the tumbling vehicle, simulating techniques to be used on future flights to rescue the LM if it were to become disabled in lunar orbit. The rest of their day was spent in the routine of checking out spacecraft systems, making minor repairs such as correcting a malfunction in the spacecraft's evaporation system, conducting experiments, and coping with the head colds they had developed.

The third day saw a few tense moments when the AC circuit breakers suddenly tripped, causing a momentary power failure in the spacecraft. The system was reset manually and everything returned to normal. The first live television broadcast from space ended the day on a happier note. The crew appeared on national TV for seven minutes, displaying hand-printed signs bearing greetings from "The lovely Apollo Room high atop everything."

More than anything else, Apollo 7 was a mission to test spacecraft durability. Only the occasional firings of the 20,500-pound-thrust SPS engine and the TV broadcasts would break the monotony of the daily routine.

The Service Propulsion System engine, necessary for entering and leaving lunar orbit, responded perfectly during its first manned trials, firing on command eight times. On October 22, the eighth SPS firing at 259 hours 39 minutes lowered Apollo 7 out of orbit. With the service module already discarded and heat shield aglow, the crew headed for their scheduled landing area in the Atlantic Ocean, splashing down 8 statute miles from the recovery aircraft carrier *Essex*.

The mission had lasted 10.8 days—longer than a journey to the moon and back. Apollo 7 had flown America's second longest manned mission to date on its "first" space flight with astronauts on board (Gemini VII had lasted 14 days). The first manned orbital space flights of Mercury and Gemini had each lasted only "three revolutions."

Apollo 7 and its millions of parts had performed superbly during its 163-orbit flight and with each revolution the cloud that had hung over Apollo for 23 months began to fade as man drew closer and closer to the moon. Apollo 7's message was clear. We were back on course and it was a very good feeling.

William Alison Anders

Birthplace	Hong Kong
Date of Birth	October 17, 1933
Height	5' 8"
Weight	145 lbs.
Eyes	Blue
Hair	Brown
Marital Status/Wife	Valerie
Daughter	Gayle
Sons	Alan, Glen, Gregory, Eric
Recreational Interests	Fishing, flying, camping, waterskiing, soccer
Service Affiliation	Captain, U.S. Air Force
Flight Record	More than 3,500 hours flying time in jet aircraft and helicopters. Logged 147 hours 1 minute in his only space flight (no EVA).
Education and Training	Bachelor of Science degree from the U.S. Naval Academy, Annapolis, in 1955. He chose an Air Force career, and after earning his wings was assigned as a fighter pilot in an all-weather interception squadron of the Air Defense Command. In 1962 he received a Master of Science degree in Nuclear Engineering at the Air Force Institute of Technology, Wright-Patterson Air Force Base, Ohio, after which he served as a nuclear engineer and instructor pilot at the Air Force Weapons Laboratory, Kirtland Air Force Base, New Mexico. He was responsible for programs studying technical management of space radiation and nuclear-power-reactor shielding and radiation effects.

Astronaut Career He was chosen with the third group of astronauts on October 18, 1963. He received the NASA Distinguished Service Medal for his only space flight, man's maiden voyage of Apollo 8 around the moon.

Anders' first flight assignment was as backup pilot to Gemini XI. On Apollo 8, December 21–27, 1968, Anders served as lunar module pilot (although no LM was carried on the mission), with veteran Gemini astronauts Frank Borman as spacecraft commander and James Lovell as command module pilot, on the Christmas voyage around the moon. That memorable flight also was the first time astronauts flew the Saturn V moon rocket.

Anders subsequently served as backup command module pilot for Apollo 11. He resigned, following completion of that mission, from NASA and active duty from the Air Force in September 1969, with the rank of Colonel, remaining in the Air Force Reserve. He became Executive Secretary of the National Aeronautics and Space Council. In 1973, he joined the Atomic Energy Commission, and with its reorganization in 1974 he became Chairman of the Nuclear Regulatory Commission. He resigned that position in the spring of 1976 to become the U.S. Ambassador to Norway. He entered private business in 1978.

Apollo 8: Breaking the Bonds

December 21–28, 1968

In a news conference held at NASA headquarters on August 19, 1968, Apollo Program Director, Lt. General Samuel C. Phillips (USAF), outlined the plans for the Apollo 8 mission.

If the Apollo 7 mission of October 11 went well, NASA expected to test the huge Saturn V on its first manned mission in December. The lunar module (Number 3) would not be ready until 1969 due to delays in checkout, and Apollo 8 would fly without it on its earth-orbiting test of the moon rocket. General Phillips also announced reassignment of the crews. The redefined Apollo 8 mission would have veteran Gemini astronauts Frank Borman as commander and James Lovell as command module pilot. Despite the lack of a lunar module, rookie astronaut William Anders' designation was LM pilot. The new Apollo 8 backup crew would be Neil Armstrong, Edwin Aldrin, and Fred Haise. James McDivitt, David Scott, and Russell Schweickart would fly on Apollo 9 with the LM.

Apollo 7 turned out to be so successful that Flight Operations Director Christopher Kraft and his team at Manned Spacecraft Center, Houston, began pressing to get the lunar-orbiting flight plan that had already been worked out in great detail assigned to the Apollo 8 mission. Their point: Why duplicate the successful Apollo 7 mission?

On October 28, NASA opened the door to a possible lunar flight, with Acting NASA Administrator Dr. Thomas O. Paine cautioning, "We will fly [only] the most advanced mission for which we are fully prepared that does not unduly risk the safety of the crew."

A little later, on November 12, 1968, the momentous decision was announced at NASA headquarters by Dr. Paine: "After a careful and thorough examination of all of the systems and risks involved, we have concluded that we are now ready to fly the most advanced mission for our Apollo 8 launch in December—the orbit around the moon." As Dr. Paine spoke, one could not help feeling that he and everyone else present were somewhat in awe of the immensity of the project he was now setting forth.

Men were going to the moon!

Each day's work in the eight years it had taken to prepare Apollo 8 had been directed toward this moment. Now that the day had finally arrived, the mission assumed a dream-like quality.

On December 21, 1968, the largest crowd to view a manned launch since that of John Glenn gathered along the roads and beaches around Cape Kennedy.

At 7:51 A.M. EST, the impact of the ignition of the Saturn V's 7.5-million-pound-thrust engines on the senses of the people in its presence left little doubt that we had at last gathered the power to break our earthly bonds and reach for the moon. The ground shook. Tremors could be felt out to a distance of 4 miles and even at that distance, the noise from the rocket blast was deafening.

The 363-foot moon rocket rose slowly at first, emerging from Pad 39A in a sea of fire. As 531,000 gallons of flaming kerosene and liquid oxygen poured through the five engines of the Saturn V's first stage, the pace began to quicken. At 2 minutes 34 seconds into the flight, the 6.2-million-pound rocket had climbed through 40 miles of atmosphere and was streaking across the skies at 6,000 miles per hour.

A split second later, the five J-2 engines of the second stage (S-II) took over, blasting away the first stage and boosting the third (S-IVB) stage, with Apollo 8 atop, higher and faster as its engines consumed 359,000 gallons of liquid hydrogen and oxygen. This burn lasted 6 minutes 10 seconds. At an altitude of 108 statute miles the S-IVB engines took command and placed the spacecraft smoothly into a 118-mile-high orbit after firing for 2 minutes and 40 seconds.

Apollo 8 coasted for two orbits around the earth as the crew carefully checked out all their systems with Ground Control. When the time drew near for a decision to fire the spacecraft on a flight path towards the moon (TLI, or translunar injection), a hush descended over Mission Control.

At 2 hours 27 minutes, while Apollo 8 was in its second orbit, Capsule Communicator (Cap Com) Mike Collins uttered the fateful words, "You are Go for TLI."

It had taken a colossus, stacked 36 stories high with 6 million pounds of highly explosive fuel and engines, to lift the 10-foot Apollo 8 command module and its propulsion system to its point of departure for the moon.

Now Borman and his crew began aligning their spacecraft and the still-attached third (S-IVB) stage into the proper position for a lunar trajectory. The huge third stage, with its nearly 80-ton explosive charge, stood poised in space like a giant cannon.

At 10:42 A.M. EST, Lovell calmly reported, "Ignition." The S-IVB engines restarted with a long burn over Hawaii lasting 5 minutes 19 seconds and boosting Apollo 8 to the 24,200-mph speed necessary to escape earth's gravity. "You are on your way," radioed Chris Kraft. "You are *really* on your way!" After the burn, the spent S-IVB stage fell away, following a path that would carry it into orbit around the sun.

As the spacecraft settled into TLI, Lovell noncha-

lantly reported, "Tell Conrad he lost his record" (referring to Conrad's altitude record of 850 miles in Gemini XI). The crew was traveling farther and faster than man had ever gone before.

The voyage out took two days. On each day at about 3 P.M. the astronauts appeared live on television screens around the world, showing spectacular views of the receding earth.

The communications network of Goddard Space Flight Center, Greenbelt, Maryland, combined with 14 land stations, four instrumented ships, and eight instrumented aircraft to maintain radio contact with Apollo 8 over the quarter-million-mile distance between earth and moon. Intelsat II and III communication satellites over the Atlantic and Pacific oceans each reserved about 100 voice circuits for communication with Apollo 8 and transmitted TV pictures from the capsule to U.S. and European audiences. Applied Technology Satellites (ATS) II and III augmented commercial transmissions.

The 85-foot antennas at Madrid, Spain, and Canberra, Australia, and the 210-foot antenna at Goldstone, California, provided a continual deep-space radio link with Apollo 8 as the earth's rotation periodically carried each successive ground station out of radio contact.

Early on the morning of December 24 the big center screen at Mission Control underwent a dramatic change. The large illuminated Mercator projection (a method of displaying a map) of the earth that had been displayed for the past three and a half years suddenly disappeared. In its place, flashed a scarred and pockmarked map with names like Mare Tranquillitatis, Mare Crisium, and many craters with such names as Tsiolkovsky, and Grimaldi. The Christmas voyagers of Apollo 8 had reached the vicinity of the moon and the appearance of the lunar map sent a wave of excitement through the control center.

As the spacecraft approached the leading edge of the moon, Cap Com Gerry Carr began the countdown. "Ten seconds to Go . . . five. . . . You are Go all the way." Apollo 8 acknowledged a Go for lunar-orbit insertion at 4:59 A.M. EST and Lovell replied, "We'll see you on the other side," as the spacecraft disappeared behind the moon.

For the first time in history, men were out of sight of (and communication with) the earth. For 34 tense minutes there would be no way of knowing whether the critical firing of the Service Propulsion System (SPS) engine would successfully establish Apollo 8 in lunar orbit or would misfunction and send the as-

An oblique view of the moon's Sea of Tranquillity as seen from the Apollo 8 spacecraft.

tronauts crashing into the moon. If the engine failed to work at all the spacecraft would whip around the moon and head back to earth like a boomerang.

As the moment arrived for Apollo 8 to emerge from behind the moon, Cap Com Gerry Carr began seeking a signal from the spacecraft. Amidst a background of nervous chatter in Mission Control, Carr began summoning the crew: "Apollo 8, Apollo 8, Apollo 8."

The calm reply of Jim Lovell, "Go ahead, Houston," broke the tension that had been mounting in the control center and the room erupted with cheering and applause.

The SPS engine had performed perfectly, slowing the spacecraft down from 5,758 mph to 3,643 mph during a 247-second burn. Apollo 8 went into an el-

liptical 168.5- by 60-mile lunar orbit at 69 hours 15 minutes into the mission. At the time of the critical firing Lovell had commented, "Longest four minutes I ever spent." Spacecraft commander Borman's response to successful orbit insertion was a businesslike, "It's not time for congratulations yet. Dig out the flight plan." A lot of work and another crucial firing of the SPS engine lay ahead before the crew could start their return home and begin breathing more easily.

The crew were the first humans to view, with their own eyes, the backside of the moon. The Cap Com began prompting the crew for an eyewitness account: "What does the old moon look like from 60 miles?"

"Essentially gray ... no color," said Lovell, "like

plaster of Paris or a sort of grayish beach sand." To the crew, the moonscape proved to be as desolate as they had anticipated. Anders observed, "You can see by the numerous craters that this planet has been bombarded through the eons with numerous small asteroids and meteoroids pockmarking the surface every square inch. The backside looks like a sand pile my kids have been playing in for some time. It's all beat up, no definition, just a lot of bumps and holes." The craters appeared rounded at their edges, with some presenting centrally located cones while others had rays emanating from them.

The second black-and-white TV telecast began at 8:40 P.M. on Christmas Eve. The first picture was a dramatic view of the earth rising above the stark lunar landscape. Then, as the TV camera panned across the moonscape, the crew of Apollo 8 shared one of the most inspirational moments of the entire space program with the estimated 1 billion people watching and listening on television and radio throughout the world.

"The vast loneliness is awe-inspiring and it makes you realize just what you have back there on Earth," began Lovell. "For all the people on earth," said Anders, "the crew of Apollo 8 has a message we would like to send you." After a momentary pause, he began reading: "In the beginning God created the Heavens and the Earth."

After four verses of the Book of Genesis, Lovell took up the reading: "And God called the light Day, and the darkness he called Night."

At the end of the eighth verse Borman picked up the familiar words: "And God said, Let the waters under the Heavens be gathered together unto one place, and let the dry land appear; and it was so. And God called the dry land Earth; and the gathering together of the waters He called seas; and God saw that it was good."

The commander added: "And from the crew of Apollo 8, we close with good night, good luck, a Merry Christmas and God bless all of you—all of you on the good earth."

After delivering its Christmas message, Apollo 8 disappeared behind the moon, as if to leave the world to reflect on the words of Genesis that had just been invoked from our past and on the future that was promised by the new technology.

The spacecraft remained in lunar orbit for about 20 hours (ten lunar orbits lasting two hours, as opposed to one earth orbit lasting 90 minutes), as the crew continued experiments and photographed pos-

sible Apollo landing sites and lunar landmarks on the approaches to these landing zones.

Early Christmas morning (1:10 A.M. EST, December 25), again behind the moon and out of contact with the earth, the crew fired the SPS engine.

The burn was perfect (3 minutes 23 seconds), but those on earth did not know whether the engine had fired properly and the crew was homeward bound until Apollo 8 came back into view.

The spacecraft was right on course as it headed back to earth, and the sixth midcourse correction was not needed. Apollo 8 left the moon at approximately 5,500 mph and gathered speed with each passing hour as it headed home under the increasing influence of earth's gravity. As the craft reached the vicinity of the earth on December 27, 1968, it was traveling at 25,000 mph. This was perhaps the most critical part of the mission. At this great speed there was no room for error. If it entered the atmosphere at too steep an angle, the ship would burn to a cinder. If the angle were too shallow, the spacecraft would skip off into deep space. In order to land safely, the crew had to "thread the eye of a needle," entering an imaginary corridor measuring 26 by 400 miles.

After discarding the service module, Apollo 8 hit the bull's-eye, heat shield first, tracing a flaming arc through the atmosphere. The craft was rolled twice so that its designed aerodynamic lift caused it to climb briefly, slowing its rate of descent.

At 24,000 feet and a speed of 300 mph, the three drogue parachutes deployed, slowing the craft down to about 140 mph. At 10,000 feet the three main orange and white (83½-foot) parachutes billowed open, gently dropping Apollo 8 into the Pacific, a mere 5,000 yards from the recovery aircraft carrier U.S.S. Yorktown. It had been 147 hours since launch and the crew was precisely on time.

Apollo 8 was the fifth Apollo craft to fly (the second manned), and the first manned operation of the Apollo system under the conditions for which it was specifically designed. The mission was an overwhelming technical achievement and during the last week of 1968 the press voted Apollo 8 story of the year.

What new things we learned about the moon from the Apollo 8 mission were secondary to the insights it gave us into ourselves as we travel together on the spaceship earth. To astronaut Lovell it appeared as "a grand oasis in the vastness of space." Perhaps that insight is the ultimate reward from our expeditions into space.

Russell Louis Schweickart

Birthplace	Neptune, New Jersey
Date of Birth	October 25, 1935
Height	6′
Weight	160 lbs.
Eyes	Blue
Hair	Red
Marital Status/Wife	Clare
Daughters	Vicki, Elin, Diana
Sons	Randolph, Russell (twins)
Recreational Interests	Backpacking, hunting, fishing
Service Affiliation	Civilian
Flight Record	More than 3,650 hours flying time (3,250 in jet aircraft). Logged 241 hours 1 minute during one space flight, of which 1 hour 7 minutes were spent in two EVA's outside the lunar module during its first manned test flight (orbiting the earth).
Education and Training	Bachelor of Science degree in Aeronautical Engineering from the Massachusetts Institute of Technology in 1956. Upon graduation Schweickart served as a pilot in the U.S. Air Force from 1956 to 1960. He was recalled to active duty for a year in 1961 in the Air National Guard. Before becoming an astronaut, he was a research scientist at the Experimental Astronomy Laboratory at MIT. He conducted research in upper-atmosphere physics and applied astronomy, as well as research

in stabilization of stellar images and star tracking, earning a Master of Science degree in Aeronautics and Astronautics in 1963 with a thesis on stratospheric radiance.

Astronaut Career He was chosen with the third group of astronauts on October 18, 1963 and was awarded the NASA Distinguished Service Medal, and the NASA Exceptional Service Medal. His first assignment as an astronaut was as lunar module pilot on Apollo 9, March 3–13, 1969. His crewmates were both veterans from Gemini flights, James McDivitt, spacecraft commander, and David Scott, command module pilot. This was Schweickart's first flight. He performed a spacewalk on and around the lunar module while docked with the command module, testing the feasibility of crew transfers from outside the space vehicles in the event the internally located docking tunnel became impassable.

The suit he was wearing for his EVA was similar to the backpacked 90-pound Portable Life-Support System that would supply air to astronauts walking on the moon.

Schweickart also assisted McDivitt in successfully flying the lunar module in space for the first time. At one point in the flight the lander, nicknamed *Spider*, was more than 100 miles from the mother ship. Rendezvous and docking with the command module had to be successful, for without a heat shield, there was no other way McDivitt and Schweickart could return it safely to earth. The performance of the courageous astronauts was flawless, rating the lunar module ready for orbital flight around the moon.

Schweickart became backup commander for Skylab 2, the first manned Skylab mission, and in addition was responsible for monitoring the development of the Apollo telescope mount (ATM) and planning the extravehicular activities for Project Skylab.

On May 1, 1974, he left the Astronaut Office at Johnson Space Center for an assignment at Headquarters NASA in Washington, D.C., to identify user needs for data produced by NASA's applications program, and to assess the socioeconomic value of the applications programs. In November 1976 he became Assistant for Payload Operations in the Office of Planning and Program Integration at Headquarters NASA.

He took a leave of absence from NASA in the summer of 1977 to assist the California governor's office.

Apollo 9: The Last Link

March 3–13, 1969

The Apollo 9 mission was a ten-day mission designed to simulate the round-trip time between earth and moon, including the time necessary for a lunar landing, a stay on the surface, and ascent. The lunar module (LM) would be powered up and powered down three times by the crew and every aspect of the lander would be closely checked in earth orbit before committing it to the planned lunar orbital flight on Apollo 10.

Veteran Gemini astronaut James McDivitt (commander) would fly the LM with Russell Schweickart (LM pilot), who would be making his first space flight. David Scott, another Gemini veteran, was assigned to fly the command module (CM). Mission planners did not want a rookie flying alone in the CM if difficulties were to occur during rendezvous and docking with the LM.

This would be only the second time (the first was

Gemini VI and VII) in the space program that two manned spacecraft would be in flight simultaneously. For ease of identification, Scott chose *Gumdrop* as the sign for his command module. The call sign for McDivitt and Schweickart in the LM was *Spider.* This custom of choosing code names such as these would continue through the remainder of Project Apollo.

The frail lander was the first true spacecraft. It had been designed to fly only in the vacuum of space and its ability to stand up to the oscillations of a Saturn V launch was a prime concern. Equally important was the ability of the Apollo command module and the lunar module to withstand the stress loads of coupled space flight.

Apollo 8 had verified, at close range, the lunar landing sites and proved out all the Apollo hardware and communications at lunar distance—except for the all-important last link, the lunar module.

The test began with the launch of Apollo 9 from Complex 39, Pad A, at 11:00 A.M. EST on March 3, 1969. The Saturn V booster carried the spacecraft combination into a 120-mile-high earth orbit. Three hours later the crew began their carefully rehearsed lunar flight drill by first separating their spacecraft from the third stage of the Saturn V. Next, they turned around and docked with the lunar module, which was still tucked into an adapter section of the third stage. Explosive bolts fired and compressed springs propelled *Spider* like a jack-in-the-box out of the rocket's third stage.

The command module and LM were now linked head to head in orbit and the crew tested the strength of their docking mechanism by firing Apollo 9's powerful engine at various angles, moving the linked craft side to side like a dog wagging its tail.

Scott radioed to Mission Control: "You can feel the whole thing shake and vibrate, but it's pretty solid."

The second day into the mission was spent tracking landmarks, photographing the earth's resources with special film and filter combinations, and doing practice maneuvers that involved firing the Apollo's main engine.

McDivitt and Schweickart entered the LM through

The lunar module *Spider* with landing gear deployed and surface probes extended from the foot pads.

the docking tunnel on the third day in orbit. They spent their time grooming *Spider* for its flight. They checked its electrical system and computer, extended its leg-like landing gear, and fired its descent engine for the first time in manned space flight. After a brief TV transmission from inside the LM, McDivitt and Schweickart returned to the command module to complete the day's experiments.

On the fourth day the crew donned pressure suits in preparation for the extravehicular exercises that had been planned. McDivitt and Schweickart returned to the LM and depressurized the craft. The extravehicular exercises would involve Scott in the command module and Schweickart in the LM.

As the two spacecraft passed 152 miles high over the Pacific Ocean, Schweickart eased through the exit hatch of the LM in the same manner that future astronauts would leave after landing on the moon. His pressure suit was not connected to the spacecraft by an umbilical life-support system. Instead, Schweickart was backpacking the kind of independent Portable Life-Support System (weighing 90 pounds) that would supply oxygen to astronauts on the moon. As he moved onto *Spider*'s "front porch," he slipped his feet into the gold-painted restraints and began to photograph Apollo 9 and the earth below. For Schweickart this moment was overwhelming and he exulted, "Boy, oh boy, what a view!"

The Portable Life Support System Schweickart was wearing was being checked out for the first time, and he had no difficulty with it during his 45-minute stay on the LM platform. As he began checking the lights that had been trained on specific parts of the spacecraft and the handholds, his crewmate Dave Scott eased open *Gumdrop*'s hatch and emerged partway into the vacuum of space. Scott wore the same type of gold-visored helmet as did Schweickart, in order to protect his eyes from the harsh glare of the sun but, unlike Schweickart, he was connected to the spacecraft by an umbilical life-support system.

Describing their experiences as they worked, the men took some photographs and retrieved thermal samples located on the spacecraft exterior. After testing the maneuverability of their pressure suits, the accessibility of sample locations, and the usefulness of the handholds and restraints, both men returned to their spacecraft.

On the fifth day of the mission, the crew prepared for the crucial flight of the LM. After entering the lunar module, McDivitt and Schweickart powered up *Spider* and cautiously separated from *Gumdrop*. As *Spider* began its first lone venture into space, McDivitt gracefully rotated her before the watchful eyes of Scott in the *Gumdrop* command module. Satisfied with the integrity of the lunar module, the crew then pulsed the engine enough to move *Spider* into a parallel orbit 3 miles distant from the command ship. The LM was on its own, but twice each orbit the two spacecraft were close enough for Scott to initiate rescue operations from the command module.

The LM crew rehearsed the possible phases of the lunar approach and departure for nearly six hours

The scorched Apollo 9 spacecraft awaiting retrieval with flotation collar in place.

while orbiting 135 miles above the earth and up to 111 miles away from and out of sight of *Gumdrop.* After the final test firing of *Spider's* descent engine, the descent stage was jettisoned and the LM's ascent engine was test-fired for the first time. McDivitt then adjusted their position 10 miles below and 80 miles behind the command module and began the approach to a rendezvous and docking, much the same as the actual event would later take place during the Apollo 11 mission.

As *Spider* approached within sight of the Apollo 9 command ship, a relieved and happy Scott welcomed back his crewmates: "You're the biggest, friendliest, funniest looking spider I've ever seen."

As they drew closer, McDivitt and Schweickart carefully guided the LM's hollow drogue into the docking probe on *Gumdrop* and when a buzzer signaled their union, McDivitt exclaimed, "Wow! I haven't heard a sound that good for a long time." By the end of the fifth day into the mission, March 7, 1969, Apollo 9 had successfully completed 97 percent of its objectives and the lunar module proved itself ready for the final test—to fly while in lunar orbit.

During the final five days, the crew's workload lightened but they still contributed valuable experiments in landmark tracking and earth photography and continued to check out the command module systems to verify the craft's readiness for the lunar landing missions.

Apollo 9 splashed down in the Atlantic within 3 miles of its prime recovery ship, the carrier *Guadalcanal* at 12:53 P.M. EST, March 13, 1969. As she settled onto the waves, there spread a renewed confidence throughout Apollo that before the year was out another *Spider* would carry two astronauts to the moon's surface.

Apollo 10: Barnstorming the Moon

May 18–26, 1969

Through the rotation system worked out for the Apollo missions by Deke Slayton, the veteran Gemini astronauts Thomas Stafford (commander), John Young (command module pilot), and Eugene Cernan (LM pilot) drew the assignment of flying the first complete Apollo spacecraft system into lunar orbit. Stafford and Young each would be making his third space flight and Cernan would be making his second. The crew had provided backup support for Apollo 7 and under the system they would skip two missions (numbers 8 and 9) and assume the prime crew slot for Apollo 10.

The flight of *Spider* on Apollo 9 was perhaps the most hazardous space venture to date. If McDivitt and Schweickart had failed to unite the LM with the command ship, they would have had no way of returning to earth and would have perished in space.

The LM, however, had proved its flying capabilities in earth orbit and all that remained now was to show that it would do the same in lunar orbit. Apollo 10 was the final rehearsal before men would be committed to landing on the moon.

At 11:49 A.M. EST, on May 18, 1969, the entire spacecraft combination was lifted into orbit from Complex 39, Pad B, by the huge Saturn V moon rocket.

The crew was given a Go for translunar injection (TLI) as they passed over Australia on their second orbit. The third-stage J-2 engine was restarted and fired for 5 minutes 42 seconds to boost the craft outward from earth's field of gravity.

At a speed of 24,250 mph, Apollo 10 was on a perfect heading, and for the second time in five months man was again visiting the moon. The command ship's service propulsion system (main engine) was positioned forward as it towed the trailing LM towards its first rendezvous with the moon.

The docking maneuver was covered by the first live TV colorcasts from space, and later the crew treated earth audiences to the first color view of their planet from thousands of miles in space. Cernan identified the Rocky Mountains, Baja California, and described Alaska as being "socked in" with cloud cover. He also pointed out a low-pressure weather system over New England.

The crew was in high spirits on the journey to the

moon. No doubt the freeze-dried diet, now standard for space flight, added to their good humor. The diet was supplemented by individually wrapped commercial bread and the makings for ham, chicken, and tuna salad. The only complaint by the astronauts was their distaste for the chlorinated drinking water.

Apollo 10's outward journey proceeded almost exactly as planned. The 24,250-mph speed at which it approached the moon was reduced hour by hour by the continued gravitational attraction of the earth to a rate of 2,000 mph. Then, as the craft entered the moon's gravitational field, it gradually picked up speed. Apollo 10 was traveling at 5,500 mph (relative to the moon) just prior to entering lunar orbit.

The route the crew had taken to reach the moon was identical to the trajectory that was planned for the Apollo 11 mission. On May 21, 1969, three days and four hours after launch, Apollo 10 fired its 16,000-pound-thrust Service Propulsion System engine for almost six minutes to reduce speed to 3,600 mph and allow the spacecraft to be captured by the moon's gravitational field. The ship was swept into an elliptical orbit 195 miles by 69 miles, which was eventually circularized to about 69 miles.

Approximately 20 minutes into the first orbit, the crew began describing the lunar terrain over which they passed. Stafford noted that they were moving out of the highlands into the mare area, the so-called dry seas. He reported a "couple of real good volcanoes." This observation was of considerable interest to astronomers who were divided as to whether crater formations were the result of meteor impacts or of volcanic activity. Young described the "volcanoes" as "all white on the outside but definitely black inside."

The first landmark the crew spotted was the Sea of Crises, bathed in lunar sunrise. Stafford commented that the sides of the ridges crossing the mare floor went "straight down, just like the Canyon Diablo in New Mexico." (All the Apollo astronauts had been

The Apollo 10 command module as viewed from the lunar module 60 miles above the moon's far side.

A helicopter from the USS *Princeton* recovers an Apollo 10 astronaut.

trained in lunar geology on field trips to areas on earth that had features similar to the moon.)

The crew found the far side of the moon, the side that is never visible to earth, well lighted by reflected light from earth (earthshine), and had no trouble finding landmarks. Cernan observed that this side was "lit up like a Christmas tree." Stafford found the detailed visibility "phenomenal."

On the third orbit of the moon, the crew turned on the TV cameras and began the first live colorcast from the moon. The opening view was the Sea of Smyth near the edge of the moon's far side. Stafford then turned the camera on the Sea of Fertility and the great crater Langrenus, with its 2-mile-high walls and rugged 7,000-foot mountain peak standing at its center.

Much of the gray-white to brownish lunar terrain was filled with craters and boulders of all sizes. The landing area intended for Apollo 11, however, appeared to be free of boulders and the craters in the area were small and shallow. There appeared to be sufficient smooth areas for a landing.

On May 22, as the second day in orbit began, the crew noticed that insulation had loosened in the docking tunnel in the LM, clogged a vent and allowed the LM to slip about 3.50 degrees out of line with the Apollo command and service modules. This caused great concern, for if the docking latches became damaged, the two crewmen flying the LM in lunar orbit might not be able to dock and return to the mother ship.

After Mission Control issued precautions to the crew, Stafford and Cernan began preparations for undocking the LM. As the instructions were acknowledged the two linked spacecraft passed behind the moon, blocking all communication with the ground for the period it was on the far side. A short time later, Stafford pulled the LM (code name *Snoopy*) away from the command module (*Charlie Brown*) and began the final check of the flight plans and hardware for the upcoming Apollo 11 lunar landing mission.

The undocking and separation maneuver began behind the moon and out of communication with Houston Mission Control. This was only the second manned flight of the LM, and at lunar distance confidence in newly acquired techniques and brand-new hardware was severely put to the test. After 36 tense minutes, Apollo reappeared on schedule with its companion *Snoopy* flying formation 50 feet away. Apollo 10 and the LM maintained their station-keeping while Houston Control checked out all the systems with the crew before Stafford and Cernan departed for the lunar surface on their planned barnstorming flight in the LM. The exchanges with Mission Control now were brief and to the point. The previously relaxed and lighthearted demeanor of the crew had vanished as they strained to complete their tasks on schedule. In edgy tones, Cernan radioed, "There are so many things to do in such a short time."

At 3:35 P.M. EST, Stafford and Cernan positioned the LM in a braking position, fired the descent engine, and parted company with the command module. Young maintained the mother ship in a state of alert, ready in an instant to begin the delicate and extremely complex rescue of the LM if problems developed.

The LM flew essentially the same approach pattern that future astronauts would take on their landing attempts. This time, however, the crew broke off their approach to the lunar surface at about 38,000 feet altitude. Almost an hour after parting with the command ship, the LM had taken the astronauts closer than any human had ever been to the moon. An excited Cernan radioed, "Hello Houston, we is down among it!" as they flew within 9.6 statute miles above Apollo 11's intended number-two landing site in the Sea of Tranquillity. They described the landing area as being "pretty smooth, like wet clay, like a dry river bed in New Mexico or Arizona." Stafford commented, "It looks like all you have to do is put your tail wheel down and we're there.... The craters look flat and smooth at the bottom. It should be real easy [for the Apollo 11 landing]."

At the low point of the LM's second swing around the moon, Stafford and Cernan jettisoned the descent stage and fired the LM's ascent engine for 15 seconds to position themselves in an 11- by 190-mile orbit that would allow a rendezvous with Young in the mother ship. It was 6:44 P.M. EST on May 22. The LM was now in a looping orbit above and behind the command module, trailing it by 368 statute miles. By 9:07 P.M. EST, they had closed to within 43 statute miles. The LM was blazing a trail back to the command module that would be followed by future astronauts ascending from the lunar surface.

The command module floated passively in orbit as Stafford and Cernan closed in to docking range. However, Young was kept busy checking the rendezvous approach of the LM every step of the way, making sextant observations and measuring the distances of separation on an ultra-high-frequency radio just in case a rescue was needed.

The rendezvous was flawless and docking was completed at 10:11 P.M. EST. As Cernan and Stafford emerged through the tunnel into the command ship 14 minutes later, Cernan declared, "Man, I'm glad I'm getting out." More than 6½ hours had transpired since Cernan and Stafford had started their descent towards the lunar surface in the LM.

The LM had performed beautifully in eight hours of independent flight. (When Houston Control heard of the successful docking, someone brought out a large cartoon of Snoopy kissing Charlie Brown. The caption read, "Smack. You're right on target, Charlie Brown.") With the tunnel sealed, the LM was jettisoned and a remote-controlled firing of its engine cast it into orbit around the sun.

The final day in lunar orbit was spent adding more data to Apollo's storehouse of lunar information.

When it came time to return to earth, the SPS engine was fired and at 5:25 A.M. EST on Friday, May 23, Apollo 10 fired out of lunar orbit and headed home. The fast return flight path would bring the crew back to earth in just 54 hours. Their course was established with such precision that the only midcourse correction needed was made only three hours before reentry. The change in velocity required was slightly more than 2 feet per second or about one part in 20,000.

The service module was cast off 15 minutes before reentry as Apollo 10 streaked towards its landing area in the Pacific, 450 statute miles east of Samoa. Splashdown occurred at 11:52 A.M. EST on May 26, 3.4 statute miles from the recovery carrier *Princeton*. The mission had lasted 192 hours 3 minutes and ended precisely on time.

As the crew boarded the *Princeton* 39 minutes later, a large sign was put up in Houston Control with "51 days to launch" inscribed on it—a reminder, as if one were needed, that the next flight out would be going all the way.

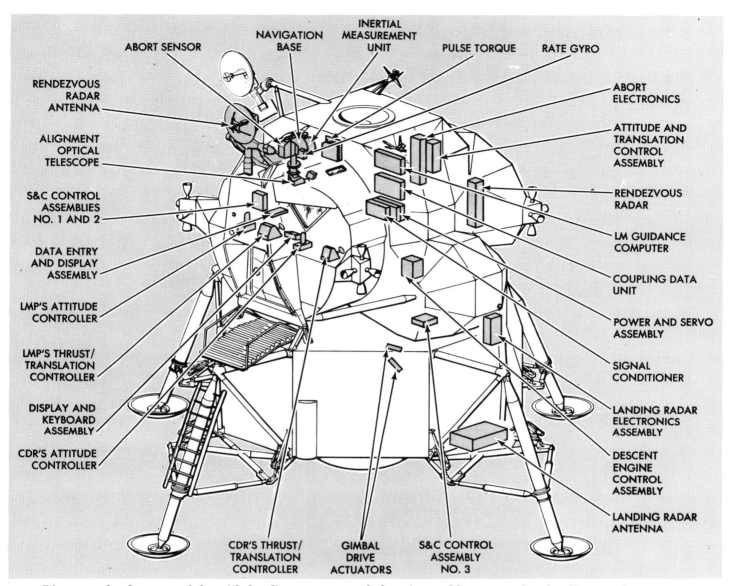

ABORT SENSOR

NAVIGATION BASE

INERTIAL MEASUREMENT UNIT

PULSE TORQUE

RATE GYRO

RENDEZVOUS RADAR ANTENNA

ALIGNMENT OPTICAL TELESCOPE

S&C CONTROL ASSEMBLIES NO. 1 AND 2

DATA ENTRY AND DISPLAY ASSEMBLY

LMP'S ATTITUDE CONTROLLER

LMP'S THRUST/ TRANSLATION CONTROLLER

DISPLAY AND KEYBOARD ASSEMBLY

CDR'S ATTITUDE CONTROLLER

ABORT ELECTRONICS

ATTITUDE AND TRANSLATION CONTROL ASSEMBLY

RENDEZVOUS RADAR

LM GUIDANCE COMPUTER

COUPLING DATA UNIT

POWER AND SERVO ASSEMBLY

SIGNAL CONDITIONER

LANDING RADAR ELECTRONICS ASSEMBLY

DESCENT ENGINE CONTROL ASSEMBLY

LANDING RADAR ANTENNA

CDR'S THRUST/ TRANSLATION CONTROLLER

GIMBAL DRIVE ACTUATORS

S&C CONTROL ASSEMBLY NO. 3

Diagram of a lunar module with landing gear extended as it would appear after landing on the moon's surface.

Apollo 11: Footprints at Tranquillity Base

July 16–24, 1969

At 12:30 P.M. on May 20, 1969, the day before Apollo 10 reached the moon, the 456-foot-high doors of the Vertical Assembly Building, where the giant moon rockets were assembled, slowly opened. Saturn booster Number 506, with its 3 million working parts, had taken five months to assemble. The various sections of the space vehicle were never together in one place before they arrived at the Vertical Assembly Building. By the time they were constructed, checked out, and readied for shipment to the Cape, most of them were already three years old. The vehicle's first stage had come from Louisiana; the second and third stages from California. They were tested and made ready in Alabama. The guidance and navigation equipment was assembled in Wisconsin and checked out in Massachusetts. The spacecraft systems came from Florida and New Hampshire and the lunar lander from New York. In one form or another, Apollo involved every section of the country in a national effort surpassed only during wartime.

The huge 363-foot rocket sat atop a crawler-transporter big enough (115 by 130 feet) to accommodate a baseball diamond. As it rode majestically through the doorway toward the launch area, there was little question but that the journey to the moon had finally begun.

The crawler had eight cleated tank-like tracks, each measuring 7 by 41 feet. An individual cleat weighed one ton. The path to Launch Complex 39, Pad A, was paved with 8 inches of Alabama river rock to distribute the 9,000-ton load (3,000-ton crawler, 6,000-ton unfueled rocket and Mobile Launch Platform) evenly. A hydraulic leveling system on the crawler kept the Saturn V to within one degree of absolute vertical.

The 3.5-mile trip to Pad A was painstakingly slow (maximum speed, 0.9 mph), taking six hours to place the towering vehicle into position. (Maximum speed was not maintained throughout the trip.) In the one month and 26 days before launch, the preparations team would pore over every aspect of the vehicle with the same painstaking care.

The crew for Apollo 11 had been officially an-

nounced on January 9, 1969, about two weeks after the splashdown of Apollo 8. Veteran Gemini astronauts, Neil Armstrong and Edwin "Buzz" Aldrin had been the backup crew for Apollo 8 and drew the assignments of Apollo 11 spacecraft commander and lunar module pilot under the usual crew rotation system.

The third crew member, Michael Collins, also was a Gemini veteran. Collins originally had been scheduled to fly with Apollo 8 but was grounded when surgery was required to repair a displaced disk of the spinal column in his neck. James Lovell left the Armstrong-Aldrin backup team to fill in for Collins on the memorable Apollo 8 Christmas mission to the moon. Now back in full health and returned to flying status, Collins would have his second chance at history as command module pilot for the scheduled Apollo 11 moon landing.

Armstrong, Aldrin, and Collins began the busiest six months of their lives, scrambling from the docking simulator at Langley, Virginia, to the centrifuge rides at Houston, then back to the Cape to the flight simulators, and so on, and so on. . . . Armstrong and Aldrin spent long hours studying maps of the moon and increasing their knowledge of photography and geology, as they prepared for their visit on the lunar surface.

In selecting a symbol to wear as a mission patch on their flight suits, the Apollo 11 crew took care not to include their names. Thousands of people had contributed to the lunar landing effort and this was *their* mission as well.

James Lovell, Armstrong's backup for the mission, suggested that an American eagle be incorporated in the design. Eventually, the crew settled for a design that showed an eagle carrying an olive branch to the moon in extended talons. The mission name Apollo 11 appeared at the top of the patch with the earth in the background. The eagle also seemed an appropriate symbol for the lunar lander, and the call sign *Eagle* was quickly adopted by Armstrong and Aldrin. Collins settled on the call sign *Columbia* for the command ship. Columbia, after Christopher Co-

The Apollo 11 Saturn V moon rocket in position at Kennedy Space Center's massive Launch Complex 39A.

lumbus, is the name that personifies the United States of America in literary and poetic usage.

(In 1865, Jules Verne had written about an imaginary trip from the earth to the moon. His spaceship carried three men and was launched from Tampa, Florida. Like Apollo 11, the ship was later recovered in the Pacific Ocean. Its name—*Columbiad*.)

With launch day two weeks away, the astronauts' physician, Dr. Charles A. Berry, placed the Apollo 11 crew in semiquarantine. Contact was limited to their colleagues in training and immediate families to avoid a last-minute interruption in the launch schedule due to a contracted illness. Even the scheduled dinner with the President of the United States on the eve of the launch was cancelled.

At 7 P.M. EST on July 10, 1969, the master clock in Firing Room 1 was started, signaling the beginning of the final countdown for Apollo 11. In a sense, however, the clock for Apollo had started ticking back in March 1955 when scientists and engineers at the Rocketdyne Division of North American Aviation first established the feasibility of developing a rocket engine powerful enough to carry men to the moon. A single-chambered F-1 engine was shown to be capable of 1 million pounds of thrust.

Five years later, on July 29, 1960, the concept of manned lunar flight had been formalized with the official announcement of Project Apollo. Abe Silverstein, Director of Space Flight Development, had first proposed the name "Apollo" because of its fitting connotations and the precedent set by Project Mercury. In Greek mythology, Apollo was the son of Zeus, ruler of the gods, and was the patron god of archers. Most importantly, he was also identified with the Sun. Apollo's twin sister, Artemis, was goddess of the Moon, the ultimate destination of Project Apollo.

In the final hours before launch, hundreds of technicians and engineers began the final examination of every component of the moon rocket. They carefully routed electrical power through the huge vehicle, testing and retesting each system as they slowly brought it to life. This launch was different from all the others. This one was special. The pad crew knew it and so did the estimated 1 million spectators who began crowding into the Cape area to witness the launch. The air was electric as everyone pondered the historic step that was about to be taken.

The astronauts, secluded in the crew's quarters near the launch area, were not unaffected by the special nature of their mission. From the moment their assignment became official, their professional and private lives came under increasing scrutiny as the rest of the world wondered what type of men fate had chosen to represent them on a journey to another world. It was not an easy task being singled out as separate and apart from the 3 billion people of one's own race.

Armstrong, Aldrin, and Collins were holding up well under the pressure of all this attention and the immensity of the task that lay ahead of them. They maintained a good attitude during their training and throughout the mission, a fact which undoubtedly had much to do with its ultimate success.

After a quiet dinner on July 15, the eve of *the launch,* the crew went to sleep, each man knowing full well that after the morrow, their lives would never again be the same.

Armstrong, Aldrin, and Collins were awakened shortly after 3 A.M. EST. It was July 16, 1969. The rehearsals were over now and the astronauts went about their preparations quietly and efficiently. At 5:27 A.M. EST the fully suited astronauts boarded the van for a ride to the Saturn V moon rocket. As the men entered the launch tower elevator for the 320-foot ride up to *Columbia,* each withdrew into his own private thoughts. The earth receded as the elevator began to rise; for the astronauts, the journey to the moon had already begun.

The launch team continued to pump fuel into all three of the Saturn stages in order to maintain a maximum load of propellant right up to lift-off. At T−4 minutes and 50 seconds, Launch Operations Manager Paul Donnelly wished the astronauts "Good luck and Godspeed," to which Neil Armstrong replied, "Thank you very much. We know it will be a good flight."

The engineers and technicians at Launch Control watched their screens intently, monitoring the "red line values" registering in front of them. These were the tolerances in temperatures and pressures they did not want to go above or below, and they stood ready to call out any deviations from the plans.

As the count approached T−3 minutes 15 seconds, the countdown came under the automatic control of the huge computers monitoring the hundreds of events going on inside the launch vehicle. At T−50 seconds the launch vehicle was automatically transferred to full internal power. Tension began to mount as technicians nervously eyed dials and the crowds began taking their final pictures before the launch. Neil Armstrong reported: "It has been a real smooth countdown."

Then, at T−17 seconds, the guidance system that

Many of the one million spectators spent the night before the Apollo 11 launch on nearby beaches.

The Apollo 11 lift-off was as awesome as its mission.

would control the rocket's flight until it reached orbit came into full internal power. The five huge F-1 engines of the Saturn V ignited at T−8.9 seconds, burning 15 tons of fuel per second as they developed the 7.5 million pounds of thrust necessary to carry their precious cargo to the awaiting moon, 218,096 miles away.

The mighty rocket strained against the four 40,-000-pound arms of the clamps holding it in place. Not until the computers sensed that the engines and the millions of parts were working properly did they order Saturn's release. "T minus 6, 5, 4, 3, 2, 1, zero! All engines running!" The voice of Jack King in Apollo-Saturn Launch Control trembled with emotion: "Lift . . . we have a lift-off!"

The buildings and the ground in the launch area trembled as the 6.5-million-pound moon rocket (the weight of 25 fully loaded air liners) thundered off the pad, making the biggest, loudest sustained noise ever created by man. Lift-off occurred at precisely 8:32 A.M. EST, and the dramatic departure reduced the crowds to silence. The flawless launch was telecast live to 33 countries on six different continents. In the U.S., an estimated 25 million viewers watched on TV.

Apollo 11 attained a 118.5-mile-high parking orbit at a point 1,400 miles downrange.

The crew spent nearly two orbits checking out equipment and communications. During the second orbit, as the spacecraft was passing northeast of Australia, Ground Control gave it a Go for insertion into a lunar trajectory. The crew refired the still-attached third stage (S-IVB) of the rocket and headed toward the moon at the required 24,200-mph velocity. Command module pilot Collins then positioned *Columbia* face to face with *Eagle* (the lunar module), which had been stored in the third stage, and completed the docking maneuver. With *Eagle* attached to its nose, *Columbia* drew away from the spent third stage and continued toward the moon.

Once on course, the crew settled into a relaxed work schedule, performing housekeeping and navigational duties. They also transmitted four color telecasts before entering lunar orbit three days later on July 19. Apollo 11 was traveling 4,000 mph (relative to the moon) as it slid behind the moon, missing it by a scant 300 miles. At 75 hours 56 minutes into the mission, while still on the moon's far side, the astronauts fired their SPS engine, establishing themselves in a 194.3- by 70.5-mile lunar orbit. During the second lunar orbit, they made a live color telecast showing spectacular views of the moon's surface and the approach to Apollo 11's Landing Site 2, the smooth-surfaced Sea of Tranquillity. Armstrong began pointing out lunar landmarks and described an unexplained glow near the crater Aristarchus that some scientists later believed was volcanic activity.

A second burn of the main engine circularized and lowered Apollo 11's orbit to an average 68 statute miles. As the crew prepared for the next day's lunar landing, pressure began to settle in. Twenty-five centuries of man's scientific and technical skills were embodied in *Columbia* and *Eagle*. They represented the limit of his technology. So far, the millions of parts and thousands of systems had worked well enough to get the space voyagers into lunar orbit. When the descent to the surface was made, *Eagle* would be pushed as never before. Would it hold up? When Armstrong and Aldrin left the bounds of human experience and crossed over into the unknown, would the surface hand them any perilous surprises? The tension mounted steadily.

On the night of July 19 the crew completed a final check of *Eagle* and reluctantly returned through the docking tunnel to the mother ship *Columbia*. Although it wasn't in the flight plan, Armstrong and Aldrin made a mental check of all the procedures for the landing and carefully set aside the necessary clothing and equipment. After covering the hatch windows and dousing the lights, the crew settled into a night of fitful sleep.

"Apollo 11, Apollo 11, good morning from the Black Team." The next morning, Ground Control awakened the crew as gently as possible. After breakfast, *Columbia* began to hum with activity as Collins assisted Armstrong and Aldrin with their preparations and then eased them into the lunar module.

After sealing themselves inside *Eagle*, Armstrong and Aldrin turned on its electrical power and made an intensive series of joint checks with Collins in *Columbia*. They paid particular attention to switch settings and the propulsion systems. The final checkout for *Eagle* was completed in an efficient and businesslike manner, 30 minutes ahead of schedule.

During the thirteenth orbit of the moon, Ground Control radioed: "You're Go for undocking." Two minutes later, Apollo 11 swept behind the moon and performed the undocking maneuver at 12:46 P.M. EST on July 20. When the two craft had separated to a safe distance, Armstrong put *Eagle* into a slow roll so that Collins could give her a good looking-over from his vantage point in *Columbia* to check her general condition and specifically to see that the four legs of

the landing gear were fully extended and locked into position.

When the two spacecraft reappeared from behind the moon, Houston Control anxiously inquired, "Hello, *Eagle*. . . . How does it look, Neil?" Armstrong replied enthusiastically, "The *Eagle* has wings!"

As *Eagle* began its final flight across the face of the moon before beginning the powered descent, Houston signaled Collins to begin increasing *Columbia*'s distance to the planned 2 miles' separation before *Eagle* fired her descent engine.

Collins radioed *Eagle*, "I think you've got a fine looking flying machine there, *Eagle*, despite the fact you're upside down." Armstrong retorted, "Somebody's upside down."

With this final attempt at breaking the tension passed, Collins radioed a pensive farewell, "Okay, *Eagle*. . . . You guys take care." Armstrong replied directly, "See you later."

At 1:12 P.M. EST, Collins fired the command ship's rockets and began to pull away from Armstrong and Aldrin.

Both spacecraft again disappeared behind the moon and 9 minutes later at 2:08 P.M. EST the onboard guidance and navigation computer automatically fired the descent engine for 29.8 seconds, placing the craft in an elliptical orbit with a low point of 50,000 feet. *Eagle* was on its way down to the lunar surface.

The suspense in Mission Control was almost unbearable as the flight controllers silently awaited word from *Eagle*.

Columbia was the first to reappear from the far side of the moon and at 2:47 P.M. EST Collins cheerfully reported to Houston, "Listen, babe. Everything's going just swimmingly! Beautiful!"

A relieved Mission Control next heard from *Eagle* as Aldrin calmly reported, "Roger. The burn was on time." He then began reading out data from the beginning of the descent-engine firing, updating Houston on the events that had transpired while *Eagle* was out of radio contact.

The lunar lander had been lowered from an initial altitude of 65.5 to 21 statute miles and was arcing steadily downward. Armstrong was "standing" on the right side of *Eagle*'s cockpit with Aldrin to his left. The two astronauts were loosely harnessed in front of the control panel and were outstretched, standing with their feet (and descent engine) toward the line of flight. Both men were facing away from the moon's surface.

The data from *Eagle* continued to "look great" to Mission Control and they gave the crew the green light for the next engine firing, the powered descent initiation (PDI), which represented the 12-minute final burn that would carry them to a soft landing.

When *Eagle* reached the 50,000-foot low point, Armstrong would have to choose between going for the landing or continuing in his orbital path back to the mother ship. As this mark was reached, a green light on the computer display panel registered "99," notifying him that he had five seconds in which to make a decision.

At 3:05 P.M. EST Armstrong pressed the Proceed button and they crossed over into the unknown, venturing closer to the moon than any human had before them.

As the astronauts entered their glide path to the landing site, communication problems developed. The situation at Houston became extremely tense as Mission Control tried to make *Eagle* aware of the problem, "*Eagle*. . . . We've got data drop-out." Houston was getting just barely enough signal to continue *Eagle* on its drive to the surface, so it used the mother ship *Columbia* a number of times to relay messages to *Eagle* through the broken and spotty transmission. Eventually, Houston resorted to coaching the crew in *Eagle* to the proper antenna alignments as the descent continued. In this way, just enough radio transmission was maintained to enable Houston to guide *Eagle* to carry out the most critical phase of the mission.

The throttleable descent engine began building up thrust gradually as *Eagle* continued its downward arc toward the landing site 250 miles away. At 2 minutes 20 seconds into the burn (descent-engine firing), the lander had slowed down to less than 3,000 mph and was passing through 47,000 feet altitude. Just then, Aldrin reported a problem to Houston, "Oh! Houston. I'm getting a little fluctuation in the AC voltage now. Could be our meter maybe, huh?" A quick reaction to the situation by Houston found everything within normal limits, and the astronauts were given a reassuring report, "Roger. Stand by. Looking good to us. You're still looking good at 3, coming up 3 minutes."

It was about now that the astronauts noticed that they were on a path that would take them beyond their intended landing site. "Our position checks downrange show us to be a little long," reported Armstrong.

Eagle passed over Sidewinder Rille at an altitude of 40,000 feet, descending at a rate of 60 mph. It was 4 minutes into the burn and the astronauts were within 80 miles of their designated landing point.

Eagle was approaching the 300-foot-high lunar landmark, Last Ridge, at a velocity of 2,100 mph when Armstrong barked, "Program Alarm! It's a 1202! Give us a reading on the 1202 Program Alarm." Again Houston reacted with reassuring speed, "Roger. We got—We're Go on that alarm."

The altitude was now 33,500 feet and the landing radar was reeling off altimeter readings for the descent in rapid succession.

At 27,000 feet altitude, Aldrin signaled another alarm, and was again reassured.

Radio transmissions from the *Eagle* were still breaking up. As they passed over Last Ridge at an altitude of 21,000 feet, the crew began to throttle down the lander. Aldrin chimed in, "throttle down . . . better than the simulator," comparing this maneuver to the hundreds of practice lunar landings he had made in flight simulators at the Cape. Houston radioed, "At 7 minutes [into the burn] you're looking great to us, *Eagle*." The spacecraft was now traveling at a lateral velocity of 818 mph and the crew was preparing for the 18-second *pitchover* maneuver, in which the lander would begin to roll slowly at an upright position (descent engine down), allowing the astronauts to view the brownish-gray plain that was their landing area.

At 7 minutes 30 seconds into the burn, *Eagle* began the pitchover maneuver. The altitude was now 16,-300 feet and the landing site was only 13 miles away. The computer was still guiding the lander.

As the lander arrived at 9,200 feet altitude, the astronauts reached their first checkpoint on their glide path, "Hi-gate" (code name P64), at 8 minutes 30 seconds into the burn. At this point, Armstrong had just 70 seconds in which to check over and redesignate a new landing site, if necessary. Their target was only 5 miles away and they were traveling toward it at less than 300 mph and dropping at a rate of less than 100 mph. They were now in the approach phase of their flight and their altitude quickly dropped to 5,200 feet.

Armstrong radioed, "Manual attitude control is good," as he reported the status of the backup control system for the lander. Capsule Communicator (Cap Com) Charlie Duke, reported, "*Eagle*, Houston. You're Go for landing. Over." The altitude was 4,200 feet and closing rapidly.

Now Aldrin anxiously reported, "Roger, understand. Go for landing. 3,000 feet. PROGRAM ALARM 1201!" Again Houston reacted with quick

Astronaut Edwin Aldrin descends the steps of the *Eagle's* ladder as he prepares to join Neil Armstrong on the lunar surface.

Aldrin prepares to deploy the Early Apollo Scientific Experiments Package (EASEP) at Tranquillity Base.

The lunar module *Eagle* with astronauts Armstrong and Aldrin aboard returns in triumph as the earth rises above the lunar horizon.

reassurance: "Roger. 1201 Alarm. We're Go. Same type. We're Go. *Eagle* looking great. You're Go."

The computer alarms that plagued Armstrong and Aldrin all through their descent to the surface were evidently the same as those experienced by Apollo 10 when the LM computer became overloaded with data and automatically postponed some of its functions. In any event, at this moment, the lives of Armstrong and Aldrin were in the hands of Steve Bales, the Flight Controller in charge of the LM computer. It was his instantaneous and weighty decisions to proceed that Houston relayed to the crew of *Eagle*. Aldrin would later recall that when he, Armstrong, and Collins were presented with Medals for Freedom by the President, Bales also received one. In Aldrin's opinion he was certainly deserving of the award because, without him, Aldrin and Armstrong might not have landed.

As Aldrin called out altitude and descent rates without interruption, Mission Control continued to guide them down—much as airline pilots are guided through bad-weather instrument landings—reassuring the astronauts at each step of the way. "Still looking very good. Still looking very good."

The lunar module approached the landing area at 540 feet altitude. This was "Lo-gate," the last checkpoint of the landing phase. Now *Eagle* was hovering directly over Site Number 2.

From the Spacecraft-to-Ground Tapes:
Aldrin: 540 feet [altitude], down at 30 [feet-per-second descent rate] . . . down at 15 . . . 400 feet down at 9 . . . forward . . . 350 feet, down at 4 . . . 300 feet, down 3½ . . . 47 *forward.* . . .

As *Eagle* hovered over the target at a height of 200 feet, the astronauts were startled to find the crater floor littered with boulders. To avoid crashing, Armstrong instantly switched to semimanual control. The computer continued to maintain control of the descent-engine firing, but now the astronaut was moving the hovering craft laterally, eagerly searching for a safe landing area as the dust began to kick up all about them. Sensing something was wrong, the flight controllers began anxiously eyeing the clock—*Eagle* should have landed by now! They're nearly out of fuel! The next 90 seconds would be an eternity for the astronauts and controllers alike.

Aldrin continued calling out rates as heavy static played havoc with his radio transmissions.

Aldrin: . . . 3½ down . . . 13 forward . . . 11 forward, coming down nicely . . . 200 feet, 4½ down . . . 5½

down . . . 5 percent . . . 75 feet . . . 6 forward . . . lights on . . . down 2½ . . . 40 feet, down 2½, kicking up some dust . . . 30 feet, 2½ down . . . faint shadow . . . 4 forward . . . 4 forward . . . drifting to right a little . . . OK. . . . down a half.

Cap Com Charlie Duke interrupted with a great urgency in his voice, "30 SECONDS!" warning the astronauts of the short fuel supply remaining!

With only 30 seconds of fuel left, Armstrong coolly lowered *Eagle* to the surface.

A blue light on the control panel flashed, indicating that the 68-inch-long probes on three of the lander's legs had made contact with the moon.

Aldrin reported, "Contact light! OK, Engine Stop. . . . Descent engine command override off . . . engine arm off." And then there was a pause. Armstrong's heart rate, which normally registered 77 beats a minute when measured at rest, was now racing at 156 beats a minute.

Adrenaline was flowing too at Houston Control as Charlie Duke inquired, "We copy you Down, *Eagle*." Armstrong replied, "Houston." There was a brief pause as he sought to contain his emotions, "Tranquillity Base here. The *Eagle* has landed!"

Duke replied with equal emotion, "Roger, Tran . . . Tranquillity. We copy you on the ground. You've got a bunch of guys about to turn blue. We're breathing again. Thanks a lot."

Armstrong: Thank you.
Houston: You're looking good here.
Armstrong: We're going to be busy for a minute.

The astronauts had only a few seconds at this point to decide whether they were going to stay or not. A quick check between the crew and Houston confirmed their status was good. *Eagle* had landed in good working order.

Aldrin: A very smooth touchdown.
Houston: Roger, *Eagle,* and you are Stay for T1 [the initial stage of the lunar landing operation lasting at least 20 minutes].
Armstrong: Roger. Understand, Stay for T1.

In recalling the landing, Armstrong later would say, "Once [we] settled on the surface, the dust settled immediately and we had an excellent view of the area surrounding the LM."

By this time, Mike Collins in *Columbia* had already passed over Tranquillity Base at an altitude of 69 statute miles and a speed of 3,700 mph and was heading for the moon's far side.

Houston: Columbia, he has landed Tranquillity Base. *Eagle* is at Tranquillity. Over.
Collins: Yes, I heard the whole thing.
Houston: Well, it's a good show.
Collins: Fantastic!
Apollo Control: The next stay-no-stay will be for one revolution [of *Columbia*].

Then Armstrong proceeded to explain his last-minute deviation from the flight plan, commenting on his manual takeover of *Eagle.*

Armstrong: Houston, that may have seemed like a very long final phase. The auto targeting was taking us right into a football-field-sized crater with a large number of big boulders and rocks for about one or two crater diameters around it. And it required us to fly manually over the rock field to find a reasonably good area.
Houston: Roger. We copy. It was beautiful from here, Tranquillity. Over.
Aldrin: We'll get to the details of what's around here, but it looks like a collection of just about every variety of shape, angularity, granularity . . . every variety of rock you could find. The colors vary pretty much depending on how you are looking relative to the zero phase length. There doesn't appear to be too much of a general color at all. However, it looks as though some of the rocks and boulders, of which there are quite a few in the near area . . . looks as though they're going to have some interesting colors to them. Over.
Houston: Roger. Copy. Sounds good to us, Tranquillity. We'll let you press on through the simulated countdown and we'll talk to you later. Over.
Aldrin: OK. This one-sixth G is just like an airplane.
Houston: Right, Tranquillity. Be advised there are lots of smiling faces in this room and all over the world. Over.
Armstrong: There are two of them up here.
Houston: Roger. It was a beautiful job, you guys.
Collins: And don't forget one in the command module.
Armstrong: Roger.

The *Eagle* came to rest on the surface at 17 minutes 42 seconds past 3 P.M. EST on July 20, 1969. The lander was only 4½ degrees off the vertical, which was more than ideal, since it could tolerate an angle up to 30 degrees without threatening to topple.

It had landed 118 miles southwest of the crater Maskelyne, to the right and just below center of the moon as it is viewed from earth. The lunar coordinates were: Latitude 0.799° North, Longitude 23.46° East. The landing was 4 miles downrange (too far to

the west), and at the time the astronauts and Houston were unsure of their exact position on the moon.

It would be necessary for the astronauts to have an exact fix on their position in order to properly align their navigation platform for blast-off from the surface. They would have to depart Tranquillity Base at a very precise time and angle in order to accomplish the rendezvous with the orbiting mother ship *Columbia.*

About 30 minutes before Collins and *Columbia* disappeared behind the moon, Houston encouraged Collins to "Say something. They [Armstrong and Aldrin] ought to be able to hear you." Collins replied, "Tranquillity Base. It sure sounded great from up here. You guys did a fantastic job!" Armstrong good-naturedly replied, "Thank you. Just keep that orbiting base ready for us up there now." To which Collins replied, "Will do." A short time later, *Columbia* swept behind the moon.

Alone in *Columbia* and a quarter-million miles from earth, Collins kept one of the loneliest vigils ever to befall a human being as his crewmates prepared to step into the pages of history on the lunar surface.

Mission Control observed later, "Not since Adam has any human known such solitude as Mike Collins is experiencing during this 47 minutes of each lunar revolution when he's behind the moon with no one to talk to except his tape recorder aboard *Columbia.*"

During an earlier press conference, Collins had half jokingly requested that Armstrong and Aldrin's moonwalk be readily available on tapes so that he could view them when he got back. Collins did not have a TV monitor on board *Columbia.*

The preparations for launch of the lunar module were completed around 5 P.M. EST. With everything in readiness for the ascent, the crew now turned their attention to the upcoming moonwalk.

Armstrong later recalled: "A number of experts had, prior to the flight, predicted that a good bit of difficulty might be encountered by people due to the variety of strange atmospheric and gravitational characteristics. This didn't prove to be the case and after landing we felt very comfortable in the lunar gravity. It was, in fact, in our view preferable both to weightlessness and to the earth's gravity."

At 9:39 P.M. EST Armstrong opened the LM hatch and slowly squeezed through the opening with Aldrin's careful guidance. Armstrong's bulky portable life-support and communications system was strapped to his shoulders. It weighed 84 pounds on earth, 14 on the moon. It allowed him to adjust the

Apollo 11 astronauts in their "isolation garments" watch pararescueman seal *Columbia's* hatch following splashdown.

pressure in his suit, as well as the temperature, and it provided him with the necessary pressurization, life-giving oxygen and carbon dioxide removal. The entire Apollo moonwalk suit weighed 180 pounds—one-sixth that weight on the moon.

Armstrong's descent down the 10-foot nine-step ladder was careful and slow. As he reached the second step, he pulled a *D*-ring, which was within easy reach, and deployed the LM's outside television camera. It was arranged to televise his progress to the lunar surface.

Armstrong came to a halt on the last step, reporting "I'm at the foot of the ladder. The LM footpads are only depressed in the surface about one or two inches . . . although the surface appears to be very, very fine-grained. As you get close to it, it's almost like a powder."

At 9:56 P.M. EST, Sunday, July 20, 1969, Armstrong put his left foot on the moon as Aldrin photographed him from inside the LM. As Armstrong made the first print placed by the weight of man on the moon, he made his memorable announcement, "That's one small step for a man, one giant leap for mankind."

Some 600 million viewers on earth, one-fifth of the world's population, watched the live TV transmission of Armstrong's historic step. Millions more

heard it on their radios or read about it in their newspapers.

Armstrong's message was clear. His step was neither an individual nor a national achievement but rather a human one. No further interpretation of this event was needed for the people around the world who, for a brief moment, were unified in their awe of what 25 centuries of human science and technology, fed by human curiosity as old as man himself, had accomplished.

Armstrong surveyed his surroundings for a while and then cautiously moved away from the LM in a slow-motion loping gait as he tested the one-sixth (of earth's) lunar gravity. "The surface is fine and powdery," he remarked. "I can pick it up loosely with my toe. It does adhere in fine layers like powdered charcoal to the sole and sides of my boots. I only go in a small fraction of an inch, maybe an eighth of an inch. But I can see footprints of my boots and the treads in the fine sandy particles.

"There seems to be no difficulty in moving around as we suspected. It's even perhaps easier than the simulations. . . ."

By now Armstrong felt more confident of his surroundings and began taking soil samples close to *Eagle.* For this he used a special bag-like device at the end of a pole. The pressure suit itself was more of a hindrance to the astronaut's mobility than the lunar gravity. Armstrong then made the following comments, "This is very interesting. It's a very soft surface, but here and there . . . I run into a very hard surface, but it appears to be a very cohesive material of the same sort." As to the landscape, he observed, "It has a stark beauty all its own. It's like much of the high desert of the United States . . . it's different, but it's very pretty out here."

Armstrong placed the small bagful of soil in a pocket on the left leg of his space suit, according to plan, to ensure the return of a sample of the moon's surface in case the mission had to be cut short.

Aldrin then emerged from the *Eagle* at 10:11 P.M. EST and backed down the ladder while Armstrong photographed him.

Armstrong continued to describe the surface, "These rocks are rather slippery." The powdery surface seemed to fill up the fine pores on the rocks, and the astronauts tended to slide over them rather easily.

Next Armstrong focused the TV camera on the stainless steel plaque attached to a leg of the lander and read the inscription: "Here men from the planet earth first set foot on the moon. July 1969, A.D. We came in peace for all mankind." Below the inscription were the signatures of the crew members and of President Richard Nixon.

Armstrong and Aldrin then spent the remainder of their stay on the lunar surface setting up three scientific experiments. For the first of these—the solar wind experiment—they erected a pole equipped with a thin sheet of aluminum to trap a sampling of the subatomic particles that are constantly emanating from the sun and showering the solar system in all directions. Scientists hoped that analysis of these solar particles could provide information on how the sun and planets were formed. The other experiments were a seismic detector sensitive enough to detect any moonquake activity below the lunar surface, as well as meteorite impact or volcanic activity, and a laser reflector which would allow scientists on earth to shoot a laser beam at the moon and calculate the exact distance between moon and earth by measuring the time it took the beam to reflect back to receivers on earth. The science package was crude compared to the instruments carried by later landing missions.

The astronauts then collected 50 pounds of lunar samples, deposited a small disk on the surface containing messages from world leaders, and continued to test their ability to move about on the lunar surface.

At 10:41 P.M. EST, the astronauts erected a 3- by 5-foot nylon flag of the United States. Its top was braced by wire to keep it extended on the airless moon. (Two other U.S. flags were carried to the moon to be returned to earth later and flown over the United States Senate and House of Representatives. Miniature flags of all 50 states, the District of Columbia, the U.S. Territories, the United Nations, and 136 foreign countries also were carried to the moon.)

At 10:48 P.M. the President of the United States spoke to the astronauts on the lunar surface by way of a radio-telephone hookup, ending the conversation with these words, "As you talk to us from the Sea of Tranquillity, it inspires us to redouble our efforts to bring peace and tranquillity to earth. For one priceless moment, in the whole history of man, all the people on this earth are truly one . . ."

The astronauts then completed their planned assignments on the surface. At 11:54 P.M. EST, July 20, 1969, after checking with Mission Control to make sure all chores were completed, Aldrin reentered *Eagle*. Armstrong joined Aldrin in the LM 15 minutes later, and at 12:11 A.M. EST, July 21, he closed the hatch, bringing to an end man's first exploration of the moon (at 111 hours 39 minutes into the mission). Armstrong had spent 2 hours 31 minutes on the surface and Aldrin 1 hour 50 minutes.

After attending to the final housekeeping details, the crew entered a sleep period at 3:25 A.M. EST.

The astronauts in *Eagle* were awakened at 10:13 A.M. EST and Aldrin described their night's sleep on the moon: "Neil has rigged himself a really good hammock . . . he's been lying on the hatch and engine cover, and I curled up on the floor."

At 12:54 P.M. EST, Monday, July 21, 1969 (124 hours 22 minutes into the mission), Armstrong fired *Eagle*'s ascent engine, blasting the astronauts into a lunar orbit which enabled them to catch up with Mike Collins in *Columbia* several revolutions later. They had spent 21 hours 36 minutes on the lunar surface in the Sea of Tranquillity.

Returning with the astronauts were the lunar samples, the aluminum foil with the solar wind particles it had collected, film from the still and movie cameras the men had carried, and the flags to be returned to earth. They left a number of items behind on the surface, reducing *Eagle*'s weight from 15,897 pounds on landing to 10,821 pounds.

The descent stage was the largest single item left behind. Other items included the plaque on the descent-stage leg, the TV camera and two still cameras, sampling tools, Portable Life-Support Systems, lunar boots, the American flag, the laser-beam reflector, and a gnomon (a device to verify colors of objects photographed).

Eagle redocked with *Columbia* while they circled behind the moon at 4:35 P.M. EST. At 11:55 P.M. EST on July 21, the astronauts fired the service module's 20,500-pound-thrust engine while again behind the moon, boosting their speed from 3,600 mph to the 6,188-mph speed necessary to break free of the gravitational pull of the moon, and headed home to earth.

On July 24, the last day of the flight, after being awakened at 5:47 A.M. EST, the crew prepared for splashdown. The service module was jettisoned at 11:21 A.M. EST and at 11:35 A.M. EST the command module made its 18,000-mph reentry into the earth's atmosphere.

Columbia splashed down at 11:51 A.M. EST in the Pacific Ocean, 949 statute miles from Hawaii and 15 statute miles from the recovery ship *Hornet.* Man's first mission to the moon ended 195 hours 18 minutes 35 seconds, or a little more than eight days, after launch. It was the most troublefree mission so far, almost completely on schedule and successful in every respect.

The lunar samples and data collected on the moon were added to an increasing store of information about that body and the solar system in general. This information was made available to scientists throughout the world in the hopes that important clues would be found to help unlock the mysteries of the origin of the solar system, of our very earth, and of life itself. The Apollo 11 mission went a long way toward providing that information. But of even greater significance was not what the astronauts saw or what they brought back with them—of greatest significance was their presence on another planet and the imprint they left on that heavenly body.

Of all man's accomplishments in space, the most important was not what he saw or what he brought back with him, but his presence on another planet, and the imprint he left on that heavenly body.

Alan LaVern Bean

Birthplace	Wheeler, Texas
Date of Birth	March 15, 1932
Height	5′ 9½″
Weight	155 lbs.
Eyes	Hazel
Hair	Brown
Marital Status/Wife	Sue
Daughter	Amy Sue
Son	Clay
Recreational Interests	Reading, painting
Service Affiliation	Lieutenant, U.S. Navy
Flight Record	More than 6,870 hours flying time (more than 4,620 hours in jet aircraft). Logged 1,671 hours 45 minutes in two space flights; EVA time includes 7 hours 46 minutes spent walking on the moon during Apollo 12, and 2 hours 41 minutes outside the orbital workshop during the Skylab 3 mission.
Education and Training	Bachelor of Science degree in Aeronautical Engineering from the University of Texas in 1955, also receiving a commission as Ensign from the Naval Reserve Officers' Training Corps program at the University. He received pilot training and was assigned to jet fighter Attack Squadron 44 at Jacksonville Naval Station for four years.

He attended the Navy Test Pilot School at Patuxent River, Maryland, where he served as test pilot and project officer for the testing of several types of naval air-

Astronaut Career craft after graduation. His assignment entailed preliminary evaluation, initial trials, final board inspections, and survey trials of the aircraft.

His last assignment prior to entry into the astronaut corps was with jet fighter Attack Squadron 172 at Cecil Field, Florida.

He was chosen with the third group of astronauts on October 18, 1963. He was awarded two NASA Distinguished Service Medals. His first flight assignment as an astronaut was as backup command pilot for Gemini X. He next served as backup lunar module pilot for Apollo 9.

Bean served as lunar module pilot for the second manned lunar landing mission, Apollo 12, November 14–24, 1969. He became the fourth man to walk on the moon. His crewmates on that flight were spacecraft commander Charles Conrad and command module pilot Richard Gordon.

Bean made his second space flight as commander for the second manned mission for Project Skylab, the Skylab 3 mission, July 28 to September 25, 1973. With him on the 59½-day, 24.4-million-mile record-setting flight (while in earth orbit) were command module pilot Jack Lousma and science pilot Dr. Owen Garriott. The crew accomplished 150 percent of its scheduled mission goals.

By the end of the flight, Bean had become the holder of 11 world records in space and astronautics.

On his next assignment, Bean served as backup spacecraft commander of the United States flight crew for the joint American-Soviet Apollo-Soyuz Test Project.

Bean retired from the Navy with the rank of Captain in October 1975 but remained with the Astronaut Office in a civilian capacity.

He is currently head of the operations and training group within the Astronaut Office, working on the development of the Space Shuttle, and hopes to be assigned to test and fly it in the future.

Apollo 12: How Times Have Changed

November 14–24, 1969

The successful first manned landing on the moon by the Apollo 11 mission had encountered no unexpected perils on the lunar surface and established the feasibility of manned scientific exploration of the moon. The moon's surface was no longer the Unknown, but rather unexplored territory.

By virtue of backing up the crew of Apollo 9, astronauts Charles "Pete" Conrad and Richard Gordon, veterans of Gemini flights, were given the assignment of Apollo 12 spacecraft commander and command module pilot, respectively. It would be Conrad's third and Gordon's second space flight. The third crew member, Alan Bean, had been backup command pilot for Gemini X, backup lunar module pilot for Apollo 9, and would be making his first space flight as Apollo 12's lunar module pilot.

Launch day, November 14, 1969, greeted the astronauts with light rain showers, broken clouds at 800 feet, and an overcast at 10,000 feet. The ground winds peaked at 14 knots but were within the acceptable limits for a launch.

The huge Saturn V moon rocket roared from Launch Complex 39, Pad A, at precisely 11:22 A.M. EST. During its ascent the rocket was struck by lightning, suddenly shutting off Apollo 12's electrical power at 36 seconds after lift-off and setting off numerous alarms within the command module. The spacecraft, however, automatically switched to backup battery power while the crew worked quickly to restore the primary power system.

Commander Conrad radioed, "We had everything in the world drop out."

Astronaut holding a container of collected lunar soil during the Apollo 12 lunar extravehicular activity (EVA). Note the checklist on his left wrist.

"We've had a couple of cardiac arrests down here too," reported a disquieted Launch Control.

"There wasn't time [for that] up here," answered Conrad.

The power system was soon restored and remained normal throughout the rest of the mission. Apollo 12 achieved its planned parking orbit of 118 by 115 miles, and after a thorough check of all systems it headed for the moon, with the lunar module (code name *Intrepid*) attached nose to nose with the command module (*Yankee Clipper*). Its destination was the Ocean of Storms.

Four and one-half days later, on November 18, Conrad and Bean entered *Intrepid* and after a detailed investigation of all switch positions and lander systems, they separated their craft from Gordon who was (at 107 hours 54 minutes into the flight) in the mother ship *Yankee Clipper*.

The burn of the descent engine carried *Intrepid* approximately 5 miles north of its planned flight path. This error was soon corrected, as well as another trajectory error that would have landed the lunar module 4,200 feet short of its target. The lunar module guidance computer had ordered compensating engine firings that brought the lander precisely on course during the final approach phase of the land-

ing. At 370 feet, as *Intrepid* passed over the right side of the target crater, the crew assumed manual control, maneuvering their spacecraft to the left and landing on the moon's Ocean of Storms at 1:55 A.M. EST on November 19 (111 hours 32 minutes into the mission).

They landed at a point only 600 feet distant from the unmanned lunar scout Surveyor III, which had arrived there 31 months earlier during a precarious automatic landing. The landing coordinates were approximately 3.036°S and 23.418°W. The site was about 1,300 miles west of where Apollo 11 had landed four months earlier. The moon's surface at this point was believed to be covered by debris thrown out millions of years ago during the formation of the crater Copernicus, located 250 miles away.

The Surveyor site was chosen for Apollo 12 because of its geologically different surface and the chance to bring back metal, electronic, and optical materials that had been exposed to the lunar environment for over two and a half years. Another unmanned spacecraft, Lunar Orbiter III (launched on February 8, 1967), made the pinpoint landing possible by its earlier feat of photographing the site in excellent detail.

Conrad later related, "When we pitched over just before the landing phase, there it was [Surveyor III], looking as if we would land practically on target. The targeting data were just about perfect, but I maneuvered [the lander] around the crater, landing at a slightly different spot than the one we had planned. In my judgment, the place we had prepicked was a little too rough." They had planned not to land closer than 500 feet to Surveyor III so as to avoid blowing dust over it with their descent engine, thus preventing them from observing it in its original state of preservation. Conrad's view during the final descent was obscured by the clouds of dust kicked up by the descent engine.

After landing, Conrad reported sighting the mother ship *Yankee Clipper* as it flew in orbit high over the landing site. Gordon, in the command module, likewise reported sighting *Intrepid* parked next to Surveyor III at the landing site.

The crew felt that Apollo 12 was a pioneering lunar expedition. The site had been studied in detail, utilizing the detailed photographs made of it by the Lunar Orbiter and by Apollo orbital flights. The courses the astronauts followed were carefully plotted to cover the maximum number of interesting geological features at the site. The astronauts also had a carefully timed schedule to follow with guidance from Houston Control. They wore checklists fastened to a sleeve of their pressure suits to guide them in their chores.

Conrad opened the *Intrepid*'s hatch at 115 hours 11 minutes into the mission. As he descended the lander's ladder, Conrad, a shorter man than Neil Armstrong, had difficulty taking the last step from the ladder. When he finally stepped down on the lunar surface, at 6:44 A.M. EST on November 19, Conrad exulted, "Whoopee! Man, that may have been a small step for Neil, but that's a long one for me." He had become only the third human to touch the moon's surface.

He described the lunar surface as soft and loosely packed, causing his boots to dig in as he walked. The sun was like a bright spotlight. He observed the condition of the lander for any damage and noted with surprise that it had landed so softly that its shock-absorbing legs had barely been telescoped under the gentle impact.

Bean next descended the ladder, stepping down on the surface 30 minutes later at 7:14 A.M. EST.

The color TV camera was unstowed along with other equipment, but quickly broke down and did not transmit pictures for the remainder of the EVA.

The crew collected contingency samples amounting to between 40 and 50 pounds of lunar material and began setting up the solar wind experiment, an exposed foil sheet deployed to catch the subatomic particles continuously streaming from the sun. They also set out the items for the ALSEP experiments (short for Apollo Lunar Surface Experiments Package). Conrad later recounted, "We learned things that we could never have found out in simulation. A simple thing like shoveling soil into a sample bag, for instance, was an entirely new experience. First you had to handle the shovel differently, stopping it before you would have on earth, and tilting it to dump the load much more steeply, after which the whole sample would fly off suddenly."

The astronauts became concerned about the clouds of dust kicking up around their feet. It was getting into everything. They worried about it clogging the working parts of their space suits and what it would do to the inside of the lunar module.

They noticed one strange surface feature, a group of small conical mounds resembling miniature volcanos. They were about 5 feet tall and about 15 feet in diameter at the base.

The astronauts concluded their first EVA after four hours and returned to the lander to rest and recheck their plans for the second EVA 16 hours later. The crew remained in their pressure suits between the EVA's to avoid unduly contaminating themselves and the lander with dust by changing out of and into the dusty pressure suits.

Both enjoyed working on the lunar surface and performed their tasks with a great deal of enthusiasm, which let them in for a lot of kidding upon their return to Houston.

The second EVA began 1 hour 40 minutes ahead of schedule at 10:55 P.M. EST, November 19 (131 hours 33 minutes into the mission). The work schedule this time was very heavy, calling for numerous visual observations, a lot more sample collections, comprehensive photographic documentation of the area around the Ocean of Storms, and, if possible, the recovery of key pieces of the Surveyor III spacecraft. Conrad later would note, "We had rehearsed that part with a very detailed mockup before the flight, and were well prepared."

The astronauts walked as far as 2,000 feet from *Intrepid*, passing the lunar features Head Crater, Bench Crater, Sharp Crater, Halo Crater, and going on to the Surveyor III site and to Block Crater before returning to the lander. They covered a total distance of about 6,000 feet on a zigzag course around their landing area. Their confidence and speed increased with experience.

Conrad reported he had fallen once but, to everyone's relief, Bean had picked him up without difficulty. It had been one of the concerns during the early planning stages that the constrictions of the pressure suits and the unique 1/6-gravity environment of the moon would make it extremely difficult if not impossible for an astronaut to get up after falling.

The entire Surveyor spacecraft appeared brown to the crew, as if something had rained on it. Although they had landed 600 feet away, the descent to the surface had kicked up and covered it with a fine layer of dust. The glass parts were unbroken and parts were retrieved, including the TV camera and soil scoop. Conrad later related, "We cut samples of aluminum tubing, which seemed more brittle than the same material on earth, and some electrical cables."

The crew also reported that the Surveyor foot-pad marks were still visible. Without climate, there is nothing on the airless moon to wear at its surface, only the constant shower of micrometeoroid dust and the occasional impact of larger meteors. Otherwise, the lunar surface the astronauts were gazing on looked much as it had when prehistoric men gazed at it from afar. As Surveyor had waited, unchanged, to be reunited with men from earth, the moon now stood before them, unchanged over hundreds of thousands of years, giving earthlings a precious glimpse into the past—a view that was possibly closely similar to that of earth in its early beginnings.

After retrieving the solar wind experiment the crew returned to the lander and sealed the hatch at 2:44 A.M. EST on November 20 (135 hours 22 minutes into the mission), concluding a 3-hour 49-minute walk on the moon.

At 9:26 A.M. EST on November 20, *Intrepid* successfully lifted off the moon and returned to *Yankee Clipper* in lunar orbit. Gordon had been kept busy in the command module performing experiments and photographing the surface, concentrating on proposed future landing sites. He paid particular attention to the Fra Mauro region of the moon, which was the scheduled landing site for Apollo 13.

The successful crew headed back to earth at 3:49 P.M. EST on November 21 (172 hours 27 minutes into the mission) after completing 44 revolutions of the moon. They brought their cargo of Surveyor III parts, 95 pounds of lunar surface samples, miniature flags of 136 nations, 50 states, and four U.S. possessions back to earth, splashing down in the Pacific Ocean at 3:58 P.M. EST on November 24, 1969, 4.03 statute miles from the recovery carrier *Hornet*.

In the framework of time, the 244-hour expedition of Apollo 12 was a unique study in contrasts. It had been a little over 10 years since the day we had struggled to hurl a volley-ball-sized satellite into earth's orbit. Only four months earlier Apollo 11 had cautiously groped at the moon's surface, landing with barely 30 seconds of fuel remaining. On the second try, we were making precision landings, and men were cavorting with confidence in a lunar setting that had changed very little since its creation.

How times have changed—how *we* have changed.

Apollo 12 astronaut visits Surveyor III during second lunar EVA. The *Intrepid* appears on the lunar horizon in the background.

John Leonard Swigert, Jr.

Birthplace	Denver, Colorado
Date of Birth	August 30, 1931
Height	5′ 11½″
Weight	180 lbs.
Eyes	Blue
Hair	Blond
Marital Status	Single
Recreational Interests	Handball, bowling, waterskiing, swimming, basketball, golf, photography
Service Affiliation	Civilian
Flight Record	More than 7,200 hours flying time (more than 5,725 hours in jet aircraft). Logged 142 hours 55 minutes in one space flight (no EVA).
Education and Training	Bachelor of Science degree in Mechanical Engineering from the University of Colorado in 1953. He served with the Air Force from 1953 to 1956. Upon graduation from the Pilot Training Program and Gunnery School at Nellis Air Force Base, Nevada, he was assigned as a jet fighter pilot in Japan and Korea. After his tour of active duty in the military, Swigert served as a jet fighter pilot with the Massachusetts Air National Guard from September 1957 to March 1960. From 1957 to 1964, he was employed as a research engineering test pilot for Pratt and Whitney Aircraft. He was a member of the Connecticut Air National Guard from April 1960 to October 1965. From 1964 to 1966, Swigert was an engineering test pilot for North American Aviation, Inc. In 1966 he was corecipient of the AIAA

Octave Chanute award for his participation in demonstrating the Rogallo Wing as a feasible land landing system for returning space vehicles and astronauts. He received a Master of Science degree in Aerospace Science from the Rensselaer Polytechnic Institute in 1965, and a Masters degree in Business Administration from the University of Hartford in 1967.

Astronaut Career He was chosen with the fifth group of astronauts on April 4, 1966. He received the Presidential Medal for Freedom in 1970 for the Apollo 13 mission. His first flight assignment as an astronaut was backup command module pilot for Apollo 13. He became the prime command module pilot for the mission 72 hours prior to launch due to Ken Mattingly's exposure to measles. The Apollo 13 mission (April 11–17, 1970) was aborted when an explosion of an oxygen tank in the service module occurred at 55 hours into the mission. The quick and decisive action of Houston and the Apollo 13 crew—Swigert, Lovell, and Haise—saved Apollo 13 from sure disaster, returning the crew safely home to earth.

Swigert accepted a position as Executive Director of the Committee on Science and Technology of the United States House of Representatives in April 1973, taking a leave of absence from NASA.

Apollo 13 astronauts Swigert, Lovell and Haise study a model of the lunar module that will soon become their lifeboat in space.

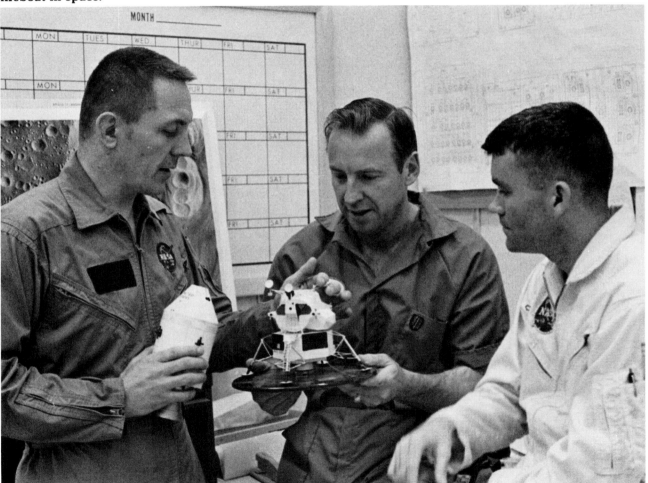

Fred Wallace Haise, Jr.

Birthplace	Biloxi, Mississippi
Date of Birth	November 14, 1933
Height	5′ 9½″
Weight	155 lbs.
Eyes	Brown
Hair	Brown
Marital Status/Wife	Mary
Daughter	Mary
Sons	Frederick, Stephen, Thomas
Recreational Interests	Flying, sailplaning (glider flying)
Service Affiliation	Civilian
Flight Record	More than 8,300 hours flying time (more than 5,400 in jet aircraft). Logged 142 hours 55 minutes in one space flight (no EVA).
Education and Training	Bachelor of Science degree with honors in Aeronautical Engineering from the University of Oklahoma in 1959. His military career began in October 1952 as a Naval aviation cadet at the Naval Air Station in Pensacola, Florida. From March 1954 to September 1956 he served as an instructor in tactics and all-weather flight in the U.S. Navy Advanced Training Command at Navy Advanced Aviation School, Kingsville, Texas, and as a U.S. Marine Corps fighter pilot with Squadrons VMF-533 and 114 at Marine Corps Air Station, Cherry Point, North Carolina. From March 1957 to September 1959, Haise was a fighter interceptor pilot with the 185th Fighter Interceptor Squadron in the Oklahoma Air National Guard.

He served with the Air Force from October 1961 to August 1962 as a tactical fighter pilot and as Chief of the 164th Standardization-Evaluation Flight of the 164th Tactical Fighter Squadron at Mansfield, Ohio.

From September 1959 to March 1963, he was a research pilot at the NASA Lewis Research Center in Cleveland, Ohio. In 1964 he received the A. B. Honts Trophy for graduating from the Aerospace Research Pilot School, Edwards Air Force Base, Class 64-A, with highest honors. He was a research pilot at the NASA Flight Research Center at Edwards, California, before joining the astronaut corps. His published papers on aviation include "The Use of Aircraft for Zero Gravity Environment" (1966).

Astronaut Career He was chosen with the fifth group of astronauts on April 4, 1966. He has been awarded the Presidential Medal for Freedom (for Apollo 13), the NASA Distinguished Service Medal, the NASA Exceptional Service Medal, and the Johnson Space Center Special Achievement Award.

His first flight assignment as an astronaut was as backup lunar module pilot for Apollo 8 and Apollo 11. He was lunar module pilot for Apollo 13, April 11–17, 1970. The planned ten-day mission was programmed for the first landing in the hilly, upland Fra Mauro region of the moon but was aborted when an oxygen tank in the service module section of Apollo 13 exploded at approximately 55 hours into the flight.

Haise and fellow crew members, James Lovell (commander) and John Swigert (command module pilot), worked closely with Houston to convert their lunar module *Aquarius* into a "lifeboat," as they successfully returned to earth after the near disaster in deep space.

He later served as backup commander for Apollo 16. From April 1973 to January 1976, he was technical assistant to the manager of the Space Shuttle Orbiter Project. He later became commander of one of the two two-man Shuttle pilot crews and piloted the Space Shuttle orbiter *Enterprise* on its free, unpowered drop-flight and landing test at Edwards Air Force Base, California, on August 12, 1977.

Haise is currently designated to command the third orbital two-man flight test of the Space Shuttle with astronaut Jack Lousma.

Apollo 13: A Successful Failure

April 11–17, 1970

The Apollo 13 prime crew of James Lovell (commander), Thomas Mattingly (command module pilot), and Fred Haise (lunar module pilot) were within one week of the scheduled launch when a backup crewman, Charles Duke, developed rubella (German measles).

Examinations of the prime crew revealed that Mattingly had no immunity to rubella, and he was removed from the Apollo 13 flight because of his contacts with Duke during training.

Lovell was one of the most experienced pilots at the time of this mission, having logged 572 hours in three space flights, beginning with pilot on the 14-day Gemini VII mission, a record not equaled until Skylab. He had graduated to command pilot for the four-day flight of Gemini XII. In 1968, he was the command module pilot for Apollo 8, the eight-day first circumlunar voyage to the moon.

As launch day, April 11, 1970, approached, Lovell was more confident than ever in his readiness and that of fellow crewman Fred Haise, with whom he had trained for this mission for two years. NASA likewise had confidence in the ability of the crew. Accordingly, Jack Swigert, the backup command module pilot, was assigned to Lovell's crew despite having had only two days of prime-crew training. Prior to this instance, the rule at NASA had been to replace the entire crew as a team rather than break it up.

As Lovell relates, "The second omen came in ground tests before launch, which indicated the possibility of a poorly insulated supercritical helium tank in the LM's descent stage. So we modified the flight plan to enter the LM three hours early, in order to obtain an onboard readout of helium tank pressure. This proved to be lucky for us because it gave us a chance to shake down this odd-shaped spacecraft that was to hold our destiny in its spidery hands. It also meant the LM controllers were in Mission Control when they would be needed most."

Another unusual circumstance was oxygen tank Number 2. This tank had been removed from the service module of Apollo 10 for modification and had been damaged in the process. After its repair and testing at the factory, it became a part of the Apollo 13 service module. It was subsequently tested during the countdown demonstration test at Kennedy Space Center beginning March 16, 1970. The tanks were emptied to about the halfway mark. Number 1 tank behaved normally, but Number 2 vented to only 92 percent capacity. The ground crew tried to cause the liquid oxygen to vent by forcing gaseous oxygen at 80 pounds pressure but without success. This discrepancy was noted in a report and two weeks before launch, on March 27, Number 1 tank again behaved normally, but Number 2 again did not respond. The contractor and NASA personnel jointly decided to heat up the liquid oxygen tank and "boil off" the excess oxygen using a tank heater. The technique worked, but it took eight hours to accomplish.

Every space flight had had its minor failures. With millions of parts involved it was too much to ask for 100 percent performance. That is why nearly every vital system had a backup. To the astronauts and launch crew, Number 2 was characterized as a discrepancy and nothing more was thought of it until it was too late.

Apollo 13 became airborne at 2:13 P.M. EST on Saturday, April 11. After a thorough checkout while in parking orbit around earth, Apollo 13 was given the green light for translunar injection.

At 4:48 P.M. EST the third stage was reignited and

Astronaut Swigert works on the "mailbox" rig to adapt the command module's lithium hydroxide cannisters for use in the lunar module.

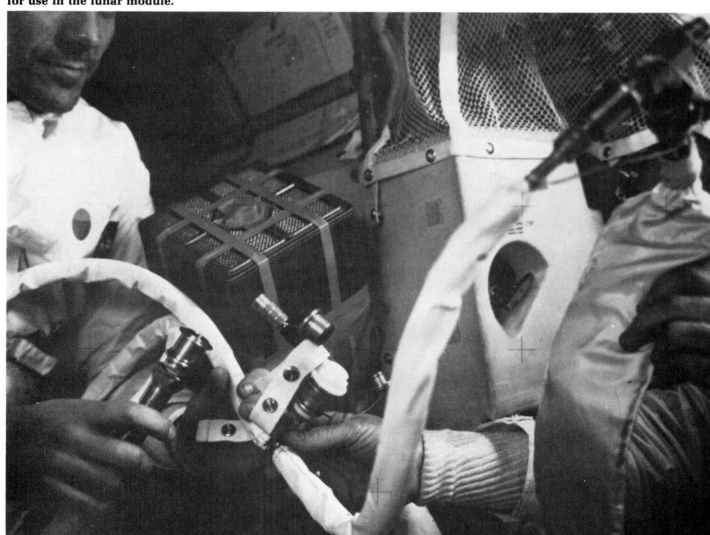

the crew was on its way to the moon and the Fra Mauro landing site. The command module, *Odyssey*, was docked with the lunar module, *Aquarius*, and Apollo 13 began to look like the smoothest flight of the program as the second day of the mission was drawing to a close.

At 46 hours 43 minutes after launch, the Capsule Communicator (Cap Com), astronaut Joe Kerwin, jokingly complained, "The spacecraft is in real good shape as far as we are concerned. We're bored to tears down here." Things were soon to change radically for the remainder of the flight.

As Lovell recalled, "At 55 hours 46 minutes, as we finished a 49-minute TV broadcast showing how comfortably we lived and worked in weightlessness, I pronounced the benediction: 'This is the crew of Apollo 13 wishing everybody there a nice evening, and we're just about ready to close out our inspection of *Aquarius* and get back for a pleasant evening in *Odyssey*. Good night'

"On the tapes I sound mellow and benign, or some might say fat, dumb, and happy. A pleasant evening, indeed! Nine minutes later the roof fell in; rather, oxygen tank Number 2 blew up, causing Number 1 tank also to fail. We came to the slow conclusion that our normal supply of electricity, light, and water was lost, and we were about 200,000 miles from earth. We did not even have power to gimbal (turn) the engine so we could begin an immediate return to earth." The time was 10:08 P.M. EST on April 13.

Haise was still in *Aquarius*. Lovell was in the tunnel between the command ship and the spider-like lunar module, holding the camera as he carefully made his way back to *Odyssey* through the TV's wire cables. Swigert was in *Odyssey*. When they heard the loud bang, Lovell and Swigert thought that Haise had made a planned valve release in *Aquarius*. As Haise reentered the command module the astronauts quickly scanned the instrument panel. One of the main electrical systems of Apollo 13 was rapidly deteriorating. At 55 hours 55 minutes into the flight, Swigert radioed, "Hey, we've got a problem here."

Next, the warning lights on the instrument panel registered the loss of two of the three fuel cells. They represented the prime source of electricity. At that point, the crew's first thoughts were of their disappointment since mission rules forbade lunar landings with only one fuel cell.

As the crew continued instrument checks, the gauges also showed one oxygen tank completely empty, and the second tank rapidly depleting.

Moments later, Lovell peered out the left-hand window and saw a blizzard of particles flying out of the service module, reporting, "We are venting something out into the—into space." It was 13 minutes since the explosion and oxygen continued escaping from the second and *last* oxygen tank in the service module. By 57 hours 24 minutes after lift-off, the oxygen pressure in the last tank approached zero.

The expanding sphere of gas surrounding Apollo 13 was reportedly seen by amateur astronomers atop a building in Houston. Lovell would later recall, "The knot tightened in my stomach, and all regrets about not landing on the moon vanished. Now it was strictly a case of survival."

Even before the discovery of the oxygen leak, the first reaction of the crew was to try to close the hatch to the tunnel. First, Swigert and then Lovell tried to lock the hatch, but it stubbornly remained open. Then, when they realized there was no cabin leak, the exasperated astronauts strapped the hatch to the command module couch.

Lovell later remarked that it was fortunate that the tunnel did remain open, "because Fred and I would soon have to make a quick trip to the LM in our fight for survival. It [was] interesting to note that days later, just before we jettisoned the LM, when the hatch had to be closed and locked, Jack did it—as easy as pie. That's the kind of flight it was."

With only 15 minutes of power remaining, Swigert fed oxygen into the reserve tank and hooked up emergency batteries to the command module navigation gyroscopes until the lunar module could be readied. Lovell and Haise succeeded in fully preparing *Aquarius* just before midnight on April 13.

The astronauts continued to remain calm as they wrestled with procedures to stabilize the spacecraft and stretch the fuel, electrical, oxygen, and water supplies.

The lunar module was now Apollo 13's lifeboat as it limped toward the moon, which still lay 20 hours and 50,000 miles ahead. The flight path had been modified before the explosion, on April 12, to facilitate a lunar landing at Fra Mauro. Although this course would have taken them on a free-return trajectory back toward the earth, but it would have left them 250 miles out—too far out to allow safe reentry. The problem now was how to get Apollo 13 back on a free-return course that would sweep them past the moon at a greater altitude (164 rather than 69 miles), bringing them back on a more direct course toward the earth.

Firing the main engine of the command ship would be too risky. There was no way to assess the damage to the service module, and it might not hold up under the stress of that firing. The descent engine of the lander was the only choice they had left.

Fortunately, the firing of the lander's descent engine in space had been practiced as a foresight by Apollo 9 during tests in earth orbit, and Lovell and Haise had practiced this procedure in the flight simulators at Kennedy Space Center. But one problem still needed solving. When should the engine be fired, in what direction, and for how long?

These critical decisions had to be made fairly soon, and Flight Director Glynn Lunney weighed the alternatives carefully as trajectory planners ran half a dozen different maneuvers through their computers.

The lunar module lifeboat theory had been discussed as a contingency procedure as far back as 1962, and just prior to the selection of the lunar orbit rendezvous method for the moon-landing missions. The theory continued to be discussed through 1963 but was dropped in 1964 after a study at the Manned Spacecraft Center concluded that "no single reasonable command-service module failure could be identified that would prohibit the use of the SPS [main engine]."

By the time of the Apollo 10 circumlunar mission, the idea of the lunar module (LM) becoming a lifeboat was again being discussed.

Fred Haise was generally thought of as the top astronaut expert on the lunar module, having spent 14 months at the Grumman plant on Long Island where the lander was built. Haise was to later remark, "I never heard of the LM being used in the sense we used it. We had procedures, and we had trained to use it as a backup propulsion device." In reality, the object had been to cover a failure of the command module's main engine to fire. According to Haise, "We never really thought and planned, and obviously we didn't have the procedures to cover a case where the command module would end up fully powered down."

Getting Apollo 13 home would require a lot of innovation and the people at Mission Control faced a difficult task.

The lunar module was designed for only a 45-hour lifetime and the astronauts had to stretch that to 90 hours. As Houston struggled with finding the best procedure for establishing the free-return trajectory, the crew inventoried their vital supplies. The oxygen supply in the LM descent tank alone would suffice, and there were two lunar pressure-suit backpacks in addition to two emergency bottles. (At reentry the crew still had more than half this oxygen reserve re-

Interior view of Apollo 13 shows cannisters in place. They cleared deadly CO_2 from the LM's atmosphere.

maining—28.5 pounds.) They estimated having just enough electrical power, 2,181 ampere hours, in the batteries on the lander—if they shut off every electrical power device not absolutely necessary. The electrical cabin heaters had to be turned off and the inside of Apollo 13 was soon reduced to 38 degrees F. The "perspiring walls and wet windows made it seem even colder," Lovell later said.

At the time of jettisoning, the lunar module had 20 percent of its electrical power remaining. There was one frightening moment, however, when one of the command module's batteries vented with such force that it momentarily went out of commission. If they had permanently lost that one, the crew would have perished.

Water was the real problem, but the crew managed to stretch out their supply so that they had enough for drinking and for cooling down some of the mechanical spacecraft systems. The crew lost a total of 31.5 pounds due to dehydration but managed to finish the flight with some water left—9 percent of the total reserve.

The real danger to the crew was carbon dioxide poisoning, but the crew was instructed by Houston on how to fit the square lithium hydroxide canisters from the command module into the round holes in the lunar module using plastic bags, cardboard, and tape, and miraculously they cleared their cabin of the dangerous levels of carbon dioxide.

The navigation system on board the lunar module was not designed to set up the midcourse corrections that Houston was about to communicate to the astronauts, but once again the flight directors and engineers on the ground came up with the answers. The computer solution called for aligning the spacecraft in the proper attitude by taking sightings on the earth, sun, and moon. Before radioing each new maneuver to the Apollo 13 crew, every move was first tried out in complete detail in flight simulators at Houston and Kennedy Space Center by their fellow astronauts.

Engineers in Downey, California, where *Odyssey* was built, ran emergency problems through computers. A 30-man team at Massachusetts Institute of Technology, where the Apollo guidance system was designed, worked through the night studying the new guidance system problems from the lunar module's point of view and working out new trajectories. Ten phone lines were kept open between Mission Control and a room staffed with 70 lunar module experts at the manufacturer's plant in Bethpage, Long Island. The President of the United States cancelled

View of the severely damaged service module as seen from the command module following jettisoning. An entire panel was blown away exposing damaged fuel cells and tanks.

his appointments to follow Apollo 13's progress and offered comfort to the wives of Lovell and Haise, and to Swigert's parents (he was unmarried) by telephone.

At 61 hours 28 minutes 43 seconds into the mission (3:42 A.M. on April 14), *Aquarius* fired its descent engine and crossed the first hurdle of the mission by placing Apollo 13 back on the planned free-return trajectory. Before disappearing behind the moon, Apollo 13 heard Mission Control confirm it for free return, estimating a splashdown in the Indian Ocean if no further engine firings were made.

Now time became the astronauts' enemy, as they tried to stretch their power and life-support supplies. The second, and critical, problem according to Apollo 13's commander Lovell, came just as the spacecraft appeared from behind the moon's far side. A second and more crucial engine firing had to be made in order to speed up their return. The new firing also would shift their landing area to the mid-Pacific, where the recovery forces were already on station.

As they came from behind the moon, Lovell barked to Swigert and Haise, who had been photographing the lunar terrain, "If we don't make this next maneuver correctly, you won't get your pictures developed!"

A swarm of debris from the ruptured service module was now traveling along with *Aquarius* and the reflection of sunlight on these bits of junk made normal visual star sightings virtually impossible. If Lovell couldn't verify the accuracy of the spacecraft's alignment, he couldn't fire the engine. The idea of sighting on the sun to check alignment accuracy put Apollo 13 over this last hurdle.

As Lovell described this critical moment, "No amount of debris could blot out that star! Its large diameter could result in considerable error, but nobody had a better plan."

He rotated the spacecraft to the position requested by Houston, and if the alignment was accurate as he sighted through the Alignment Optical Telescope, the sun would be at dead center of that sextant. "It had to be. And it was!" recalled Lovell. The space-to-ground tapes of this part of the mission, according to Lovell, sounded like a song from *My Fair Lady*:

Lovell: OK. We got it. I think we got it. What diameter was it?
Haise: Yes. It's coming back in. Just a second.
Lovell: Yes, yaw's coming back in. Just about it.
Haise: Yaw is in. . . .

Lovell: What have you got?
Haise: Upper right corner of the sun. . . .
Lovell: We've got it!

"If we raised our voices, I submit it was justified," Lovell later said of this moment. "The cheer of the year went up in Mission Control."

Flight Director Gerald Griffin, a man not easily shaken, said later of the flight: "Some years later I went back to the log and looked up that mission. My writing was almost illegible, I was so damned nervous. And I remember the exhilaration running through me: My God, that's kinda the last hurdle—if we can do that, I know we can make it. It was funny, because only the people involved knew how important it was to have that platform properly aligned."

The error in alignment was less than a half degree. At 9:41 P.M. on April 14, the second engine firing boosted Apollo 13 on a faster return trajectory to the Pacific landing point. The crew was not home free, but things began looking better with each hour that passed.

Haise radioed about three hours later, "*Aquarius* has really been quite a winner."

After jettisoning and photographing the damaged service module at 138 hours 2 minutes into the flight on April 17, the crew began final preparations for splashdown, which was now only four hours away.

The crew transferred to the command module, and at 141 hours 30 minutes into the mission, the lunar module was jettisoned. Houston Control acknowledged separation, "Farewell, *Aquarius* and we thank you."

Apollo 13 splashed down gently in the Pacific Ocean southeast of American Samoa and only 4 miles from the recovery ship *Iwo Jima*. Recovery reported: "I have astronaut Haise aboard, and his condition is excellent. . . ." It would be nine months before Apollo 14 would fly.

From the moment the announcement of Apollo 13's emergency was made, millions of people from around the nation and around the world began to focus their attention on the drama that was unfolding out in space. *Men* were in trouble, deep in the darkness of space. They were not just American astronauts anymore. And for the moment, the family of man prayed for its men. From the vantage point of space, the predicament of Apollo 13 looks strikingly similar to our own dilemma here on our own spaceship—Earth. Our air is becoming foul, our resources depleted. Will we learn from this new perspective? Only time will tell.

Stuart Allen Roosa

Birthplace	Durango, Colorado
Date of Birth	August 16, 1933
Height	5′ 10″
Weight	160 lbs.
Eyes	Blue
Hair	Red
Marital Status/Wife	Joan
Daughter	Rosemary
Sons	Christopher, John, Stuart
Recreational Interests	Hunting, fishing
Service Affiliation	Captain, U.S. Air Force
Flight Record	More than 5,300 hours flying time (more than 4,700 hours in jet aircraft). Logged 216 hours, 2 minutes in one space flight (no EVA).
Education and Training	Studied at Oklahoma State University and the University of Arizona. He was graduated with honors and a Bachelor of Science degree in Aeronautical Engineering from the University of Colorado in 1960.

He entered the Air Force in 1953 and received a commission after graduation from the Air Force Aviation Cadet Program at Williams Air Force Base, Arizona. He was later assigned as a fighter pilot at Langley Air Force Base, Virginia, where he flew F-84f and F-100 jet aircraft. After graduation from the University of Colorado and from the Air Force Institute of Technology Program, he served two years as Chief of Service Engineering at Tachikawa Air Base in Japan.

He was a maintenance flight test pilot at Olmsted Air Force Base, Pennsylvania, from July 1962 to August 1964, flying F-101 jet aircraft.

Following graduation from the Air Force Aerospace Research Pilot School in September 1965, he remained at Edwards Air Force Base, California, as an experimental test pilot until May 1966.

Astronaut Career He was chosen with the fifth group of astronauts on April 4, 1966. He received the NASA Distinguished Service Medal and the Johnson Space Center Superior Achievement Award. His first flight assignment as an astronaut was as command module pilot for the Apollo 14 moon-landing mission January 31–February 9, 1971. With him on this third landing mission was veteran astronaut Alan Shepard (commander) and Edgar Mitchell (lunar module pilot), making his first flight. Roosa remained in lunar orbit in the command ship *Kitty Hawk* as Shepard and Mitchell visited the Fra Mauro landing site that had been targeted for the aborted Apollo 13 mission.

Roosa later served as backup command module pilot for the Apollo 16 and 17 missions. He then was assigned to the Space Shuttle program and on February 1, 1976, resigned from NASA and retired from the Air Force with rank of Colonel. He is presently in private industry.

Flying a parabolic curve, an Air Force KC-135 jet aircraft creates a moment of weightlessness for Apollo 14 astronaut Edgar Mitchell.

Edgar Dean Mitchell

Birthplace	Hereford, Texas
Date of Birth	September 17, 1930
Height	5′ 11″
Weight	180 lbs.
Eyes	Green
Hair	Brown
Marital Status/Wife	Louise
Daughters	Karlyn, Elizabeth
Recreational Interests	Handball, swimming, scuba diving, sailplaning (glider flying)
Service Affiliation	Commander, U.S. Navy
Flight Record	More than 4,000 hours flying time (more than 1,900 hours in jet aircraft). Logged a total of 216 hours 2 minutes in one space flight, of which 9 hours 23 minutes were spent walking on the moon during two EVA's.
Education and Training	Bachelor of Science degree in Industrial Management from the Carnegie Institute of Technology in 1952. After graduation he entered the Navy and was commissioned in 1953, after completing his basic training at the San Diego Recruit Depot. He was commissioned as an Ensign in May 1953 after completing instruction at the Officer Candidate School at Newport, Rhode Island. He completed flight training in July 1954 at Hutchinson, Kansas, and was subsequently assigned to Patrol Squadron 29, based in Okinawa.
	From 1957 to 1958 he flew Navy A3 aircraft while assigned to Heavy Attack Squadron 2 aboard the aircraft carriers U.S.S. *Bon Homme Richard* and U.S.S. *Ticonderoga*. He was a research project pilot with Air Development Squadron 5 until 1959.

Mitchell received a Bachelor of Science degree in Aeronautical Engineering from the U.S. Naval Post Graduate School in 1961, and a Doctor of Science degree in Aeronautics and Astronautics from the Massachusetts Institute of Technology in 1964.

He became Chief of the Project Management Division of the Navy Field Office for the Manned Orbiting Laboratory program in 1964 and served in that capacity till 1965, whereupon he attended the Air Force Aerospace Research Pilot School at Edwards Air Force Base, California, graduating first in his class. Prior to becoming an astronaut he was an instructor at the school.

Astronaut Career He was chosen with the fifth group of astronauts on April 4, 1966. He was presented the Presidential Medal for Freedom in 1970, the NASA Distinguished Service Medal, and the Manned Spaceflight Center Superior Achievement Award (1970).

His first flight assignment as an astronaut was as a member of the astronaut support crew for Apollo 9. He then became backup lunar module pilot for Apollo 10.

Mitchell made his first space flight on Apollo 14, January 31–February 9, 1971, when he and veteran astronaut Alan Shepard (commander) visited the landing site in the Fra Mauro region of the moon that was intended for the aborted Apollo 13 mission. He became the sixth man to walk on the moon.

The third crew member, Stuart Roosa (command module pilot), remained in lunar orbit in the mother ship *Kitty Hawk* as Shepard and Mitchell descended in the lunar module *Antares*.

This mission saw the first use of the Mobile Equipment Transporter (MET), a two-wheeled rickshaw-like device used for transporting equipment and samples across the lunar surface. Other mission firsts were the use of a shortened lunar orbit rendezvous technique and the use of color TV with the new vidicon tube on the lunar surface.

Mitchell later became backup lunar module pilot for Apollo 16.

He retired from NASA and the Navy with the rank of Captain in October 1972 to enter private business. He has written a book, *Psychic Exploration: A Challenge for Science.*

Apollo 14 astronauts Shepard and Mitchell during geology training in Arizona.

Joe Henry Engle

Birthplace	Abilene, Kansas
Date of Birth	August 26, 1932
Height	6'
Weight	155 lbs.
Eyes	Hazel
Hair	Blond
Marital Status/Wife	Mary
Daughter	Laurie
Son	Jon
Recreational Interests	Flying (including World War II fighter aircraft), big-game hunting, athletics
Service Affiliation	Captain, U.S. Air Force
Flight Record	More than 7,700 hours flying time (more than 5,680 in jet aircraft). He has flown more than 135 different types of aircraft during his career, including 25 different fighters. Three of his sixteen flights in the rocket-powered X-15 research aircraft exceeded an altitude of 50 miles, the altitude that qualifies a pilot for Astronaut Wings.
Education and Training	Bachelor of Science degree in Aeronautical Engineering from the University of Kansas in 1955. He received his commission in the Air Force through the Air Force Reserve Officers' Training Corps at the University of Kansas and entered flight training in 1957. After earning his wings, he served with the 474th Fighter Day Squadron and the 309th Tactical Fighter Squadron at George Air Force Base, California. His overseas assignments were in Spain, Italy, and Denmark. He graduated from the U.S. Air Force Experimental Test Pilot School and the Air Force

Aerospace Research Pilot School in 1962. Upon graduation, Engle remained at Edwards Air Force Base as a test pilot in the Fighter Test Group.

In June 1963, he was selected as a test pilot for the U.S. Air Force-NASA X-15 research rocket aircraft.

Astronaut Career He was chosen with the fifth group of astronauts on April 4, 1966. He had previously received the Air Force Astronaut Wings for his achievements as a test pilot in the X-15 program and also was named the Air Force Association's Outstanding Young Officer in 1964. The American Institute of Aeronautics and Astronautics awarded him the Lawrence Sperry Award in 1966 for his experimental research in aerodynamics as test pilot of the X-15.

Engle's first flight assignment as an astronaut was as backup lunar module pilot for the Apollo 14 mission. He subsequently became commander of one of the two two-man crews assigned to fly the Space Shuttle powerless approach and landing test flights at Edwards Air Force Base, California. Engle flew the Space Shuttle orbiter *Enterprise* on its second unpowered drop-flight and landing test at Edwards Air Force Base, California, on September 13, 1977. During the flight, he turned, banked, and rolled the prototype spacecraft from side to side and glided the 75-ton shuttlecraft to a perfect landing.

He will serve as backup commander for OFT-1, the first orbital flight test of the Space Shuttle spacecraft, now scheduled for 1979–80, and will command the second orbital two-man flight of the Space Shuttle with Richard H. Truly.

Apollo 14: An Era Ends

January 31–February 9, 1971

The crew for Apollo 14, Alan Shepard, spacecraft commander, Stuart Roosa, command module pilot, and Edgar Mitchell, lunar module pilot, were selected on August 6, 1969, just after the successful moon landing by Apollo 11.

The mission was tentatively scheduled for the moon's Littrow region with an October 1970 launch date. But the explosion of the oxygen tank aboard Apollo 13 called for several alterations in the Apollo 14 spacecraft. The Fra Mauro region of the moon, originally targeted for Apollo 13, was shifted to Shepard's mission, and the launch date eventually was moved to January 1971.

Engineers redesigned the area involved in the explosion to lessen the possibilities of any future reoccurrence and added an extra oxygen tank, battery, and water supply, sufficient to see astronauts through a three-day return trip to earth should the primary supplies again be destroyed near the moon.

The prime crew used the extra weeks to augment their training. Shepard and Mitchell each spent more than 300 hours walking in desert areas and simulators that resembled the lunar surface. Roosa spent nearly 1,000 hours practicing in the Apollo command module flight simulators.

A well-prepared crew lifted off Launch Complex 39, Pad A, at 4:03 P.M. EST on January 31, 1971. An estimated half-million persons were eyewitnesses to the launch, including the Vice President of the United States, the royal couple from Spain, and the first man to walk on the moon, astronaut Neil A. Armstrong.

The Saturn V placed the spacecraft in a 117.4- by 113.8-mile parking orbit. Astronaut Roosa had problems docking with the lunar module, but during the sixth try was able to link the command module *Kitty Hawk* with the lander *Antares* and pull away towards the moon. The astronauts had chosen the name *Kitty Hawk* as a tribute to the first manned powered flight in 1903 by the Wright brothers at Kitty Hawk, North Carolina. The lander was named *Antares* for the star on which it would orient itself just before descending to the Fra Mauro landing site.

Apollo 14 entered lunar orbit three and a half days later, at 1:55 A.M. EST on February 4 (82 hours 37 minutes after lift-off). Roosa radioed Mission Con-

Astronaut Shepard assembles lunar hand tools during first Apollo 14 EVA. Modularized Equipment Transporter (MET) stands to his right.

trol: "You're not going to believe this—it looks just like the map." Shepard continued, describing the scene out his window, "Really quite a sight. No atmosphere at all. Everything is clear up here. Really fantastic!" To Mitchell, the moon looked like "a plaster mold that somebody has dusted with grays and browns." Talking about the contrast between darkness and light on the surface, Mitchell described "some fairly high crater walls and high country, with those long shadows; it really looks rugged. It looks like you could walk along that surface into the darkness and fall into nothing."

In all previous Apollo lunar flights, the command ship had come no closer than 70 miles to the moon's surface. At that altitude, the lunar module would cast off and begin its descent to the landing site. The hilly terrain at Fra Mauro would necessitate a different approach by Apollo 14. The astronauts first fired their spacecraft into an elliptical 70- by 193-mile-high lunar orbit. After two such orbits, another firing dropped the spacecraft into a 50,000-foot by 70-mile

elliptical orbit, bringing the mother ship closer than any previous Apollo command module had been to the lunar surface. Apollo 14 was now clearing the highest peaks of the lunar mountain ranges by only 7 miles. Mitchell later recalled that this first close look at the moon was for him, emotionally, one of the most touching experiences of the flight.

Twenty-two hours after attaining lunar orbit, Shepard and Mitchell departed (at 104 hours 28 minutes into the flight) from the mother ship and headed for the lunar surface in *Antares*. By leaving at the lowest point in this new orbit (50,000 feet), Shepard gained about 14 seconds of extra fuel capacity, allowing him to hover a little longer. The Fra Mauro landing site was more rugged than the sites of the Apollo 11 and 12 landings, and extra fuel might just be needed.

As *Antares* arched towards the lunar surface, the onboard landing radar which controls the descent rate by continuously measuring the decreasing altitude failed to lock on to the lunar surface (failed to register) at the prescribed altitude of 30,000 feet. At 22,713 feet, with a little encouragement from Mitchell, the landing radar finally began to register, prompting him to exclaim, "Whew! That was close!"

Antares then descended smoothly to the surface, coming to rest on an 8-degree slope. Passing high overhead in the command ship *Kitty Hawk,* Roosa reported sighting *Antares.* He later described it as showing up "as a white spot, obviously something foreign to the lunar surface reflecting light . . . you couldn't see a shape . . . but with no doubt, the LM was there."

The landing at Fra Mauro occurred at 4:17 A.M. EST on February 5, only 30 to 60 feet short of the planned landing site. Considering that this was only the third manned mission to touch down on the moon, the precision of the landing was almost as overwhelming as the fact they had gotten there at all.

At touchdown, Mitchell began to report, "We seem to be sitting in a bowl. It's choppy, undulating. There is a large depression to our right to the north of us, which forms another bowl. And I can see several ridges and rolling hills of perhaps 35 to 40 feet in height."

The first EVA was delayed by 49 minutes due to a malfunction of the radio communications system built into the helmet of Shepard's pressure suit and backpack. With the problem solved, Shepard descended the lander's ladder, stepping onto the moon at 9:53 A.M. EST, February 5 (at 114:30 hours into the mission). Shepard, the first American in space, became the fifth man to walk on the moon. As he stood on the moon, this astronaut who had fought his way back to flight status after an ear ailment grounded him in 1963, put his emotions into words as he reported to Houston, "I'm on the surface. It's been a long way, and I'm here." Mitchell descended six minutes later, becoming the sixth man to walk on the moon.

The lunar coordinates of their landing site were 3° 40′ South Latitude by 17° 28′ West Longitude.

The crew collected 43 pounds of contingency lunar samples and deployed the TV, communications, and scientific equipment. They roamed as far as 500 feet from *Antares* while setting the scientific experiments in place (from the ALSEP package) and after 4 hours and 49 minutes concluded their first EVA by reentering the lander and sealing the hatch behind them.

After a long rest period, the astronauts again resuited and began their second EVA at 3:11 A.M. EST

on February 6 (131:48 hours into the mission). The astronauts had the Modularized Equipment Transporter with them this time. It was a rickshaw-like device in which the astronauts pulled their tools, cameras, and samples with them across the moon. As Shepard later described "Our planned traverse [walk] was to take us from *Antares* . . . due east to the rim of Cone Crater . . . because scientists wanted samples and rocks from the crater's rim. The theory is that the oldest rocks from deep under the moon's surface were thrown up and out of the crater by the impact" of the meteor which formed it millions of years ago.

Like the Apollo 12 astronauts, Shepard and Mitchell were plagued by the dust they kicked up. In preparation for the first use of the motorized moon rover on Apollo 15, the two astronauts conducted experiments that would be helpful to those astronauts in controlling dust.

The trip had been mapped out to Cone Crater, which took them along a nearly 1,000-yard path. The walk wound its. way through rugged terrain and progress was slower and more laborious than expected. Houston curtailed their trek to the crater, fearing they would become dangerously overtired. Besides, the unevenness of the terrain made it difficult for the crew to navigate by landmarks. Shepard would later recall, "Ed and I had difficulty in agreeing on the way to Cone, just how far we traveled, and where we were. Later estimates indicated we were perhaps only 30 feet or so below the rim."

The two disappointed and tired astronauts made their way back to *Antares* after covering an estimated total of 3 miles on the lunar surface. Their second EVA had lasted 4 hours 35 minutes and ended at 136:26 hours into the mission when they reentered the lander with their 50 pounds of lunar samples and sealed the hatch behind them.

Approximately six hours later at 1:49 P.M. on February 6, *Antares* blasted off the surface of the moon after a 33-hour 31-minute stay on the surface. It returned to lunar orbit, employing a new maneuver that would save time and fuel in achieving the rendezvous and docking with the mother ship, *Kitty Hawk.* The new technique was the "first-orbit rendezvous" maneuver developed during Project Gemini. Because of its complexity, the technique had not been incorporated into the moon missions until Apollo 14.

Antares was reunited with *Kitty Hawk* about two hours later at 3:35 P.M. (144:12 hours into the mission) instead of the usual four to five hours. This time docking occurred normally, on the first try.

Antares was jettisoned at 5:48 P.M. (146:25 hours into the mission) and at 8:39 P.M. on February 6 (146:25 ground elapsed time—GET, or hours into the mission), *Kitty Hawk* rocketed out of lunar orbit and headed for home. After nearly three days of coasting flight, Apollo 14 splashed down in the Pacific Ocean, 4.6 statute miles from the recovery carrier *New Orleans,* on February 9, 1971—216 hours 42 minutes after launch.

Apollo 14 marked the end of what space engineers designated the *H* missions. That series was followed by the *J* missions which had substantially advanced stay capacities on the moon. The *J* series landing crafts had enlarged propellant tanks, additional battery power, more life-support supplies, and provisions for the mechanized Rover vehicles. The Apollo 15, 16, and 17 missions allowed three separate moonwalk periods of up to seven hours each, thus doubling the mission exploration time attained by the Apollo 14 astronauts. Apollo 11 had shown that man could reach the lunar surface and perform useful research there. Apollo 12 and 14 proved we could get there with precision and conduct scientific experiments with relative ease. But, the proving days were over, and Apollo 15 would mark the beginning of man's greatest chapter in the history of exploration.

Tracks left by the Modularized Equipment Transporter (MET) wind their way to the lunar module *Antares*.

Alfred Merrill Worden

Birthplace	Jackson, Michigan
Date of Birth	February 7, 1932
Height	5′ 10½″
Weight	153 lbs.
Eyes	Blue
Hair	Brown
Marital Status	Divorced, subsequently remarried
Daughter	Alison
Son	Merrill
Recreational Interests	Bowling, skiing, waterskiing, swimming, handball, automobile racing
Service Affiliation	Captain, U.S. Air Force
Flight Record	More than 3,667 hours flying time (more than 2,900 in jet aircraft). Logged 295 hours 12 minutes in one space flight, of which 38 minutes were spent in deep-space EVA.
Education and Training	Bachelor of Science degree from the United States Military Academy, West Point, in 1955. He chose an Air Force commission upon graduation, undergoing flight training at Moore Air Force Base and Laredo Air Force Base, Texas, and at Tyndall Air Force Base, Florida. He served as a pilot and armament officer from March 1957 to May 1961 with the 95th Fighter Interceptor Squadron at Andrews Air Force Base, Maryland. In 1963, he received Master of Science degrees in Aeronautical and Astronautical Engineering from the University of Michigan. He attended the Randolph Air Force Base Instrument Pilots Instructor School in 1963. He also was a graduate of the Empire Test Pilots School in Farnborough, England,

having completed training there in February 1965. Worden subsequently attended the Air Force Aerospace Research Pilot School at Edwards Air Force Base, graduating in September 1965, and remained there as an instructor.

Astronaut Career Worden was chosen with the fifth group of astronauts on April 4, 1966. He is a recipient of the NASA Distinguished Service Medal. His first flight assignment as an astronaut was as a member of the astronaut support crew for the Apollo 9 mission. He later became backup command module pilot for the Apollo 12 flight.

Worden served as command module pilot for his first and only space flight, Apollo 15, July 26–August 7, 1971. Fellow crewmates on that flight were David Scott (commander) and James Irwin (lunar module pilot). Apollo 15 was the fourth manned lunar-landing mission, visiting the moon's Hadley Rille area at the base of the Apennine Mountains which are located on the southeast edge of the Mare Imbrium (Sea of Rains). Worden remained in lunar orbit in the command ship *Endeavor* as Scott and Irwin descended to the surface aboard *Falcon*. Mission firsts included: the first use of a motorized vehicle on the lunar surface (Rover 1), first use of a lunar surface navigation device (mounted on the rover), the first subsatellite launched in lunar orbit (an 80-pound scientific satellite, 31 inches long and 14 inches in diameter and carrying three experiments), and the first EVA from a command module during a transearth coast, performed by Worden as he retrieved film cassettes from the panoramic mapping cameras (EVA time 38 minutes).

In September 1972, he was assigned to NASA Ames Research Center, Moffett Field, California, as Director of Advanced Research and Technology. He resigned from NASA and the Air Force with the rank of Lt. Colonel on September 1, 1975, to enter private business. He has written a book of poetry entitled *Hello Earth: Greetings from Endeavor,* and a children's book, *A Flight to the Moon.*

Astronaut Al Worden spacewalks while retrieving film cassettes from cameras located in the service module during Apollo 15's return to Earth (171,000 nautical miles away).

James Benson Irwin

Birthplace	Pittsburgh, Pennsylvania
Date of Birth	March 17, 1930
Height	5′ 8″
Weight	160 lbs.
Eyes	Brown
Hair	Brown
Marital Status/Wife	Mary Ellen
Daughters	Joy, Jill, Jan
Son	James
Recreational Interests	Skiing, paddleball, handball, squash, tennis, fishing, diving, camping
Service Affiliation	Major, U.S. Air Force
Flight Record	More than 7,015 hours flying time (more than 5,300 in jet aircraft). He has logged 295 hours 12 minutes in one space flight, of which 18 hours 35 minutes were spent walking on the surface of the moon. Irwin also is credited with 38 minutes' EVA time due to the open hatch in the command module during Worden's EVA on Apollo 15.
Education and Training	Bachelor of Science degree in Naval Science from the United States Naval Academy, Annapolis, in 1951. Upon graduation, he chose a commission in the Air Force and received flight training at Hondo Air Base and Reese Air Force Base, Texas.

In 1957, Irwin received Master of Science degrees in Aeronautical Engineering and Instrumentation Engineering from the University of Michigan.

Irwin attended the Air Force Experimental Test Pilot School, graduating in 1961. He subsequently attended the Air Force Aerospace Research Pilot School in 1963 and served with the F-12 Test Force at Edwards Air Force Base, California.

He was also with the AIM 47 Project Office at Wright-Patterson Air Force Base, Ohio. His last assignment prior to entering the astronaut corps was as Chief of the Advanced Requirements Branch at Headquarters Air Defense Command.

Astronaut Career He was chosen with the fifth group of astronauts on April 4, 1966. He was awarded the NASA Distinguished Service Medal.

He was crew commander of lunar module LTA-8 (Lunar Test Article). This vehicle finished the first series of thermal vacuum tests on June 1, 1968.

His first flight assignment as an astronaut was as a member of the astronaut support crew for Apollo 10. He then became backup lunar module pilot for the Apollo 12 flight.

Irwin served as lunar module pilot for Apollo 15, July 26–August 7, 1971, accompanying (commander) David Scott to the Hadley Rille–Apennine area of the moon aboard the LM *Falcon,* while command module pilot Alfred M. Worden orbited high overhead in *Endeavor.* Irwin was the eighth man to walk on the moon.

He resigned from NASA and the Air Force with the rank of Colonel in July 1972 to form a religion-oriented foundation called The High Flight Foundation. He has also written a book entitled *To Rule the Night.*

Apollo 15: Exploration at Its Greatest

July 26–August 7, 1971

David R. Scott, spacecraft commander, Alfred M. Worden, command module pilot, and James B. Irwin, lunar module pilot, had earned the assignment of prime crew for Apollo 15 by virtue of their role as backup crew for Apollo 12. Scott, a veteran astronaut from the Gemini program and Apollo 9, would be making his third space flight. Worden and Irwin would be making their first space flights.

The crew launched on time at 8:34 A.M. EST on July 26, 1971, from Complex 39, Pad A, before an estimated audience of 1 million viewers. The Saturn V moon rocket carried the astronauts into a 106.5- by 105.3-mile-high parking orbit. After achieving docking with the lunar module *Falcon,* the command module *Endeavor* streaked towards its rendezvous with the moon three days later.

On July 29, Apollo 15 swept behind the moon, firing itself into lunar orbit at 3:05 P.M. EST after 78 hours and 31 minutes of relatively routine space flight.

Scott described his first closeup view of the moon, "This is really profound . . . it's fantastic!" To him the Apennine Mountains looked unreal. "They stand out in tremendous relief. They appear to be smooth or rounded. But they are cratered and in many places

rough in texture. We don't see any jagged peaks. They don't look like . . . any other mountains we've seen on earth."

Just 22 hours later, at 1:13 P.M. EST on July 30 (100:39 GET—ground elapsed time), Scott and Irwin, aboard *Falcon,* separated from *Endeavor* in preparation for a descent to the foot of those Apennine Mountains that had caused Scott such wonderment.

Four hours later, at 5:15 P.M. EST, Scott reported, "OK Houston, the *Falcon* is on the plain at Hadley." The lander had touched down in the moon's Hadley-Apennine region on the plain called Palus Putredinis (Marsh of Decay), 656 yards north-northwest of the planned target area (lunar coordinates 26° 5' North Latitude, 3° 39' East Longitude). Unknown to Houston, the lander's engine had stirred up so much dust that the landing site had been completely obscured during the last 50 feet of the descent. The astronauts reported that except for instruments, they had been flying blind during the last seconds of touchdown. This was the most difficult to date of the Apollo landing sites, but was chosen because it allowed sampling of three different types of lunar topography—a mare basin (the lunar plain upon which they sat, Palus Putredinis), the lunar rille (a 600- to 1,200-

Apollo 15 astronaut Jim Irwin at Hadley Base. Lunar module *Falcon* and "rover" are in background.

foot-deep gorge called Hadley Rille), and the 15,000-foot-high mountain front of the Apennines.

After cabin depressurization at 106:43 hours (GET), Scott looked out of the upper hatch and described and photographed the area for 33 minutes. The area was hilly, but not rocky or rugged. There were very few boulders strewn about the numerous craters that were present.

At 8:13 A.M. EST on July 31 (119:39 GET), Scott climbed down the ladder to become the seventh man to walk the moon. This EVA would be the first of three exploratory missions that would begin the era of motorized exploration of the moon's surface.

Stowed on the lander for the first time was a collapsible, stripped-down version of a dune buggy, the Lunar Roving Vehicle. Each of the four wheels had its own battery-powered motor. The wheels were oversized and made of wire mesh. The rover came

complete with an earth-controlled color TV camera and a directional antenna to transmit the spectacular color views and voice descriptions to viewers throughout the world.

Irwin soon followed Scott to the surface and the two astronauts began deploying equipment and taking the contingency sample collections.

The crew then unstowed the rover from its bay on the side of the lander, and at 121:45 hours (GET), the two astronauts rode off at the speed of 5 mph. The first portion of this trip was devoted to putting the rover through its paces. Scott, the driver, reported, "The rover handles quite well. It negotiates small craters quite well although there is a lot of roll. The steering is quite responsive . . . and I can maneuver pretty well. . . . There is no accumulation of dirt in the wire wheels." The latter observation was very important. If the wheels had become clogged, the rover might have bogged down in the lunar dust and become useless. At their second stop, the color TV camera aboard the rover treated television viewers to a spectacular view down into Hadley Rille itself.

With six bags of rocks, four of soil, and two double-core tube samples loaded aboard the rover, Scott and Irwin headed back to *Falcon* to deploy the Apollo Lunar Surface Experiment Package (ALSEP). The first EVA had been strenuous for the crew and was ended 28 minutes earlier than scheduled after the men had spent 6 hours and 33 minutes exploring the surface.

During that first EVA, Scott summarized his feelings as an explorer in this way: "As I stand out here in the wonders of the unknown at Hadley, I try to realize there is a fundamental truth to our nature. Man must explore. And this is exploration at its greatest." The motorized vehicle greatly enhanced their ability to cover wide areas of lunar surface and provided views that the astronauts described as "fantastic," "breathtaking," and "spectacular."

After resting inside *Falcon*, recharging and repairing their life-support backpacks, and reviewing their plans for the second EVA, the crew exited the lander at 6:49 A.M. EST on August 1 (142:15 GET). They powered up the rover and headed for the Apennine Mountain front. Things were progressing so smoothly that Mission Control restored the 28 minutes deleted from the previous day's EVA. Eventually another 15 minutes were added to that and the astronauts were able to explore nearly 8 miles along the base of the Apennine Mountains.

The lunar excursion included stops at Spur Crater, Dune Crater, Hadley Plains, and the area between Spur and Window craters. Among the 16 bags of documented rock samples, 8 bags of soil, 6 large rocks, and one core sample, one find evoked excitement in astronauts and scientists alike. A thrilled Scott reported, "I think we found what we came for!" He described a crystalline rock with plagioclase. "As a matter of fact, oh boy, I think we might have ourselves something close to anorthosite." He was referring to a material possibly representative of the formation of the solar system itself. The crystalline stone, since nicknamed the "Genesis rock," was found lying on an Apennine slope. It was later estimated to be more than 4 billion years old.

An exhilarated Scott and Irwin returned to the lander at 149:27 hours into the mission, closing out a very productive second EVA after 7 hours and 12 minutes of work on the moon's surface.

The third and final EVA began at 3:52 A.M. EST on August 2 (163:18 GET), approximately 1 hour 45 minutes late due to the changes that had occurred in the carefully planned schedule on the prior two days. The programmed lift-off time was unalterable, and accordingly the third EVA was shortened to four and a half hours. The astronauts motored west from *Falcon* and began to explore 7.8 miles along the rim of the gorge called Hadley Rille. Along the way the astronauts stopped at Scarp Crater, "The Terrace" near Rim Crater, and Rim Crater itself, collecting samples and taking photographs as they went. Scott tripped over a rock and fell but experienced no difficulty in getting up. The EVA was capped by the cancellation of a pair of space stamps issued by the U.S. Postal Service, depicting astronauts aboard a rover, and commemorating United States achievements in space.

Scott followed this with the memorable demonstration of the Galilean principle that two objects of different weights will fall at the same speed if unhindered by the friction of the atmosphere. While Irwin filmed the experiment, Scott held a geologist's hammer and a falcon feather aloft in either hand. As predicted, both struck the moon's surface at the same instant.

The crew then positioned the rover at a safe distance from the lander so that it could record the blast-off from the moon's surface for the first time. The final reading of the rover's odometer showed that it had traveled about 17.5 miles through three days of EVA. The men loaded the samples aboard the lander—the samples now totaled 170 pounds—and sealed the hatch (20 minutes later than planned) at 168:08 GET after 4 hours 50 minutes on the lunar surface. The crew had spent a record 18 hours 35 minutes exploring the lunar surface.

Meanwhile, Worden, orbiting high above in the command ship *Endeavor*, had completed lunar and astronomic photographic observations during Scott and Irwin's epic three-day sojourn on the moon. He had discovered fields of cinder cones made by volcanic eruptions and noted layering on the interior walls of several craters. This latter discovery also suggested volcanic activity.

As Worden prepared *Endeavor* for rendezvous, Scott and Irwin lifted off the lunar surface in *Falcon* amidst a shower of colorful sparks. Millions of viewers were able to witness the launch thanks to the rover's color TV camera. Lift-off occurred at 12:11 P.M. EST on August 2 (171:34 GET), ending a 66-hour 55-minute stay on the moon.

Docking was completed successfully at 173 hours

36 minutes into the mission in full view of the TV audience. *Endeavor* remained in lunar orbit two more days, during which time an 80-pound scientific subsatellite was launched at 3:13 P.M. EST on August 4—the first such operation in lunar orbit.

Endeavor rocketed out of lunar orbit at 4:23 P.M. EST on August 4 (223:49 GET) and started home after 74 orbits of the moon.

Splashdown occurred in the mid-Pacific 6.3 statute miles from the recovery ship *Okinawa* at 3:47 P.M.

EST on August 7, 12 days 7 hours 12 minutes after lift-off, ending the most ambitious and scientific exploration yet of the lunar surface. During the mission, the freedom of movement demonstrated by the astronauts as they roamed the lunar surface was mind-boggling. The accomplishment of Apollo 15 vividly demonstrated man's unlimited ability to explore. At the time, his will to explore seemed equally unlimited.

Astronaut Irwin beside lunar rover. Mount Hadley is in the background.

Thomas Kenneth Mattingly II

Birthplace	Chicago, Illinois
Date of Birth	March 17, 1936
Height	5′ 10″
Weight	140 lbs.
Eyes	Blue
Hair	Brown
Marital Status/Wife	Elizabeth
Son	Thomas K., III
Service Affiliation	Lieutenant, U.S. Navy
Flight Record	More than 5,565 hours flying time (more than 3,390 hours in jet aircraft). Logged 265 hours 51 minutes in one space flight, of which 1 hour 24 minutes were spent in deep-space EVA.
Education and Training	Bachelor of Science degree in Aeronautical Engineering from Auburn University in 1958. He then received a commission as Ensign in the Navy and earned his wings in 1960. He was then assigned to Attack Squadron VA-35 and flew A1H aircraft from the aircraft carrier U.S.S. *Saratoga* from 1960 to 1963. In July 1963 he served in squadron VAH-11 aboard the U.S.S. *Franklin D. Roosevelt,* where he flew A3B aircraft for two years. Mattingly subsequently entered the Air Force Aerospace Research Pilot School at Edwards Air Force Base, California.
Astronaut Career	He was chosen with the fifth group of astronauts on April 4, 1966. He was a recipient of the NASA Distinguished Service Medal, the Johnson Space Center Certifi-

cate of Commendation (1970), and the Johnson Space Center Group Achievement Award (1972).

On early assignments as an astronaut he was a member of the astronaut support crews for the Apollo 8 and 11 missions. He was astronaut representative in the development and testing of the Apollo space suit and backpack.

Mattingly was the designated command module pilot for the Apollo 13 mission but was removed from flying status 72 hours prior to launch because of an apparent exposure to German measles. He was replaced on that flight by astronaut John L. Swigert, Jr.

Mattingly did fly on the fifth lunar landing mission, Apollo 16, as command module pilot with John Young (spacecraft commander) and Charles Duke (lunar module pilot). While orbiting the moon in the command ship *Casper,* he extended the photographic and geochemical mapping of a belt around the lunar equator.

He is currently serving in a support position to the operational development of the Space Shuttle as Assistant for Technical Coordination to the Chief of the Astronaut Office with the rank of Commander, U.S. Navy.

Astronaut Mattingly in Apollo spacesuit.

Charles Moss Duke, Jr.

Birthplace	Charlotte, North Carolina
Date of Birth	October 3, 1935
Height	5′ 11½″
Weight	155 lbs.
Eyes	Brown
Hair	Brown
Marital Status/Wife	Dorothy
Sons	Charles, Thomas
Recreational Interests	Hunting, fishing, reading, golf
Service Affiliation	Captain, U.S. Air Force
Flight Record	More than 4,147 hours flying time (more than 3,632 in jet aircraft). Logged 265 hours 51 minutes in one space flight, of which 20 hours 14 minutes were spent walking on the moon. In addition, 1 hour 24 minutes of EVA was credited to Duke when the command module hatch was opened to allow Mattingly to perform his deep-space EVA.
Education and Training	Bachelor of Science degree in Naval Sciences from the U.S. Naval Academy, Annapolis, in 1957. Upon graduation, he chose the Air Force as a career. He completed primary flight training at Spence Air Base in Georgia, and then went to Webb Air Force Base in Texas for basic training where he graduated in 1958 with honors. He again was a distinguished graduate at Moody Air Force Base, Georgia, where he completed advanced training in F-86 L jet aircraft. Upon completion of this training, he served three years as a fighter pilot with the 526th Fighter Interceptor Squadron at Ramstein Air Base, Germany.

In 1964, Duke graduated from the Massachusetts Institute of Technology with a Master of Science degree in Aeronautics and Astronautics.

He attended the Air Force Aerospace Research Pilot School, graduating in September of 1965, and stayed on there as an instructor. Duke was teaching control systems and flying in the F-101, F-104, and T-33 aircraft when he was selected to be an astronaut.

Astronaut Career He was chosen with the fifth group of astronauts on April 4, 1966. He was awarded the NASA Distinguished Service Medal and the Johnson Space Flight Center Certificate of Commendation (1970).

He served as a member of the astronaut support crew for the Apollo 10 mission. His first flight assignment was as backup lunar module pilot for Apollo 13.

On his first space flight Duke served as lunar module pilot of Apollo 16, April 16–27, 1972. Spacecraft commander John Young accompanied him to the lunar surface in the LM *Orion*. They landed on the moon's Cayley Plains, where Duke became the tenth man to walk on the moon. Astronaut Thomas Mattingly remained in lunar orbit aboard the command ship *Casper*.

Mission firsts were: placement of the first cosmic ray detector on the moon, the first lunar observatory with the far ultraviolet camera, and the longest inflight EVA (by Mattingly) from a command module during transearth coast (1 hour 24 minutes).

Duke became the backup lunar module pilot for Apollo 17 and later Deputy Manager for Advanced Planning in the Office of Manager for Operations Integration.

Duke resigned from NASA and the Air Force with the rank of Colonel on January 1, 1976, to enter private business.

Apollo 16: A Message from Descartes

April 16–27, 1972

On April 16 at 12:54 P.M. EST, Apollo 16 lifted off from Pad A of Launch Complex 39, Kennedy Space Center. An estimated half-million people were eyewitnesses to the launch, with approximately 38 million viewers watching it on television. The astronauts on board were John W. Young, spacecraft commander, Thomas K. Mattingly II, command module pilot, and Charles M. Duke, Jr., lunar module pilot. This would be the fourth space flight for John Young, who had flown two Gemini missions and Apollo 10, and the first for Mattingly and Duke. The crew had won their assignment to this mission by virtue of their role as backup crew for Apollo 13.

Apollo 16's code name for the command module was *Casper*, a reference to the comic strip character "Casper, the Friendly Ghost." The lunar module was nicknamed *Orion* after the constellation named for the mythical hunter, Orion.

Their destination was the lunar highlands near the Cayley Plains in the moon's Descartes region. Some scientists believed this area to be the oldest region on the moon, and the mission of the crew was to collect rocks and soil samples in the highland area adjacent to the crater Descartes.

The huge Saturn V launch vehicle placed Apollo 16 in the customary (109.3- by 103.6-mile) parking orbit and after a complete checkout of all systems, Apollo 16 headed for the moon.

The spacecraft attained lunar orbit at 3:23 P.M. EST on April 19. Young, who had orbited the moon in Apollo 10, said it was "just as fantastic as it ever was." He described black mounds which looked like volcanic craters with white central peaks. The central peak of Tsiolkovsky Crater appeared to him like "a white marshmallow in a sea of hot chocolate." The crew also described whitish fracture patterns that looked like chalk scribbling and surface markings that reminded them of chicken tracks.

Mattingly said Humboldt Crater had "every contrast in color on the moon." Material from a crater at Descartes looked like cinder fields, and the submerged craters looked like coral atolls of the South Pacific.

At 1:08 P.M. EST (96:14 GET) on Thursday April 20, Young and Duke separated the lander *Orion* from the command ship after a thorough check of all its systems. Both spacecraft flew in formation after the undocking, and as they came from behind the moon, Mattingly suddenly reported a malfunction in the command ship's backup steering system.

Shortly after the two spacecraft had separated in moon orbit, Mattingly performed a routine test of his primary and secondary steering systems. The primary system responded perfectly, but when the secondary system was used to steer the command ship's main engine, the Service Propulsion System rocket engine, it vibrated when steered from side to side. A failure of both steering systems would be catastrophic.

Houston delayed the start of *Orion's* descent to the surface for six hours while it wrestled with the problem. Apollo 16's predicament was studied with great intensity at several facilities across the country. In searching the records of previous flights, it was found that similar oscillations had occurred on Apollo 9 with no dangerous results. Actual engine tests were conducted at Tullahoma, Tennessee, and simulations were run at Kennedy Space Center and the Manned Spacecraft Center in Houston. The conclusion was that the problem was minor.

The delay in the landing, however, forced major changes in the flight plan for the remainder of the mission. Flight directors at Houston instructed Mattingly to forego the planned orbital change for the intended photographic experiments and shortened the mission itself from 12 to 11 days. After the flight, Young recalled those agonizing six hours in moon orbit when the landing seemed uncertain, and referred to it as a real "cliff hanger."

Despite the landing delay, the crew was able to carry out nearly every major assignment, thanks to a careful rescheduling of duties. Of the total 33 major experiments of Apollo 16, only one, the heat-flow experiment, was not accomplished.

Orion touched down on the moon's Cayley Plains near the Descartes Mountains (lunar coordinates 8° 54' South Latitude, 15° 30' East Longitude) approximately 150 miles southwest of Apollo 11's Tranquil-

lity Base at 9:23 P.M. EST on Thursday, April 20 (104:30 GET). Duke exclaimed, "Wow! Down! Old *Orion* is finally here, Houston. Fantastic! All we have to do is jump out of the hatch and we've got plenty of rocks."

Descartes Base was the southernmost site visited on the moon by Apollo astronauts and had a much higher elevation than any of the other landing sites. It was about 8,000 feet higher than Tranquillity Base, where Apollo 11 had landed. Duke and Young described the site as rolling country surrounded by mountains and covered with big boulders. The site appeared rockier, more hilly, and more cratered than the previous landing sites. The soil was firm, with rocks strewn over 30 percent of the area and small craters covering 70 percent of it. The sunlight was so bright that it washed out the colors on the surface, making the soil appear white.

Because of the six-hour delay in lunar orbit the lander was powered down to conserve electrical power and the first EVA was rescheduled to follow the sleep period.

The first EVA began at 11:59 A.M. EST on April 21 (119:05 GET). Young was followed shortly by Duke onto the surface, but because of a problem with the lander's antenna, the first steps of the astronauts on the moon failed to get beamed back to earth. Finally, TV pictures were obtained showing a view of the flat-topped Smoky Mountain to the north and Stone Mountain to the south.

The two astronauts then deployed the Apollo Lunar Surface Experiments (ALSEP) Package. Young tripped over the heat experiment cable, pulling it from its connector. It was never repaired due to the lack of time.

The crew then unstowed the rover (Lunar Rover 2) and began their exploration in earnest, visiting Flag, Spook, Plum, and Buster Craters and collecting 44 pounds of sample material including a number of white rocks. One crystalline rock coated with bluish glass appeared to have the same texture as the anorthosite "Genesis rock" collected by Apollo 15. Other rocks were flecked with green and black glass, some were black and gray, and one weighed 14 pounds.

EVA Number 1 terminated at 126 hours 16 minutes into the mission after 7 hours 11 minutes 11 seconds spent exploring the surface. One of the highlights of this first EVA had been the first astronomical observation ever made from a heavenly body other than the earth. The astronauts had set up a far ultraviolet camera/spectroscope to photograph ultraviolet

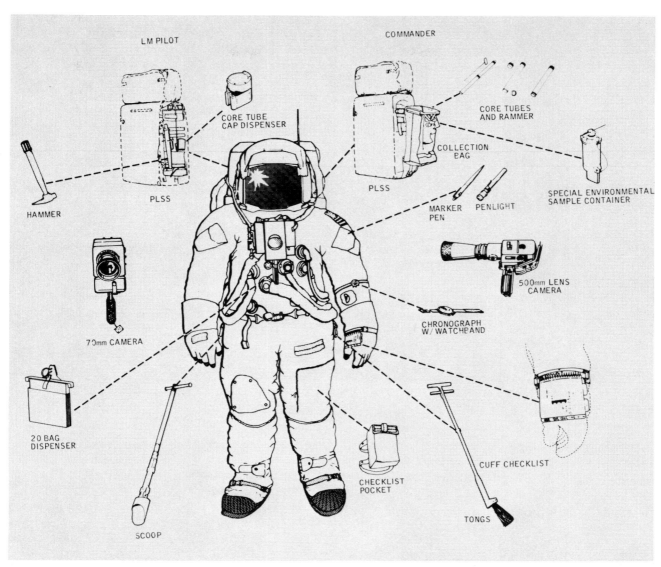

LM PILOT

CORE TUBE
CAP DISPENSER

COMMANDER

CORE TUBES
AND RAMMER

PLSS

COLLECTION
BAG

PLSS

SPECIAL ENVIRONMENTAL
SAMPLE CONTAINER

HAMMER

MARKER
PEN

PENLIGHT

500mm LENS
CAMERA

70mm CAMERA

CHRONOGRAPH
W/ WATCHBAND

20 BAG
DISPENSER

CHECKLIST
POCKET

CUFF CHECKLIST

TONGS

SCOOP

Diagram of spacesuit showing Portable Life-Support System (PLSS) backpack and accessories worn by astronauts during extravehicular activities on the moon.

emissions from clouds of hydrogen and other gases around the earth and deep in space. Ultraviolet light is filtered out by the earth's atmosphere, making valuable observations like those gained by the astronauts impossible from earth. They also set up a cosmic ray detector.

The astronauts ate, slept, and replenished their backpacks with oxygen and other supplies before starting their second EVA at 11:33 A.M. EST on April 22 (142:51 GET). This time they explored Survey Ridge and drove their rover up the 20-degree slope of Stone Mountain (named by them for a mountain in Georgia). After stopping a few times for rock sam-

ples, the two astronauts left the rover and began walking up the terraced side of the 1,600-foot mountain till they were about 700 feet above *Orion* and their landing site. As he looked down, Duke exclaimed, "What a view!" "Absolutely unreal!" replied Young.

On this second EVA the crew took surface samples near the rays of craters with a felt-like device, which could enable scientists to understand why the relatively thin upper layers of these areas reflect more sunlight than the other moon surfaces. They also took samples in areas that were constantly in darkness. If these "shadowed soil" samples had

Apollo 16 astronaut John Young collecting lunar samples at the rim of Plum crater during the first EVA. The rover can be seen at the opposite rim.

Astronaut Young using lunar surface rake and a set of tongs to gather lunar samples near North Ray crater during third Apollo 16 EVA. Rover is parked in background.

never been exposed to sunlight, investigators might be able to analyze volatile compounds from the moon's original material.

The crew returned to *Orion* 20 minutes later than planned due to an extension in their schedule. They sealed the hatch at 150 hours 14 minutes into the mission after setting an EVA endurance record of 7 hours 23 minutes 26 seconds.

The last of the three EVA's began 30 minutes early at 10:27 A.M. EST on Sunday April 23 (165:45 GET). Young and Duke drove their battery-powered rover a distance of 3 miles from their lander to the rim of the 3,000-foot-diameter North Ray Crater, the largest crater to be directly explored in the Apollo program. After leaving the rover, they proceeded to the rim of the huge crater with the loping gait that had become a trademark of all the moonwalkers as they negotiated the 1/6-gravity (as compared to earth) environment.

The astronauts could not see the bottom of the crater because its walls sloped inward. Before they left North Ray Crater, the crew recorded the magnetic forces at this site. To everyone's surprise, they found the highest readings of magnetism (313 gammas) so far encountered on the moon, indicating a lunar history of faster spinning and/or a hotter core than the current theories had held.

With the end of EVA Number 3, at 4:05 P.M. EST on Sunday, April 23 (it had lasted 5 hours 40 minutes 14 seconds), the crew concluded a record 20 hours 14 minutes 54 seconds of scientific investigation and exploration on the lunar surface, covering a total of 16.8 miles.

The deployment of the Apollo 16 automated geophysical research station (from the ALSEP package) 300 feet from their landing site brought to 20 the number of automated scientific instruments transmitting information from the moon to earth. Its station complemented three other active stations set up by astronauts: on the Ocean of Storms (Apollo 12, November 1969), in the Fra Mauro region (Apollo 14, February 1971), and at the Hadley-Apennine site (Apollo 15, August 1971). The Apollo 11 station was relatively primitive and had since ceased to function.

The Apollo 16 station included sensing devices to observe moonquakes, to detect and measure magnetic fields, and to study the moon's interior and some of its physical properties.

A highly satisfied crew blasted off the lunar surface with a record 213 pounds of lunar samples at 8:26 P.M. EST on April 24 (175:44 GET), climbing high above the lunar surface to their reunion with Ken Mattingly in the command ship *Casper*.

While Young and Duke were on the surface, Mattingly made a surprising discovery of his own as he performed observations from his lofty perch aboard *Casper*. He located a radioactive hot spot on the eastern edge of the Ocean of Storms, south of the Apollo 12 landing site, which was subsequently identified as thorium, potassium, and uranium.

After Young and Duke's return to the command ship, the crew launched a scientific subsatellite, similar to the one launched by Apollo 15, into lunar orbit.

On April 24, at 9:15 P.M. EST (200:33 GET), Apollo 16 left lunar orbit to begin the voyage home to earth after 65 lunar orbits.

Apollo 16 was the twenty-sixth manned space flight. In that time, eight flights had gone to the moon and five of those flights had landed on its surface. Not quite 11 years had passed since the first 15-minute U.S. manned space flight. Yet, this and the preceding flights had demonstrated over and over again the enormous capabilities in engineering and science that the United States had acquired and developed in that short span of time.

Before Apollo 16 splashed down in the Pacific Ocean at 2:44 P.M. EST on April 27, just 3 miles from the recovery ship *Ticonderoga* (11 days and 2 hours after launch, or 290:08 GET), spacecraft commander John Young reflected on just this point. Mission Control was conducting an in-flight press conference with the crew on April 26 while the spacecraft was still 123,000 miles from earth on its homeward journey.

In quoting René Descartes, the seventeenth-century French mathematician and philosopher, after whom that region of the moon where Apollo 16 had landed is named, Young transmitted this following message to Houston Control and the global radio and television audience: "Well, let me say just one thing. . . . Mr. Descartes said it. He said there is nothing so far removed from us as to be beyond our reach or so hidden that we cannot discover it. I really guess the story of our mission, so far, is that we've been out testing this theory."

Ronald Ellwin Evans

Birthplace	St. Francis, Kansas
Date of Birth	November 10, 1933
Height	5′ 11½″
Weight	160 lbs.
Eyes	Brown
Hair	Brown
Marital Status/Wife	Janet
Daughter	Jaime
Son	Jon
Recreational Interests	Golfing, boating, swimming, fishing, hunting
Service Affiliation	Lt. Commander, U.S. Navy
Flight Record	More than 2,500 hours flying time (more than 2,200 hours in jet aircraft). Logged 301 hours 52 minutes in one space flight, of which 1 hour 6 minutes were spent in one spacewalk (EVA).
Education and Training	Bachelor of Science degree in Electrical Engineering from the University of Kansas in 1956. He graduated with a commission as an Ensign through the Navy Reserve Officers' Training Corps program. He received his wings in June 1957.

He participated in two WestPac aircraft carrier cruises while a pilot with Fighter VF Squadron 142. He was a combat flight instructor (F-8 aircraft) from January 1961 to June 1962.

He received a Master of Science in Aeronautical Engineering from the U.S. Naval Postgraduate School in 1964. When notified of his selection as an astronaut in 1966, Evans was on sea duty in the Pacific. He was assigned to Fighter Squadron VF-51, flying F-8 aircraft from the carrier U.S.S. *Ticonderoga* during a seven-month period in Vietnam combat operations.

Astronaut Career He was chosen with the fifth group of astronauts on April 4, 1966. He received the NASA Distinguished Service Medal (1973), and the Johnson Space Center Superior Achievement Award (1970). His first flight assignment as an astronaut was as backup command module pilot for Apollo 14. His only space flight was as command module pilot on Apollo 17. His crewmates on that last moon-landing mission were Eugene Cernan and Harrison Schmitt. Cernan was the last man to walk on the moon.

Evans performed a spacewalk on the return flight from the moon.

He later served as backup command module pilot for the Apollo-Soyuz Test Project. He retired from the Navy on April 30, 1976, with the rank of Captain, and from NASA on March 15, 1977, to enter private industry.

Astronaut Cernan and an "upside down" Evans performing a little hi-jinks in space before *America*'s on-board camera.

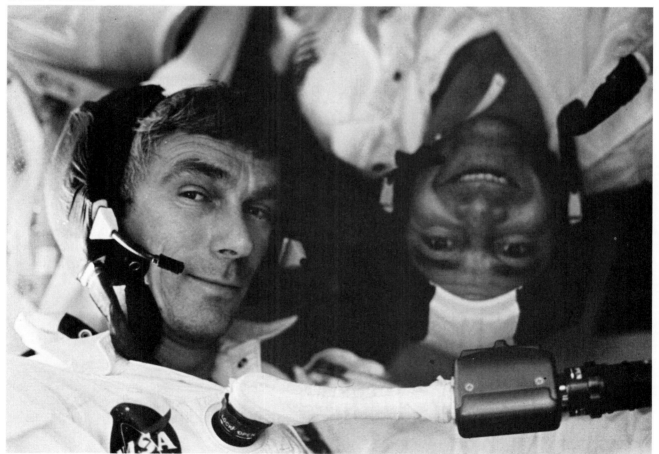

Harrison Hagan Schmitt

Birthplace Santa Rita, New Mexico
Date of Birth July 3, 1935
Height 5' 9"
Weight 165 lbs.
Eyes Brown
Hair Black
Marital Status Unmarried
Service Affiliation Civilian
Flight Record He entered the astronaut corps as a nonpilot and was taught to fly after his selection. He logged more than 2,100 hours flying time, most of which has been jet aircraft and also spent time in helicopter training and flying the lunar lander test vehicle in training for the moon landing.

He has logged 301 hours 52 minutes in one space flight, of which 22 hours 4 minutes were spent walking the lunar surface. He is also credited with 1 hour 6 minutes of EVA time due to the open hatch in the command module during Evans' EVA.

Education and Training Bachelor of Science degree in Geology from the California Institute of Technology in 1957. He studied at the University of Oslo in Norway, 1957–58, after receiving a Fulbright Fellowship. In 1958 he was awarded a Kennecott Fellowship in Geology, and later held a Harvard Fellowship, 1959–60, a Harvard Traveling Fellowship in 1960, and a Parker Traveling Fellowship, 1961–62. In 1963 he received a National Science Foundation Postdoctoral Fellowship, Department of Geological Sciences at Harvard University.

He received a Ph.D. in Geology from Harvard University in 1964. He was also a teaching fellow at Harvard.

Dr. Schmitt did geological work for the Norwegian Geological Survey in Oslo and for the U. S. Geological Survey in New Mexico, Montana, and Alaska.

Before joining NASA, Dr. Schmitt was project chief for phototelescopic mapping of the moon and planets for the U.S. Geological Survey's Astrogeology Center in Flagstaff, Arizona. As an astrogeologist for the U.S. Geological Survey, he instructed the NASA astronauts during their geological field trips.

Astronaut Career He was chosen with the fourth group of astronauts, the scientist-astronauts on June 28, 1965. He received the NASA Distinguished Service Award and the Manned Spacecraft Center Superior Achievement Award. He was trained by NASA to pilot jet aircraft and completed that phase of his training in 1966.

His first flight assignment was as backup lunar module pilot for Apollo 15. He made his first and only space flight on the last manned moon-landing mission, Apollo 17. He descended to the moon's Taurus-Littrow region with astronaut Eugene A. Cernan aboard the lunar module *Challenger*. He was the twelfth man to walk on the moon.

Mission highlights were the largest payload of lunar samples, the longest duration of EVA and staying time on the lunar surface, and the final walk on the moon by a human—Cernan. Schmitt was the first scientist-astronaut to fly in space and the only one to walk on the moon.

He later became Chief of the Scientist Astronaut Office, Science and Applications Directorate at Johnson Space Center before being named NASA's Assistant Administrator for Energy Programs in May 1974. He resigned that position on August 30, 1975, to enter politics and is currently a U.S. Senator from the state of New Mexico (elected on November 2, 1976).

Apollo 17: The Passing of the Torch

December 7–19, 1972

Apollo 17 was launched from Kennedy Space Center's Complex 39, Pad A, at 12:33 A.M. EST on December 7, 1972. It was the first nighttime manned launch. As it disappeared into the black night sky, a curtain of darkness descended over the launch complex as if to signal the end of the Apollo expeditions to the moon.

This was the last time for a long time—possibly forever—that man would visit the moon. Spacecraft commander Eugene Cernan, a veteran of Gemini and the Apollo 10 flight, was making his third flight into space and his second visit to the vicinity of the moon. He would be the eleventh man to walk on the lunar surface. More importantly, he also would be the last. Joining him on the moon's surface was lunar module pilot Dr. Harrison Schmitt, a geologist. It was the first space flight for this scientist astronaut and he would have the distinction of being the first from his group to fly in space. The command module pilot was Ronald Evans and this was his first space flight also. Evans would remain in orbit in the command module *America* when Cernan and Schmitt descended to the moon's surface aboard the lunar module *Challenger*.

After a relatively troublefree translunar flight, Apollo 17 attained lunar orbit at 2:47 P.M. EST on December 10. Cernan announced their arrival, "*America* has arrived on station for the challenge ahead." He described the site moving by below him as "still just as impressive." This was reference to the flight Cernan had made in the Apollo 10 lunar module when he and Stafford descended to within 38,000 feet of the moon in May of 1969.

Cernan and Schmitt touched *Challenger* down on their Taurus-Littrow landing site at 2:55 P.M. EST on December 11, and began man's longest stay on the surface of the moon—74 hours 59 minutes 38 seconds. Cernan descended onto the lunar surface at 7:05 P.M. EST on December 11, declaring, "I'd like to dedicate the first step of Apollo 17 to all those who made it possible." Schmitt followed soon after and took pictures of Cernan as he unfurled a U.S. flag that had flown in the Mission Operations Control Room since Apollo 11 and said, "We very proudly display it on the moon, to stay for as long as it can, in honor of all those people who have worked so hard to put us here . . . and to make the country—the United States—and mankind something different than it was."

The Taurus-Littrow landing site (lunar coordinates 20° 12′ 16″ North and 30° 45′ 0″ East) was chosen for Apollo 17 because its makeup appeared to range from the most ancient highlands to young mantling material that overlay an older basalt (lava) subfloor. As it turned out, the expedition indeed turned out to be a journey through time, as Cernan and Schmitt sampled and described highlands material that was probably 4 billion years old, basalts possibly 3 billion years old, and overlying rubble estimated at from 1 to 2 billion years old.

A second reason for choosing this site was the observation of conical mounds in this vicinity by Al Worden during the Apollo 15 mission. He identified them as similar to the cinder cones formed by volcanic activity on earth. In their first EVA, Cernan and Schmitt drove the rover to the vicinity of Steno Crater, sampling and making observations on the way. Their first trip lasted 7 hours and 11 minutes.

Their second EVA began 1 hour and 20 minutes late. The first task they performed was to repair the damaged wheel fender on their rover using tape and spare maps. The rigged fender functioned perfectly.

It was on this trip, as they explored Lunar Station 4 on their program (Shorty Crater), that Schmitt found the orange soil which he excitedly described as possibly younger than 25 million years. Later examination showed it to be a disappointing 3.75 billion years old and in line with current estimates that, geologically, the moon's major activity must be measured in billions rather than in millions of years. The reddish soil was composed mostly (90 percent) of tiny orange-tinted glass spheres and fragments. The

particles were mostly finer than 50 microns (1/500 inch) and contained about ten times as much zinc as other lunar soil samples. It was a relatively recent deposit, without any of the other bits of rubble mixed in with it. The constant meteorite bombardment by particles from outer space accounts for the observed stirring of the lunar surface material. The core samples taken around Shorty Crater also indicated its possible volcanic origin.

The heat-flow measurements made by the Apollo 15 ALSEP instruments in the Hadley-Apennine area greatly surpassed all expectations, considering the quantity of radioactive elements thought to be present in the moon. Scientists wanted to see if this was just a local hot spot or if the moon was indeed warmer than earlier estimates. The Taurus-Littrow heat-flow instruments produced measurements similar to the data from Hadley-Apennine, lending support to the feeling that the moon was not as cold or inert as first suspected. Similar readings from the ALSEP instruments at the other landing sites also began to add additional support to this belief.

Residual magnetism detected in the moon rocks also suggested a molten core as well as a lunar history of faster spinning than first theorized.

The second EVA established a new endurance record—7 hours and 37 minutes—for a single manned excursion on the surface, during which time the astronauts covered 12 miles. The EVA ended on December 13 at 2:05 A.M. EST.

Cernan and Schmitt began the third EVA on the moon at 5:26 P.M. EST on December 13.

They retrieved the cosmic-ray detector and collected 145.9 pounds of lunar samples while riding the rover. They ended their final excursion on the moon at 42 minutes after midnight on December 14, after spending 7 hours 16 minutes on the surface.

Before entering *Challenger* for the last time Cernan and Schmitt made a final telecast from the moon's surface. Cernan proceeded: "To commemorate not just Apollo 17's visit to the Valley of Taurus-Littrow, but as an everlasting commemoration of what the real meaning of Apollo is to the world, we'd like to uncover a plaque that has been on the leg of our spacecraft." He read the inscription: "Here man completed his first exploration of the moon, December 1972 A.D. May the spirit of peace in which we came be reflected in the lives of all mankind."

Schmitt gave his own meaning to Apollo 17 one month later when he and the other two astronauts addressed a joint session of Congress on January 22,

Astronaut Schmitt is dwarfed by huge, split lunar boulder during third Apollo 17 EVA at Taurus-Littrau landing site.

Apollo 17 astronaut Cernan returning to lunar rover after deploying U.S. flag.

1973: "I would first like to tell you about a place I have seen in the solar system," he began, "the Valley of Taurus-Littrow.... The Valley as I think of it now, however, has been unchanged by being a name on a distant planet, while change has governed the men who named it. The Valley has been less altered by being explored than have been the explorers. The Valley has been less affected by all we have done than have been the millions who, for a moment, were aware of its towering walls, its visitors, and then its silence.

"... The moon's evolution took place before that portion of earth history familiar to us; namely, prior to 3 billion years ago. [The moon that we view now] is a window into our own past which was beyond our expectations only a few years ago. Now we have insight into events in the early history of the earth ...

"I have spoken of just one facet of the revolution in knowledge that your Apollo program brought to the world. Possibly more important than factual knowledge, however, was the overall act of obtaining that knowledge. In doing so, man has evolved into the universe ... mankind (has) found that its reach could include the stars."

Cernan and Schmitt left the moon with a record 250 pounds of lunar samples at 5:55 P.M. EST on December 14 after an incredible 22 hours 4 minutes 4 seconds of exploration on the surface, during which they covered 22 miles in their rover. They returned to *America* and their crewmate Ron Evans, who told the returning astronauts, "Good to have you all back up here."

While Cernan and Schmitt were on the surface, Evans had observed a series of small dark round humps with smooth surfaces in Aitken Crater on the moon's far side. These resembled the volcanic domes found on earth. His sighting was the first evidence of recent possible volcanic activity on the far side of the moon.

Apollo 17 splashed down in the Pacific at 2:25 P.M. EST, on December 19, 1972, 4 miles from the recovery ship *Ticonderoga,* ending the longest Apollo mission—12 days 13 hours 51 minutes.

Of real significance was an event that occurred before the astronauts had left the surface of the moon.

It was during the third and final EVA, when Cernan dedicated a moon rock to all the youth of the world, represented by 80 teenage science students (from 79 nations on six continents) who were participants in the NASA-sponsored International Youth Science Tour. The students were at the Manned Spacecraft Center, Houston, watching the EVA, live, when Cernan made the announcement. It was a fitting tribute for the final manned expedition on the lunar surface, for it would be the responsibility of this new generation to continue to carry humanity forward. Symbolically, the torch had been passed— and so had the dream that went with it.

Apollo 17, the last lunar manned flight, is greeted by earth-rise just prior to leaving for home.

Project Skylab and Beyond

PROJECTS MERCURY, Gemini, and Apollo had shown that man could accurately navigate through space, across expanses as great as lunar distances. For short durations of time, he could explore, perform scientific experiments, and other useful tasks. With the huge Saturn V moon rockets, he could lift massive amounts of materials with which to build habitats in space. But, in 1973, the question still remained, could man live indefinitely in space?

On May 14, 1973, at 12:30 P.M. EST, the last Saturn V launch vehicle to be fired at Kennedy Space Center roared off Launch Complex 39, Pad A (modified to two stages instead of the three-stage moon rocket configuration). It carried Skylab 1, the orbital workshop, into an initial 272.2-mile-high circular orbit.

Nine astronauts occupied this first space station in three-man shifts. Each shift spent weeks at a time in an attempt to demonstrate that man could live and work in the weightlessness of space for long periods without any compromise to health.

During their stay they engaged in numerous activities that were designed specifically for improving man's life on earth. The Skylab crew evaluated systems and techniques aimed at monitoring the earth's resources and environmental programs. Remote sensing devices aboard Skylab provided an effective technique for measuring natural resources on a global scale and provided an effective means by which man could inventory earth's finite resources.

During the nearly ten months of the Skylab Program, it flew over the entire United States and covered about 75 percent of the earth's surface every five days. Its 37 cameras systematically photographed the terrain below for geographic mapping purposes, and were used to record weather observations. Remote studies also were conducted on crops, forest cover, vegetation health, types of soils, the potential reservoir of water found in the earth's snow fields, and geological features associated with mineral deposits. Oceanographic observations included global sea-surface temperatures, studies of wind and sea conditions, and the location and mapping of promising fishing areas.

Skylab also was used as an orbiting astronomical observatory. Telescopes trained on the sun provided increased knowledge about the multitude of solar influences on earth's environment. Much of what happens on the earth depends on the sun. Weather alone can have a determining impact on the productivity of a crop at harvest, and even its ultimate survival. It exerts a strong influence on the food supply of nations. Study of the sun might someday also unlock the secret of controlled atomic fusion, which could provide a tremendous source of clean power for use on earth. Atomic fusion is the source of the sun's energy.

The medical experiments performed by the Skylab crews not only provided knowledge about man's adaptability to life in space, but the physical reactions of the crews to the new environment provided insights into the fundamental workings of the human body that later had direct applications to medical practice here on earth.

Past space flights by the U.S. and Russia had hinted at certain biological changes. On their return to earth, the crews exhibited some disorientation, as

well as changes in the body's chemical balances. There was a measurable loss of calcium from bones and a reduction in cardiovascular efficiency. Each manned Skylab mission had an astronaut-doctor aboard who could perform the in-flight physical examinations on the crew that had been previously accomplished remotely through telemetry and postflight physicals. He was also rated to perform dentistry as well as remove an appendix. A battery of medical tests—they included blood tests and urine analysis, as well as psychological, cardiovascular, and metabolic analyses—were performed during flight. These contributed immeasurably to the understanding of man's adaptability to space flights.

In addition, experiments employing industrial processes performed in weightlessness and the "perfect vacuum" of space provided valuable information on the possibility of new materials as well as new manufacturing processes. Tests were conducted in an attempt to cast perfect spheres and accomplish pure crystalline growth for certain structures. Attempts also were made at developing high-strength materials.

The Skylab orbital workshop, where the crew ate, slept, and worked in a shirt-sleeve environment, provided 10,426 cubic feet of living space. If the airlock module (622 cubic feet) and the multiple docking adapter (1,140 cubic feet) were included, the total habitable volume of the Skylab orbital workshop zoomed to over 12,000 cubic feet, providing the volume of an average three-bedroom house. It was 50 times larger than the crew compartment of the Apollo command module, which measured only 210 cubic feet. If one included the crew compartment on the lunar module, only another 157 cubic feet were added. In 1973, the 36-cubic-foot crew compartment occupied by John Glenn during his Mercury 11 flight years earlier was unthinkable!

The combined weight of the command ship and lunar module used to explore the moon was approximately 98,500 pounds. Skylab weighed 164,869 pounds and was 106 feet long. Its shape was essentially the same as the third stage of the Saturn V rocket, but after it reached orbit, it sprouted wing-like solar panels that provided the electrical power for Skylab's systems.

The Skylab living quarters (the aft compartment) included a modest bathroom, a kitchen with a cen-

Lift-off of the Skylab space station atop a modified Saturn V rocket.

trally located table, and a large porthole for viewing the earth.

The bedroom contained a sleeping bag for each crew member, which was hung along partitions. Each suspended sleeping bag came equipped with a light, headphones for listening to music, and a flame-proof curtain for privacy.

Since there was no up or down in the weightless environment of Skylab, handholds were strategically located on walls and ceilings throughout the space station.

Shoes had special cleats for insertion into the specially designed aluminum grillwork of the floor. Thus an astronaut's feet stayed in place, leaving his hands free for work.

The second floor (forward compartment) opened up into a spacious room large enough for exercising and recreational activities like playing catch or handball.

There was additional space in the airlock module and the multiple docking adapter unit attached to the laboratory workshop to provide areas for solitude.

In an emergency, Skylab had an alternate docking port to receive a rescue command module from earth. The rescue ship would be a modified Apollo command module that required a crew of only two and was capable of transporting five astronauts back to earth.

Before Skylab flew, NASA invited the nation's high school students to submit proposals for experiments to be performed during the mission. Twenty-five experiments were chosen out of the 3,400 submitted. They ranged from how plants will grow in zero gravity to astronomical problems like measuring the x-ray emissions from the planet Jupiter. The most intriguing of these was an experiment conducted with a spider to see how it would spin its web in zero gravity.

The Skylab space station in earth orbit with solar panels extended. The makeshift "parasol sunshade" is visible over rear section.

Paul Joseph Weitz

Birthplace	Erie, Pennsylvania
Date of Birth	July 25, 1932
Height	5′ 10″
Weight	180 lbs.
Eyes	Blue
Hair	Blond
Marital Status/Wife	Suzanne
Daughter	Cynthia
Son	Matthew
Recreational Interests	Hunting, fishing
Service Affiliation	Lt. Commander, U.S. Navy
Flight Record	More than 5,500 hours flying time (4,400 hours in jet aircraft). Logged 672 hours 50 minutes in one space flight, of which 2 hours 11 minutes were spent in two EVA's in the vicinity of the orbital workshop.
Education and Training	Bachelor of Science degree in Aeronautical Engineering from Pennsylvania State University in 1954. He received his Navy commission through the Reserve Officers' Training Corps at the University, and was assigned to destroyer duty aboard the U.S.S. *John A. Bole.* After a year's service he attended flight training and was awarded his wings in September 1956.

From 1956 to 1960 he was an A-4 Tactics Instructor with Squadron VA-44 at the Naval Air Station in Jacksonville, Florida. While on duty with Squadron VX-5 from September 1960 to June 1962, at China Lake, California, he served as a project officer for various air-to-ground delivery tactics projects.

Weitz spent the next two years at the U.S. Naval Postgraduate School and was then assigned to Squadron VAH-4 at the Naval Air Station, Whidbey Island, Washington, in June 1964, serving as a detachment officer-in-charge.

Astronaut Career Weitz was chosen with the fifth group of astronauts on April 4, 1966. He received the NASA Distinguished Service Medal.

Weitz served as a member of the astronaut support crew for Apollo 12. His first space flight was as pilot for the first manned mission to occupy the orbital workshop, Skylab 2, May 25 to June 22, 1973. With him on the flight were veteran astronaut Charles Conrad (spacecraft commander) and Joseph Kerwin (science pilot), who also was making his first space flight.

The crew was credited with salvaging the orbital workshop for use of future crews by erecting a makeshift sunshade to solve the workshop heating problem and getting a jammed solar array wing fully extended to bring the electrical power up to normal.

Weitz retired from the Navy with the rank of Captain on June 1, 1976, after 22 years of service. He remains with NASA as a civilian astronaut. His current assignment is head of the Astronaut Office's design support group, currently involved in the development of NASA's Space Shuttle program.

Skylab 2 astronaut Weitz is given an examination in space by crewmate Kerwin.

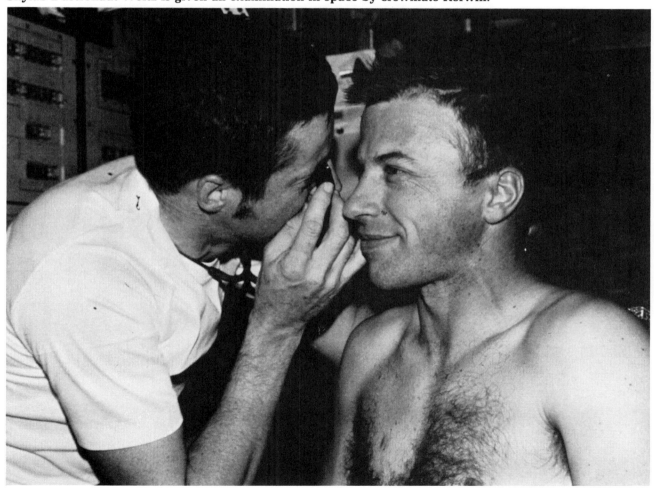

Joseph Peter Kerwin

Birthplace	Oak Park, Illinois
Date of Birth	February 19, 1932
Height	6'
Weight	175 lbs.
Eyes	Blue
Hair	Brown
Marital Status/Wife	Shirley
Daughters	Sharon, Joanna, Kristina
Recreational Interests	Reading, classical music
Service Affiliation	Lt. Commander, U.S. Navy
Flight Record	More than 3,400 hours flying time (more than 2,540 hours in jet aircraft). Logged 672 hours 50 minutes in one space flight, of which 3 hours 23 minutes were spent in EVA's outside the orbital workshop.
Education and Training	Bachelor of Arts degree in Philosophy from the College of the Holy Cross, Worcester, Massachusetts, in 1953, and a Doctor of Medicine from Northwestern University Medical School, Chicago, Illinois, 1957. Upon graduation from medical school, he entered the Navy Medical Corps. He attended the U.S. Navy School of Aviation at Pensacola, Florida, graduating as a Naval Flight Surgeon in December 1958. He completed flight training at Beeville, Texas, in 1962, earning top honors in his class.

He served two years as Flight Surgeon with Marine Air Group 14 at Cherry Point, North Carolina. Later, he was assigned as Flight Surgeon for Fighter Squadron 101 at Oceana Naval Air Station, Virginia Beach, Virginia. He subsequently served as Staff Flight Surgeon for Air Wing 4, Naval Air Station, Cecil Field, Florida.

Astronaut Career He was chosen with the fourth group of astronauts, the science astronauts, on June 28, 1965. He was awarded the NASA Distinguished Service Medal and the Johnson Space Center Commendation Medal (1970). He was also the recipient of the Johnson Space Center Special Achievement Award (1978).

His first space flight was the first manned mission to occupy the orbital workshop, Skylab 2, May 25 to June 22, 1973. With him on that flight were veteran astronaut Charles Conrad (spacecraft commander) and Paul Weitz (pilot), who was also making his first space flight.

The crew was able to salvage the orbital workshop for the two manned Skylab missions remaining. They were able to solve the overheating problem by erecting a makeshift sunshade and releasing the jammed solar power wing to provide Skylab with adequate electricity.

He was a participant in the Outlook for Space study, and was assigned to Space Shuttle development and is Chief of the Life Science Astronaut Office. In April 1978, he was named head of the Operations Mission Development Group within the Astronaut Office and is responsible for supervisory astronaut office planning for all Shuttle missions subsequent to orbital flight tests. His current rank is Captain, U.S. Navy.

Skylab 2: The First Manned Mission

May 25–June 22, 1973

Astronauts Pete Conrad, Dr. Joseph Kerwin, and Paul Weitz lifted off Complex 39, Pad B, on a Saturn IB launch vehicle at 8 A.M. EST, May 25. The launch had been delayed twice while officials tried to assess the seriousness of the damage that had occurred to the Skylab orbital workshop during launch, when it lost the meteoroid shield and suffered a damaged solar panel. Temperatures inside soared to 125° F., requiring a shifting of the workshop to keep it out of the sun's full glare.

Conrad, a veteran of Gemini and Apollo, would be making his fourth space flight and was spacecraft commander. Weitz, pilot, and Kerwin, science pilot, were making their first flights into space.

The crew flew aboard an Apollo command module similar to ones flown in the moon missions, with the exception of the adapter modification installed on the spacecraft for docking with Skylab's orbital workshop.

Rendezvous was accomplished in the fifth revolution and the crew made a fly-around inspection tour of the workshop with Weitz standing in the open hatch of the command module while Kerwin held his legs. Conrad was at the controls.

The scientific airlock was found to be clear, one solar panel completely gone, and the other only slightly extended. It was jammed by an aluminum strap. Weitz was unable to dislodge or cut this strap during the 75-minute stand-up EVA.

At 10:50 P.M., after five attempts, the crew redocked with Skylab (the orbital workshop). They spent the night of May 25 in their command module.

The next day, the crew entered and activated the workshop, which was registering 90 to 100 degrees F.

Astronaut Dr. Joseph Kerwin administers a dental check-up to an extremely cooperative, weightless Charles Conrad during the Skylab 2 mission.

At 3:30 P.M. EST, Conrad and Weitz began their EVA and deployed a makeshift "parasol sunshade" that had been devised only two days before by officials on the ground. By June 4 the temperature inside Skylab had dropped to a comfortable 75 degrees F.

The crew performed a power-limited schedule of experiments and observations on board the space station while a solution for freeing the jammed solar power wing was worked out in Mission Control. On day 14 of the mission, Conrad and Kerwin went outside the spacecraft and during an EVA lasting 4 hours and 10 minutes, they freed the solar panel. Within hours the electrical power supply was up to a sufficient level to allow the mission to proceed as it was originally planned.

Splashdown came at 28 days 50 minutes, on June 22, 1973, 830 miles southwest of San Diego, California, at 8:50 A.M. EST. The crew was recovered by the aircraft carrier *Ticonderoga*. The astronauts were found to be wobbly but otherwise in good health after spending four weeks in the weightlessness of space.

Kerwin, himself a physician, later remarked, "It was a continuous pleasant surprise to me to find out how easy it was to live in zero G [weightlessness], and how good it felt." However, the first Skylab crew recommended an increase in the exercise routine for the succeeding crews.

Accomplishments:

1. Some 80 percent of the planned solar data was obtained, including one major scientific accomplishment, the monitoring of a solar flare.

2. They completed 11 out of 14 of the planned earth-resources studies.

3. All 16 medical experiments were conducted and the progress of man's adaptation to weightlessness was charted for the first time during space flight.

4. Five student investigations were completed.

5. It was the longest manned space flight to date—28 days 50 minutes.

Astronaut Conrad in the shower enclosure. Skylab crew members had to save the warm water; only three quarts were provided.

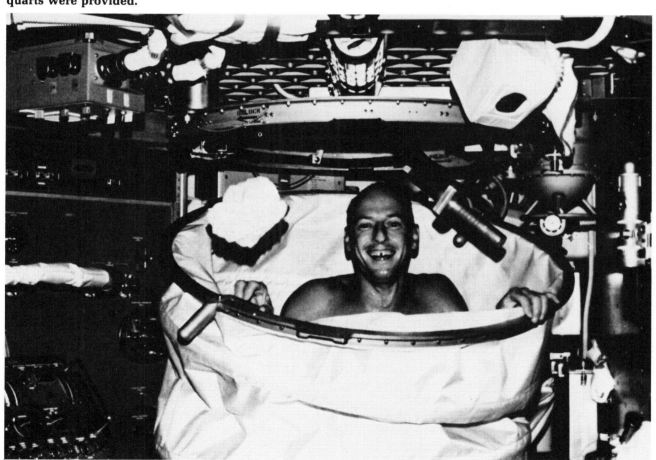

Jack Robert Lousma

Birthplace	Grand Rapids, Michigan
Date of Birth	February 29, 1936
Height	6′
Weight	195 lbs.
Eyes	Blue
Hair	Blond
Marital Status/Wife	Gratia Kay
Daughter	Mary
Sons	Timothy, Matthew
Recreational Interests	Golf, hunting, fishing
Service Affiliation	Captain, U.S. Marine Corps
Flight Record	More than 5,000 hours flying time (more than 3,300 in jet aircraft and 240 hours in helicopters). Logged 1,427 hours 9 minutes in one space flight, of which 11 hours 1 minute were spent in two separate EVA's outside the orbital workshop.
Education and Training	Bachelor of Science degree in Aeronautical Engineering from the University of Michigan in 1959. He then entered the Marine Corps and received his wings in 1960 after completing training at the U.S. Naval Air Training Command. He was then assigned to Squadron VMA-224, 2nd Marine Air Wing, as an attack pilot and later served with Squadron VMA-224, 1st Marine Air Wing, at Iwakuni, Japan.

In 1965 he graduated from the U.S. Naval Postgraduate School with the degree of Aeronautical Engineering. Lousma was assigned as a reconnaissance pilot at the Marine Air Station, Cherry Point, North Carolina, when he was selected as an astronaut.

Astronaut Career He was chosen with the fifth group of astronauts on April 4, 1966. He was awarded the Johnson Space Center Certificate of Commendation (1970) and the NASA Distinguished Service Medal (1973).

He served as a member of the astronaut support crews for the Apollo 9, 10, and 13 missions. Lousma's first space flight was as pilot on the second manned Skylab mission, Skylab 3, July 28 to September 25, 1973. With him on the 59½-day flight were veteran astronaut Alan L. Bean (spacecraft commander) and Owen K. Garriott (science pilot) who was also making his first space flight.

The crew completed 150 percent of their mission goals while completing 858 revolutions of the earth, traveling 24,400,000 miles in orbit. They returned to earth with a massive amount of data, including 16,000 photographs and 18 miles of magnetic tape documenting earth-resources observations.

Lousma served as backup docking module pilot of the United States flight crew for the Apollo-Soyuz Test Project mission, July 15–24, 1975.

He is currently assigned to Space Shuttle development and will serve as pilot of the third orbital flight test of the Space Shuttle with astronaut Fred Haise.

His current rank is Lt. Colonel, U.S. Marine Corps.

NASA technician Al Rockford attends to Skylab 3 astronaut Jack Lousma on launch day.

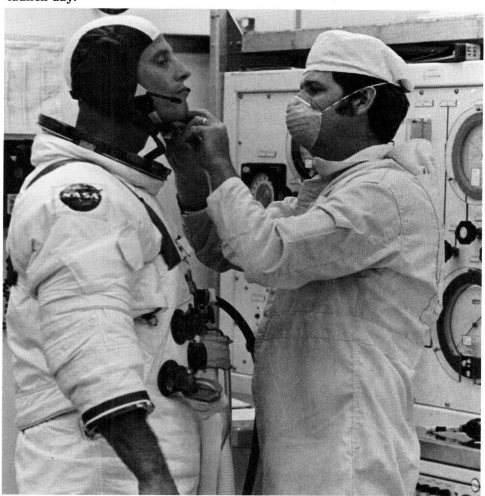

Owen Kay Garriott

Birthplace	Enid, Oklahoma
Date of Birth	November 22, 1930
Height	5′ 9″
Weight	140 lbs.
Eyes	Blue
Hair	Brown
Marital Status/Wife	Helen
Daughter	Linda
Sons	Randall, Robert, Richard
Recreational Interests	Skiing, sailing, scuba diving
Service Affiliation	Civilian
Flight Record	More than 3,700 hours flying time (more than 1,890 hours in jet aircraft, the remainder in light aircraft and helicopters). In addition to NASA ratings, he holds FAA commercial pilot and flight instructor certification for instrument and multi-engine aircraft. He has logged 1,427 hours 9 minutes in one space flight, of which 13 hours 42 minutes were spent in three separate EVA's outside the orbital workshop.
Education and Training	Bachelor of Science degree in Electrical Engineering from the University of Oklahoma in 1953. He served as an electronics officer while on active sea duty with the U.S. Navy from 1953 to 1956 aboard several U.S. destroyers at sea. Garriott received a Master of Science degree and a Ph.D. in Electrical Engineering from Stanford University in 1957 and in 1960, respectively. He was awarded a National Science Foundation Fellowship at Cambridge University and at the Radio Re-

search Station at Slough, England, 1960–61. He taught electronics, electromagnetic theory, and ionospheric physics as an Associate Professor in the Department of Electrical Engineering at Stanford University from 1961 to 1965. He has performed research in ionospheric physics since obtaining his doctorate and has written or collaborated on more than 30 scientific papers and one book on this subject.

Garriott had been a consultant to the Manned Space Science Division of NASA's Office of Space Sciences and Applications, as well as Lockheed Corporation's Space Physics branch. He served as Secretary to the U.S. Commission, International Scientific Radio Union, and was regional editor of *Planetary and Space Sciences*. He remains a Consulting Professor at Stanford University.

Astronaut Career He was chosen with the fourth group of astronauts, the scientist astronauts on June 28, 1965. He was a recipient of the NASA Distinguished Service Medal in 1973.

After selection, he completed his 53-week training course in 1966, at Williams Air Force Base, Arizona. His first space flight was as science pilot for the second manned mission to occupy the orbital workshop, Skylab 3, July 28 to September 25, 1973. With him on the flight were veteran astronaut Alan Bean, commander, and Jack Lousma, pilot, who also was making his first space flight.

Garriott accomplished, at that time, a record-breaking 13 hours 42 minutes of extravehicular activity for a flight during three separate EVA's. The Skylab 3 crew accomplished 150 percent of its mission goals.

Since his flight, Garriott served as Deputy and then Director of Science and Applications and as the Assistant Director for Space Science at the Johnson Space Center.

Dr. Garriott returned to the Astronaut Office to continue training for future flights in the Space Shuttle program.

Scientist-astronaut Garriott during EVA at the Apollo telescope mount of the Skylab space station (Skylab 3).

Skylab 3: The Second Manned Mission

July 28–September 25, 1973

The second Skylab crew lifted off at 6:11 A.M. EST from Pad B of Launch Complex 39 on July 28, 1973. Riding the Saturn IB into earth orbit were astronauts Alan Bean, commander, Jack Lousma, pilot, and Dr. Owen Garriott, science pilot. Bean was a veteran of the Apollo 12 moon mission. Lousma and Garriott were making their first space flights.

The crew experienced motion sensitivity for the first few days, but as they adapted to weightlessness, the astronauts recovered with no aftereffects.

A serious problem occurred early in the mission that threatened its cancellation. Two of the four clusters of rockets that "steer" a command module in flight developed leaks. The problem was considered so serious as to warrant around-the-clock preparations to ready a command module for rescue. The two remaining clusters, however, continued to function perfectly and were adequate to steer the command ship. The rescue operations were called off.

By the tenth day, the crew together had reached a work efficiency level of 19 combined hours a day on scientific experiments. A week later, their output rose to 27–30 combined man hours of experiments per day. Twenty-six earth-resources-experiment passes had been planned, but the crew wound up accomplishing 39. They studied weather conditions including the drought in Africa and tropical storms.

Mission planners had scheduled 206 hours of solar viewing. The crew logged 305 hours, which included the viewing of two major solar flares.

The medical experiments planned were an ambitious 327 runs. All told, 333 were accomplished, including the first orbital demonstration of astronaut maneuvering equipment.

The crew managed to complete 10 of the 12 student investigations during this mission, including the spider experiment.

Besides the students' experiments, many of Skylab's experiments were being conducted for numerous government agencies, industrial organizations, and academic investigators. Skylab's earth-resources experiments alone involved 100 American and 42 foreign groups from the categories just mentioned.

At lift-off of Skylab 1, more than 270 scientific and technical investigations were scheduled for one or more of the three manned Skylab missions and even, in some cases, for automated experiments between crew rotations.

The Skylab 3 crew splashed down in the Pacific at 5:20 P.M EST on September 25, 1973, 250 miles southwest of San Diego, California. They were recovered by the aircraft carrier *New Orleans*.

Accomplishments of Skylab 3:

1. Three EVA sessions were undertaken. The first, the longest to date, a 6-hour 31-minute excursion to deploy experiments and adjust the sunshade on August 6. Lousma later reported, "We took our time. We did not get tired at any time, even when we didn't have water cooling [in the pressure suit] to assist us."

2. The list of experiments completed exceeded the planned workload by 50 percent.

3. The observation and recording of one of the biggest solar flares seen on a Skylab mission.

4. At 59 days 11 hours 9 minutes, they achieved the longest-duration, manned space flight to date.

The Saturn 1B launch vehicle is moved toward Complex 39-B in preparation for the Skylab 3 mission.

Gerald Paul Carr

Birthplace	Denver, Colorado
Date of Birth	August 22, 1932
Height	5' 9"
Weight	155 lbs.
Eyes	Blue
Hair	Brown
Marital Status/Wife	JoAnn
Daughters	Jennifer, Jamee, Jessica
Sons	Jeffrey, John, Joshua
Recreational Interests	Sailing, racquetball, hunting, fishing, woodworking, restoring vintage automobiles
Service Affiliation	Major, U.S. Marine Corps
Flight Record	More than 5,940 hours flying time (more than 5,290 in jet aircraft). Logged 2,017 hours 16 minutes in one space flight, of which 15 hours 51 minutes were spent in three EVA's outside the orbital workshop.
Education and Training	Bachelor of Science degree in Mechanical Engineering from the University of Southern California in 1954. He entered the U.S. Navy in 1949 and in 1950 was appointed a midshipman, in the Naval Reserve Officers' Training Corps. He enrolled in the University of Southern California and upon graduation in 1954 re-

ceived his commission. He subsequently reported to the U.S. Marine Corps Officers' Basic Training School at Quantico, Virginia. He received flight training at Pensacola, Florida, and Kingsville, Texas. He was then assigned to Marine All-Weather Fighter Squadron 114 where he gained experience in the F-9 and F-6A Skyray. He received a Bachelor of Science degree in Aeronautical Engineering from the U.S. Naval Postgraduate School in 1961 and a Master of Science degree in Aeronautical Engineering from Princeton University in 1962. He then served with Marine All-Weather Fighter Squadron 122 from 1962–1965, piloting the F-8 Crusader in the United States and Far East. He has also flown F-4, T-1, T-28, T-33, T-38, H-13 aircraft and ground-effect machines. His last assignment prior to selection as an astronaut was with the Test Directors Section, Marine Air Control Squadron 3. He carried out testing and evaluation of Marine tactical data systems.

Astronaut Career He was chosen with the fifth group of astronauts on April 4, 1966. He was awarded the NASA Distinguished Service Medal in 1974 and the NASA Group Achievement Award in 1971. He was a member of the astronaut support crews and served as Cap Com for the Apollo 8 and 12 missions. He participated in the development and testing of the lunar roving vehicle which was used on the lunar surface by Apollo 15 to 17 flight crews.

Carr served as commander of the third and final manned mission of the orbital workshop, Skylab 4, November 16, 1973 to February 8, 1974. At 84 days 1 hour 16 minutes, it was a record-making space flight in terms of duration. Carr was accompanied by astronauts William R. Pogue (pilot) and Dr. Edward G. Gibson (science pilot). All three astronauts were making their first space flights on this 34.5 million-mile, 1,214-orbit flight. The crew logged 338 hours of operation of the Apollo telescope mount, which made extensive observations of the sun's solar activity.

He retired from the U.S. Marine Corps on September 1, 1975, with the rank of Colonel but remains active as a NASA astronaut currently assigned to the Space Shuttle development program.

Carr served as head of the design support group within the Astronaut Office responsible for areas involving space transportation system design, simulations, testing, and safety assessment.

Skylab 3 astronaut Carr flying a back-mounted maneuvering unit in the weightless environment of their orbiting space station.

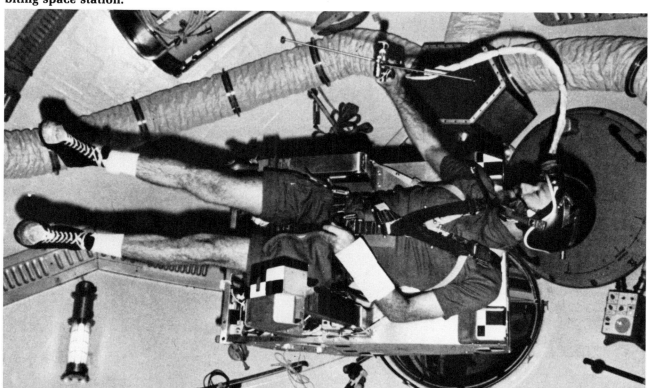

William Reid Pogue

Birthplace	Okemah, Oklahoma
Date of Birth	January 23, 1930
Height	5′ 9″
Weight	160 lbs.
Eyes	Blue
Hair	Brown
Marital Status/Wife	Helen
Daughter	Layna
Sons	William, Thomas
Recreational Interests	Jogging, paddle ball, handball, gardening, studying Biblical history
Service Affiliation	Major, U.S. Air Force
Flight Record	More than 7,200 hours flying time (more than 4,200 in jet aircraft). He flew 43 combat missions during the Korean War. He has logged 2,017 hours 16 minutes in one space flight, of which 13 hours 37 minutes were spent in two EVA's outside the orbital workshop.
Education and Training	Bachelor of Science degree in Education from Oklahoma Baptist University in 1951 after which he enlisted in the Air Force. He received his commission in 1952. Pogue served with the Fifth Air Force during the Korean War, from 1953 to 1954, flying fighter bombers into combat. From 1955 to 1957 he was a member of the U.S. Air Force Thunderbirds precision flying team.

He gained proficiency in more than 50 types of American and British aircraft and is qualified as a civilian flight instructor. He received a Master of Science degree in Mathematics from Oklahoma State University in 1960. Pogue served in the Mathematics Department as an assistant professor at the U.S. Air Force Academy, in Colorado Springs, Colorado, from 1960 to 1963. In September of 1965, he completed a two-year tour as test pilot with the British Ministry of Aviation under the U.S. Air Force–Royal Air Force Exchange Program after graduating from the British Empire Test Pilots School in Farnborough, England.

In October 1965 he was assigned as an instructor at the Air Force Aerospace Research Pilot School, Edwards Air Force Base, California.

Astronaut Career He was chosen with the fifth group of astronauts on April 4, 1966. He was the recipient of the NASA Distinguished Service Medal (1974) and the Johnson Space Center Superior Achievement Award (1970). He served as a member of the astronaut support crews for Apollo 7, 11, and 14 missions.

Pogue was pilot of Skylab 4, the third and final manned visit to the Skylab orbital workshop. Launched November 16, 1973, the mission concluded February 8, 1974. At 84 days 1 hour 16 minutes, it was the longest manned space flight up to that time. Pogue was accompanied on the record-setting 34.5-million-mile flight (in earth orbit) by Gerald Carr (commander) and Dr. Edward G. Gibson (science pilot). They successfully completed 56 experiments, 26 science demonstrations, 15 subsystem detailed objectives, and 13 student investigations during their 1,214 revolutions of the earth. Pogue and his Skylab 4 crewmates shared the world record they had set for individual time in space (2,017 hours 15 minutes 32 seconds). Pogue retired from the U.S. Air Force with the rank of Colonel on September 1, 1975, and became a civilian astronaut with NASA on April 18, 1976. He is currently Crew Training Representative in the Operations and Training Group within the Astronaut Office. He is also assigned to the Earth-Resources Program Office.

Edward George Gibson

Birthplace	Buffalo, New York
Date of Birth	November 8, 1936
Height	5' 9"
Weight	160 lbs.
Eyes	Brown
Hair	Brown
Marital Status/Wife	Julie
Daughters	Jannet Lynn, Julie Ann
Sons	John, Joseph
Recreational Interests	Distance running, swimming, photography, flying, motorcycling
Service Affiliation	Civilian
Flight Record	More than 3,900 hours flying time (more than 1,820 in jet aircraft). Logged 2,017 hours 16 minutes in one space flight, of which 15 hours 22 minutes were spent in three EVA's outside the orbital workshop.
Education and Training	Bachelor of Science degree in Engineering from the University of Rochester in June 1959, and a Master of Science degree in Mechanical Engineering (Jet Propulsion) from the California Institute of Technology in June 1960. He received a Ph.D. in Engineering with a minor in physics from the California Institute of Technology in June 1964. He studied at C.I.T. under a National Science Foundation Fellowship and an R. C. Baker Fellowship.

While studying at C.I.T. Gibson was a research assistant in the fields of jet propulsion and classical physics. His technical publications are in the fields of plasma physics and solar physics. He was Senior Research Scientist with the

Applied Research Laboratories of Philco Corporation at Newport Beach, California, from June 1964 until coming to NASA. While at Philco, he did research on lasers and the optical breakdown of gases. While with NASA he wrote a textbook on solar physics entitled *The Quiet Sun* (1965).

Astronaut Career He was chosen with the fourth group of astronauts, the scientist astronauts on June 28, 1965. He was awarded the Johnson Space Center Certificate of Commendation (1970) and the NASA Distinguished Service Medal (1974). He completed a 53-week course in flight training at Williams Air Force Base, Arizona, and earned his Air Force wings. Since then he has flown helicopters and T-38 jet aircraft. He served as a member of the astronaut support crew and as Cap Com for the Apollo 12 lunar landing. He also participated in the design and testing of many elements of the Skylab orbital workshop.

Gibson's first space flight was as science pilot of the third and final manned mission of the orbital workshop, Skylab 4, November 16, 1973 to February 8, 1974. This was the longest manned flight to date, lasting 84 days 1 hour 16 minutes. His area of responsibility for that flight was in the area of solar physics, comet observations (the mission observed Comet Kohoutek during the flight), stellar observations, earth-resources studies, space medicine, physiology, and flight surgeon activities. Dr. Gibson was accompanied on that record-setting 34.5-million-mile flight (1,214 revolutions of the earth) by Gerald Carr (commander) and William Pogue (pilot). All three astronauts were making their first space flights.

He resigned from NASA in December 1974 to do research on Skylab solar physics data as a Senior Staff Scientist with the Aerospace Corporation of Los Angeles, California. Beginning in March 1976 he served for one year as a consultant to ERNO Raumfahrittechnik Gmbh, in West Germany, on spacelab design under the sponsorship of a U.S. Senior Scientist Award from the Alexander von Humboldt Foundation. He returned to NASA and the Johnson Space Center in March 1977 as Chief of Scientist Astronaut Candidates to participate in Space Shuttle development for the Astronaut Office.

A view of the Skylab space station as seen from the Apollo command module during the final "fly-around" before returning home (Skylab 4).

Skylab 4: The Final Manned Mission

November 16, 1973–February 8, 1974

The third manned, and final, Skylab mission began with lift-off at 9:01 A.M. EST of the Saturn IB launch vehicle from Complex 39, Pad B. It was November 16, 1973.

It was the first manned flight of an Apollo command module without a veteran astronaut on board. Astronauts Gerald Carr, commander, William Pogue, pilot, and Dr. Edward Gibson, science pilot, would all be making their first space flights.

Upon boarding Skylab, the crew found a welcoming note on the teleprinter: "Jerry, Ed and Bill, welcome aboard the space station Skylab. Hope you enjoy your stay. We're looking forward to several months of interesting and productive work. (Signed) Flight Control."

After that welcome, the crew settled down to continue the observations and experiments carried on by the two previous crews.

The highlight of the mission was the appearance of the newly discovered Comet Kohoutek. Dimly visible

One of the most spectacular solar flares (upper left) ever recorded spanning 367,000 miles across the Sun's surface. (Photographed aboard Skylab during last manned mission).

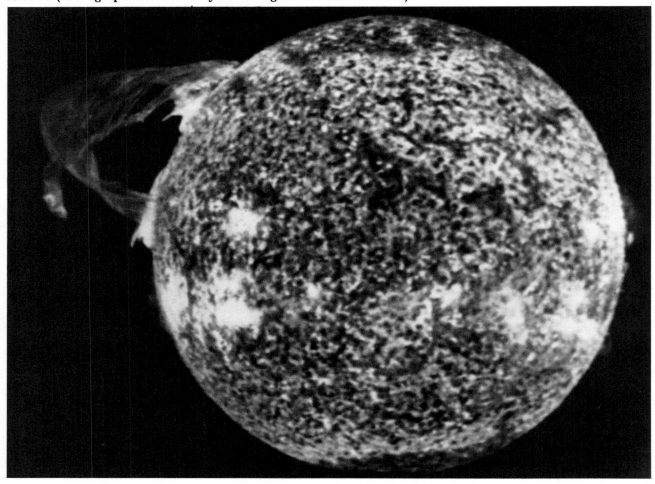

The island of Hawaii photographed during the Skylab 4 mission.

from earth, the comet put on a spectacular show for the astronauts. Pogue began an extensive photographic study of the comet, making 121 observations and separate documentations as it approached, looped around, and retreated from the sun.

Earthbound viewers were disappointed in that it never reached its predicted brightness, but the crew's reaction was different. "Hey, I see the comet! There's the tail. Holy cow!" exclaimed Gibson as he began his spacewalk of December 29 to photograph Kohoutek. Carr, also outside the space station, agreed. "Beautiful!" The comet had looped around the sun the day before and, at that time, Dr. Lubos Kohoutek used the Houston communication facilities to ask that the crew try to observe certain characteristics of his namesake. "The comet's got a spike and a tail," Gibson confirmed. "It is yellow and orange . . . just like a flame."

The crew experienced the physical growth that had been experienced by previous Skylab crews, but this was the first flight on which proper measuring devices were flown. A height increase of 1 to 2 inches was accompanied by a loss of some muscle mass as the body adjusted to weightlessness, redistributing the body fluids accordingly.

In zero gravity, the body's calves and thighs re-duce in size as fluids move up from the legs. Without the pull of gravity, the spinal column stretches and the chest and abdomen reduce. The trim look is not lasting, however, and the crew returned to normal shortly after their return to earth.

Splashdown occurred at 10:17 A.M. EST on February 8, 1974, 175 miles southwest of San Diego, California. The crew had landed 3 miles from their recovery ship *New Orleans.*

Accomplishments of Skylab 4:

1. The crew were the first human beings to study a comet in outer space.

2. The longest orbital spacewalk to date was made by Carr and Pogue on Christmas Day, 1973. It lasted 7 hours 1 minute.

3. They accomplished the longest-duration space flight to date—84 days 1 hour 16 minutes. It was so successful that the original planned 60 days of the mission was extended by 24 days.

4. All three Skylab missions had shown that man had not yet and may never reach the upper limits of his ability to safely live and work in space. Dr. C. A. Berry, former NASA director of life sciences, who had medically overseen the astronauts since 1958, had this view: "From what we know today, there is no reason to bar a 2-year [manned] mission to Mars."

Vance Devoe Brand

Birthplace	Longmont, Colorado
Date of Birth	May 9, 1931
Height	5′ 11″
Weight	175 lbs.
Eyes	Gray
Hair	Blond
Marital Status/Wife	Joan
Daughters	Susan, Stephanie
Sons	Patrick, Kevin
Recreational Interests	Jogging, skin diving, skiing, canoeing
Service Affiliation	Civilian
Flight Record	More than 5,910 hours flying time (more than 4,860 in jet aircraft). Has flown 390 hours in helicopters and been checked out in more than 30 types of military aircraft. Logged 217 hours 28 minutes in one space flight (no EVA).
Education and Training	Bachelor of Science degree in Business from the University of Colorado in 1953. He received a commission and became a naval aviator in the U.S. Marine Corps, serving from 1953 to 1957. He spent a 15-month tour in Japan as a jet fighter pilot and continued in the Marine Corps Reserve and Air National Guard jet fighter squadrons until 1964.

He received a Bachelor of Science degree in Aeronautical Engineering from the University of Colorado in 1960. As a civilian he was employed by the Lockheed Aircraft Corporation from 1960 to 1966, working initially as a flight test engineer on the P3A Orion aircraft. In 1963 Brand graduated from the U.S. Naval Test Pilot

School and was assigned to Palmdale, California, as an experimental test pilot on Canadian and German F-104 development programs. He received a Master's degree in Business Administration from the University of California at Los Angeles in 1964.

Prior to selection as an astronaut, Brand worked at the West German F-104G Flight Test Center at Istres, France, as an experimental test pilot and leader of a Lockheed flight test advisory group.

Astronaut Career He was selected with the fifth group of astronauts on April 4, 1966. He received the Johnson Space Center Certificate of Commendation in 1970, the NASA Exceptional Service Medal in 1974, and the NASA Distinguished Service Medal in 1975. He first served as a crew member for the thermal vacuum chamber testing of the prototype command module and was a support crewman for the Apollo 8 and 13 missions. He later served as backup command module pilot for Apollo 15 and backup commander for the Skylab 3 and 4 missions.

His first space flight was as command module pilot for the Apollo-Soyuz Test Project mission, July 15–24, 1975. He was accompanied by veteran astronaut Thomas Stafford, spacecraft commander, and Donald Slayton, Apollo docking module pilot. Slayton, one of "the Original Seven" Mercury astronauts, also was making his first space flight. The American crew rendezvoused and docked, in the world's first joint international space flight, with a Soviet Soyuz spacecraft manned by cosmonaut Aleksey Leonov, the first human to walk in space (Soyuz commander) and Valeriy Kubasov (Soyuz flight engineer). The link-up tested a unique new docking system and paved the way for future international cooperation in space. There were 44 hours of docked, joint activities which included four crew transfers between Apollo and Soyuz.

It was the last Apollo spacecraft to fly in space and the last manned U.S. space flight until the Space Shuttle is launched on orbital test flights in 1979–80. Brand will serve as commander of the fourth two-man crew assigned to fly the Space Shuttle in earth orbit. He will be accompanied by astronaut Charles G. Fullerton.

Apollo-Soyuz Test Project: End of the First Space Age

July 15–24, 1975

In reality, the mission began with the lift-off, at 7:20 A.M. EST on July 15, 1975, of Soyuz 19 from the Baikonur Cosmodrome at Kazakhstan, a sandy, hilled area of North Central Asia near the Aral Sea, 1,400 miles southeast of Moscow in the Soviet Union. Aboard Soyuz 19 were veteran Soviet cosmonaut Aleksey A. Leonov, commander, and cosmonaut Valeriy N. Kubasov, flight engineer. As second pilot of the Soviet Union's Voskhod 2, Leonov became the first human (on March 18, 1965) to walk in outer space. Kubasov had flown on one previous Soyuz flight.

On schedule, seven and one-half hours after the Soyuz launch, at 2:50 P.M. EST, a Saturn IB rose from Launch Complex 39, Pad B, at Kennedy Space Center, carrying the last Apollo command module to fly in space. On previous flights, Apollo had flown in quests of exploration. Its last flight would be in the quest for peace.

Astronaut Thomas Stafford, veteran of Gemini and Apollo space flights, was spacecraft commander. With him on his first space flight was Donald "Deke" Slayton, docking module pilot. Slayton was the last active astronaut of the legendary "Original Seven," chosen back in 1959 at the beginning of our manned space program. In November 1963, he was appointed Director of Flight Crew Operations of the Astronaut Office, where he acted as the guiding hand behind

Lift-off of the Saturn 1B launch vehicle for the Apollo-Soyuz Test Project carrying the last manned Apollo spacecraft to fly in space.

the astronaut crew assignments throughout the highly successful Gemini, Apollo, and Skylab programs. Now the "teacher" was making his space flight.

Vance Brand, command module pilot, would also be making his first space flight.

After the Apollo command ship separated from its Saturn booster it performed a docking maneuver with the special docking module (mounted on the second stage of the Saturn rocket) that would be used for the docking maneuver in history's first *international* manned space flight.

With the docking module attached to its nose, Apollo flew in space for two days before the docking maneuver was carried out. It was the active partner in the joint operation and on July 17, at 10:52 A.M. EST, Stafford's crew pulled alongside the Soyuz and the two spacecraft flew in a joint station-keeping formation. At 11:09 A.M. EST on that same day, the Apollo crew eased the universal docking assembly at the far end of the docking module into the receptacle carried by Soyuz and completed the historic international link-up.

The passive Soyuz docking target was on its thirty-fifth orbit and Apollo was in its thirtieth orbit. The Apollo was the active partner in the mission due to its broader capabilities.

The docking was televised to viewers on earth via a TV camera pointed out the Apollo window. As the two ships approached and then came together with a slight jar, Stafford exclaimed, "We have succeeded!" The Soyuz commander replied, "Good show, Tom, Soyuz and Apollo are shaking hands now."

Three hours later, at 2:19 P.M EST, the two spacecraft commanders, Stafford and Leonov, shook hands in the connecting tunnel between the spacecraft and embraced each other with the traditional Russian bear-hug welcome.

Then, Stafford and Slayton moved into the Soyuz spacecraft and received a message of congratulations from Soviet party leader Leonid I. Brezhnev and a radio call from President Ford at the White House. There followed a televised ceremonial exchange of flags and momentoes of the occasion.

Before returning to their spacecraft for a sleep period, Stafford and Slayton shared a meal of borscht (squeezed from a tube), turkey, cranberry sauce, apple and plum sticks, and apple juice. The visit ended with the astronauts sealing their Apollo hatch at 5:51 P.M. EST on July 17.

Each spacecraft had been the workhorse of their (U.S. and Soviet) respective space programs, carry-

ing more men into space than any other vehicle built by its country. The larger Apollo spacecraft had been designed to transport men to the moon, while the smaller, lighter Soyuz spacecraft had been designed for earth-orbiting missions.

The Apollo command module is basically controlled by the astronauts on board, who can determine when and where it will go. On the other hand, the Soyuz spacecraft is controlled almost entirely from the ground.

The connecting link between the two craft, the docking module, was built by the United States. The basic shape of the module was cylindrical, forming a 10-foot 4-inch by 4-foot 8-inch aluminum corridor weighing 4,436 pounds. The docking module carried communications equipment including radio and television, containers of atmosphere-replenishing gases, and research equipment including a small electric furnace.

The atmospheres of the two spacecraft were very different. The Apollo craft's atmosphere was made up of pure oxygen at 5 pounds per square inch (one-third the normal atmospheric pressure). The two-gas atmosphere of the Soyuz spacecraft consisted of a mixture of nitrogen and oxygen at 14.7 pounds per square inch. To speed the transfer process, the difference in spacecraft atmospheres was reduced by lowering the atmospheric pressure of Soyuz to 10 pounds per square inch and maintaining the same absolute oxygen content. Crew transfers required spending a few minutes in the docking tunnel to adjust to the different atmospheres between the two spacecraft. A too-rapid transfer from the higher-pressure nitrogen atmosphere of the Soyuz to the lower-pressure Apollo atmosphere would cause nitrogen gas to bubble in the blood system, creating an illness similar to the "bends" experienced by deep-sea divers who rise too rapidly from ocean depths.

On July 18, cosmonaut Leonov transferred to the Apollo spacecraft as astronaut Vance Brand visited cosmonaut Kubasov in the Soyuz spacecraft at 4:45 A.M. EST.

A third and fourth crew transfer were completed on July 18 before the last farewell handshake was made at 3:49 P.M. EST on that same day.

On July 19 the two crews performed the first undocking maneuver at 7:03 A.M. EST, and redocked the two spacecraft 31 minutes later in a final test of the international docking systems and maneuvers. At 10:26 A.M. EST on July 19, the Apollo and Soyuz undocked for the last time, each radioing a farewell in the other crew's language (the format throughout

Apollo astronauts Stafford and Slayton pose with an "inverted" cosmonaut Leonov for the onboard camera.

the mission was for the astronauts to speak only in Russian, and the cosmonauts to communicate only in English).

The Soyuz remained in orbit another two days, returning to Soviet soil with a landing in Kazakhstan at 5:50 A.M. EST on July 21 (recovery was on land).

The Apollo spacecraft remained in orbit until July 24 when it splashed down at 4:19 P.M. EST, in the Pacific Ocean 270 miles west of Hawaii, 4.5 statute miles from the recovery ship *New Orleans*.

The Soyuz flight had lasted 5 days 22 hours 30 minutes (97 orbits) and the Apollo flight had lasted 9 days 1 hour 29 minutes (138 orbits).

The mission marked the first successful testing of a universal docking system and was a milestone in the development of rescue capabilities of astronauts and cosmonauts stranded in space. It was also a major advancement towards the international ex-

ploration of space. The Apollo crew carried out 23 scientific and technical experiments, while the Soyuz crew completed six. In addition, five joint experiments were carried out during the 44 hours of docked, joint activities. All the major mission objectives were accomplished as the crews established six records for docked and group flight.

The Apollo splashdown completed the last flight for that spacecraft. In its seven years of service it had carried 38 Americans through space in 15 separate flights. These included nine missions to the moon, of which six led to landings by a total of 12 men on the lunar surface.

The Apollo spacecraft also served as the "space taxi" for the three different crews that manned the Skylab space station between 1973 and 1974.

At a 6 A.M. news briefing on the last day of the Apollo-Soyuz mission, Capsule Communicator Karol

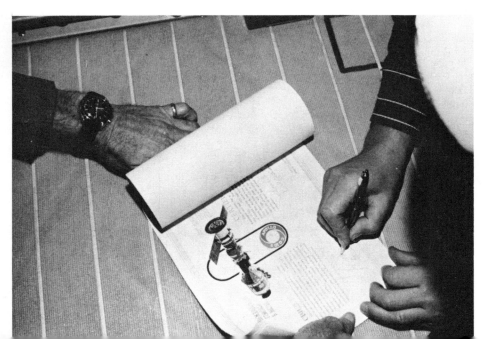

Cosmonaut Kubasov adds his signature on the Soviet side of the official joint certificate marking the historic docking in space of the Apollo and Soyuz spacecraft during ceremonies in orbit.

Bobko was talking to the assembled reporters and writers. As a "new generation astronaut," his observations were very fitting: "I was a little surprised that one of the questions asked the other day was How long do you think it will be before we'll [Soviets and Americans] start to explore a planet? and I thought to myself that here we are—we have started together to explore a planet, and that planet we started to explore together is the planet Earth."

As he journeyed into space, perhaps the greatest contribution to man's understanding of himself and his relationship to the earth was the distant view of his home planet—absent of boundaries, except for the land and the seas and the brilliant blue sphere against the blackness of space. On the grand scale of the universe, life, as we know it, exists in a dimension no greater than the film of a soap bubble, in just as delicate a balance.

A member of the recovery team standing contemplatively on the last Apollo spacecraft to fly in space.

ASTRONAUT CANDIDATES
SELECTED JANUARY, 1978

BLUFORD   BRANDENSTEIN   BUCHLI   COATS   COVEY   CREIGHTON   FABIAN

FISHER   GARDNER   GIBSON   GREGORY   GRIGGS   HART   HAUCK

HAWLEY   HOFFMAN   LUCID   McBRIDE   McNAIR   MULLANE   NAGEL

NELSON   ONIZUKA   RESNIK   RIDE   SCOBEE   SEDDON   SHAW

SHRIVER   STEWART   SULLIVAN   THAGARD   VAN HOFTEN   WALKER   WILLIAMS

Epilogue: Space— The Eternal Frontier

ON JULY 1, 1978, a group of 35 new astronaut candidates reported to Johnson Space Center, Houston, Texas. They joined the 28 astronauts currently on flight status in training for the Space Shuttle program.

After two years of training and evaluation at the Johnson Space Center, successful candidates will become astronauts and enter the Shuttle training program, leading to selection of a flight crew.

A year earlier, on August 12, 1977, the *Enterprise,* a prototype of the Space Shuttle orbiter spacecraft, had been successfully tested in its first freeflight in the earth's atmosphere. The delta-winged spacecraft (about the size of a DC-9 jet liner) was carried aloft by a modified 747 airliner. At an altitude of 24,000 feet above NASA's sprawling Dryden Flight Research Center, in the Mojave Desert, the astronaut crew aboard the *Enterprise* fired the three explosive bolts that held the two ships together, separated from the 747, and in a five-minute powerless flight, returned the 90-ton glider softly to earth in an airplane-like landing on a jet-sized runway. The flight simulated the last few minutes of future Shuttle space missions.

On tests beginning in late 1979, the Shuttle will blast off like a rocket and, after completing a mission in earth-orbit that could last up to a month, return to earth like a glider.

Unlike unmanned spacecraft of the past, which were one-time vehicles, the Shuttlecraft are being designed to make 100 round trips into space before requiring a major overhaul. It is also being designed so that the forces of acceleration at launch and deceleration at reentry are mild enough (a mild 3-G maximum force) to be easily withstood by the average healthy individual. In addition, the Shuttle is constructed and pressurized so that passengers such as scientists, engineers, and others will be able to ride into space in ordinary clothing.

NASA presently plans 560 Shuttle flights between 1980 and 1992 at a rate that will eventually reach more than one a week.

The successful flight of *Enterprise* on August 12 in effect marked the beginning of a new era, a *Second Space Age,* holding the promises of space flight on a routine basis and space travel open to everyone.

A new frontier is opening up to us. It is eternal, offering infinite resources and an endless challenge to mankind's restless spirit. Accepting this challenge will require a great effort—meeting it will insure our greatness.

ACTIVE ASTRONAUTS

Allen

Bobko

Crippen

Fullerton

Hartsfield

Henize

Lenoir

Lind

McCandless

Musgrave

Overmyer

Parker

Peterson

Thornton

Truly

Glossary of Space Terms

Ablation. The removal of surface material or coating from an object by vaporization, melting, or other erosive process in order to reduce surface heat. The heat shield of a spacecraft provides thermal protection by ablation, during the buildup of aerodynamic heat upon reentry. See AERODYNAMIC HEATING, HEAT SHIELD.

Abort. To cut short an activity, such as a launch operation or a space flight.

Acceleration. The rate of change of velocity. See G, GRAVITATION, GRAVITY, INERTIA, MASS.

Acquisition. 1. The process of locating the orbit of a satellite or the trajectory of a space probe so that tracking or telemetry data can be gathered. 2. The process of pointing an antenna so that it is properly oriented to allow gathering of tracking or telemetry data from a satellite or space probe. See TELEMETRY.

Adapter. Any device designed primarily to fit or adjust one piece of equipment to another; such devices can be used to alter spacecraft for uses other than those for which they were designed.

Aerodynamic Heating. The heating of a body produced by passage of air or other gases over the body; caused by friction and by compression processes, especially at high speeds. See ABLATION, HEAT SHIELD.

Aerodynamics. The science that deals with the motion of air and other gaseous fluids and of the forces acting on bodies (a) when the bodies move through such fluids or (b) when such fluids move against or around the bodies.

Aerodynamic Vehicle. A device, such as an airplane, glider, etc., capable of flight only within a sensible *atmosphere* and relying on aerodynamic forces to maintain flight. The term is used when it is desirable to differentiate from a vehicle designed solely for space flight. See ATMOSPHERE.

Aeroembolism. 1. The formation or liberation of gases in the blood vessels of the body, as brought on by a too-rapid change from a high atmospheric pressure to a lower one. 2. The disease or condition caused by the formation of gas bubbles (mostly nitrogen) in the body fluids. Also called *decompression sickness*; the victim feels neuralgic pains, cramps, and swelling, which can at times result in death. Astronauts were placed on pure oxygen prior to space flights in order to purge nitrogen from their blood vessels. See DECOMPRESSION SICKNESS.

Aerospace. (From *aeronautics* and *space*.) Of or pertaining to both the earth's *atmosphere* and *space*.

Agena Launch Vehicle. An upper-stage rocket, originally developed for the Air Force as an advanced research project. It was named for the star Agena in the constellation Centaurus because the rocket was an upper stage "igniting in the sky." A later version, the Agena D (succeeding the A, B, C versions) was adapted atop an Atlas rocket and served as the rendezvous and docking target for Project Gemini.

Anoxia. A complete lack of oxygen available for physiological use within the body. Compare HYPOXIA.

Apogee. That point in earth orbit at which the satellite is farthest from the earth. See ORBIT, PERIGEE.

Artificial Gravity. A simulated gravity established

within a space vehicle by rotation or acceleration. See GRAVITATION, GRAVITY.

Artificial Horizon. A gyroscopically operated flight instrument that indicates pitching and banking attitudes in an aircraft or spacecraft with respect to a reference horizon by means of the relative position of lines or marks on the face of the instrument, representing the craft and the horizon. See ATTITUDE, PITCH, ROLL, YAW.

Astrobiology. The study of living organisms on celestial bodies other than the earth. See EXOBIOLOGY.

Astrodynamics. The practical application of *celestial mechanics, astroballistics,* propulsion theory, and allied fields to the problem of planning and directing the flightpaths of space vehicles. See BALLISTICS, BALLISTIC TRAJECTORY, CELESTIAL MECHANICS, GRAVITATION.

Astrophysics. A branch of astronomy that deals with the physical properties of celestial bodies such as luminosity, size, mass, density, temperature, and chemical composition.

Atlas Launch Vehicle. The Atlas rocket was an adaptation of the Air Force Atlas Intercontinental Ballistic Missile. A modified Atlas launched the four manned orbital flights of Project Mercury and the Agena target vehicle of Project Gemini for rendezvous and docking. It was the workhorse of both the early manned and unmanned space program and an updated version is still in use today. It was named for the mighty god of ancient mythology who carried the world on his shoulders. At the time, Atlas was the US's mightest rocket.

Atmosphere. The envelope of air surrounding the earth; also the body of gases surrounding or comprising any planet or celestial body.

Atmospheric Braking. The action of slowing down an object such as a spacecraft entering the atmosphere of the earth by using the drag exerted by air or other gas particles in the atmosphere. See DRAG.

Atmospheric Pressure. The pressure at any point in an atmosphere due solely to the weight of the atmospheric gases.

Attitude. The position or orientation of an aircraft or spacecraft, either in motion or at rest, as determined by the relationship between its axes and some reference line or plane. See AXIS, PITCH, ROLL, YAW.

Attitude Control. 1. The regulation of the attitude of an aircraft or spacecraft. 2. A device or system that automatically regulates and corrects the orientation of a spacecraft in relation to one or more of its three axes of motion. See ATTITUDE, AXIS, PITCH, ROLL, YAW.

Axis. (plural *axes*) A straight line about which a body rotates. For example, the earth's axis of rotation is an imaginary line drawn through the center of the earth from the north to the south pole. See ATTITUDE, ATTITUDE CONTROL, PITCH, ROLL, YAW.

Backup. An item available to replace the primary item if it fails to perform properly.

Ballistics. 1. The science that deals with the motion, behavior, and effects of projectiles, especially bullets, rockets, or the like. 2. The science or art of designing and hurling projectiles so as to achieve the desired performance. See ASTRODYNAMICS, BALLISTIC TRAJECTORY, CELESTIAL MECHANICS, GRAVITATION.

Ballistic Trajectory. The flightpath followed by a body being acted upon only by gravitational forces and the resistance of the atmosphere, or medium, through which it passes. See ASTRODYNAMICS, BALLISTICS, CELESTIAL MECHANICS, GRAVITATION.

Beam. A ray or collection of focused rays of radiated energy. A beam of radio waves can be used as a navigation aid.

Biosensor. A sensor used to provide information about a life process. See BIOTELEMETRY, SENSOR.

Biotelemetry. The remote measuring and evaluation of life functions in spacecraft or biosatellite. See BIOSENSOR, SENSOR.

Blackout. A fadeout of radio communications due to ionospheric disturbances. A vehicle entering the atmosphere at high speeds creates a disturbance characterized by shock waves and a boundary layer of charged particles (plasma sheath) around its exterior, causing an interruption of radio or telemetry transmissions. See IONIZATION, TELEMETRY.

Boilerplate Model. A replica of a flight vehicle, the structure or components of which are heavier than the flight model.

Boil-Off. The vaporization of a liquid, such as super-cooled liquid oxygen or hydrogen, whose temperature reaches its boiling point upon exposure to the normal atmosphere. A common event during fueling and launching of liquid-fueled rockets. See LIQUID FUEL, LOX, PROPELLANT.

Booster. Short for booster engine or booster rocket. A launch vehicle or rocket.

Booster Engine. An engine that adds its thrust to the thrust of the sustainer engine. An engine of a booster rocket.

Booster Rocket. 1. A rocket motor or engine, either solid- or liquid-fueled, that assists the normal propulsive system (sustainer engine) of a rocket or aircraft in some phase of flight. 2. A rocket used to set a vehicle in motion before the main engine takes over.

Burn. An expression used to describe the time period between the beginning and end of a rocket engine firing. In flight usually referred to as the first burn or second burn, etc.

Celestial Mechanics. The study of the theory of the motions of heavenly bodies under the influence of gravitational fields. See ASTRODYNAMICS, BALLISTICS, BALLISTIC TRAJECTORY, GRAVITATION.

Centrifuge. A large motor-driven apparatus with a long arm, at the end of which human and animal subjects or equipment can be revolved and rotated at various speeds to simulate the forces of acceleration (G-forces) experienced in high-performance aircraft, rockets, and spacecraft.

Chemical Fuel. A fuel that depends on an oxidizer for combustion or for development of thrust, such as liquid or solid rocket fuel or internal-combustion-engine fuel. Distinguished from nuclear fuel. See LIQUID FUEL, LOX, PROPELLANT.

Circumlunar. A flightpath or trajectory around the moon.

Cislunar. Of or pertaining to the area between the earth and the moon. See TRANSLUNAR, CIRCUMLUNAR.

Coasting Flight. The flight of a rocket between burn-out or thrust *cutoff* of one stage and ignition of another. See *BURN*, *CUTOFF*.

Configuration. When referring to the makeup of a space vehicle, a specific type of rocket or craft that differs from others of the same model by virtue of the arrangement of its components or by the addition or omission of auxiliary equipment.

Console. An array of controls and indicators for the monitoring and control of a particular sequence of actions, as in the checkout of a rocket, a countdown action, or a launch procedure. See CONTROL.

Contingency Lunar Sample. A lunar surface sample taken by an astronaut at the earliest possible moment after stepping out onto the lunar surface. It was taken as a precaution to insure the return of at least some lunar material should an emergency cut short the planned lunar mission.

Control. (Central Control) The facility from which specific activities of a space mission are directed. See LAUNCH COMPLEX.

Control Rocket. The rocket engine of a launch vehicle or spacecraft that is used to make small changes in its speed, direction of flight, or orientation.

Cosmic Dust. Fine, dustlike solid matter, sized smaller than a millimeter (smaller than a micrometeorite) moving through interplanetary space.

Cosmic Rays. The extremely high-energy particles traveling through space. They are considered fragments of atoms (mostly protons—hydrogen nuclei) and bombard the earth from all directions—*cosmic radiation*. Solar cosmic rays originate from the Sun and galactic cosmic rays from outside the solar system. See SOLAR WIND.

Countdown. A step-by-step process that culminates in a climactic event, each step being performed in strict sequence in accordance with a specific schedule. The count is in inverse numerical order. This method is used to prepare a large or complicated rocket vehicle for launch or for firing tests. See HOLD, RECYCLE.

Cutoff. The instance of shutting off the propellant flow in a rocket or stopping the combustion of the propellant. See PROPELLANT.

Deceleration. Sometimes called *negative acceleration*. The act of causing to move with decreasing speed.

Decompression Sickness. A disorder experienced by deep-sea divers and pilots alike caused by reduced atmospheric pressure and the formation of gas bubbles (usually nitrogen) in the body and pain in the extremities. Also called the "bends." See AERO-EMBOLISM.

Docking. The act of coupling two or more orbiting objects in space.

D-Ring. A ring with one flat side.

Drag. A retarding force acting upon a body moving through a fluid causing it to slow down. See ATMOSPHERIC BRAKING.

Drogue Parachute. A parachute used specifically to pull a larger parachute out of stowage.

Dropout. Any discrete variation in signal strength during the reproduction of recorded data which results in loss of data.

Dynamic Load. A force caused by dynamic action or movement. In aircraft, rockets, or spacecraft, the force exerted on its structures due to acceleration, winds, landing, or rocket firings.

Dynamic Stability. Steadying characteristics of an aircraft or rocket that cause it to return to its original state of steady flight when a disturbing force makes its flight unsteady. See AERODYNAMICS.

Eccentric Orbit. An orbit which is not, at all times, perfectly circular or equidistant from the surface of the object it is orbiting. See ORBIT.

Electromagnetic Radiation. Energy propagated through space in the form of an advancing disturbance in electric and magnetic fields existing in space. Sunlight, for example.

Escape Tower. A trestle tower placed on top of a spacecraft which connects the craft to the escape rocket which would separate from the rocket in the event of dangerous conditions during countdown, lift-off, or early flight.

Escape Velocity. The speed a body must attain to escape from the gravitational field of a planet or star. See GRAVITATION.

Exobiology. That field of biology which deals with the effects of extraterrestrial environments on living organisms and with the search for extraterrestrial life. See ASTROBIOLOGY.

Explorer. Explorer I was launched on January 31, 1958, by the US Army. It was America's first satellite and the US's contribution to the International Geophysical Year (IGY). Explorer I was credited with making the major discovery of IGY, the Van Allen Radiation Belt, which girdles the earth.

Extra Vehicular Activity (EVA). Any activity performed by a suited astronaut while operating in the vacuum of space.

Eyeballs In, Eyeballs Out. Expressions used by test pilots to describe the experiences of physiological acceleration. A force like the push from behind experienced by astronauts during launch (positive *G-forces*) is called *eyeballs in*. A force like a push on the front of the body (a backward-acting force) like the firing of *retrorockets* to slow down a spacecraft is called *eyeballs out*. See RETROROCKET.

Fix. In navigation, a position determined without reference to any former position. It can be visual, electronic, or radio, depending on the means of establishing it.

Flyby. An interplanetary mission in which the vehicle passes close to the target planet but does not impact it or go into orbit around it.

Fly-by-Wire. An electronic communication system between pilot and guidance components—the latter governed by built-in sensors which respond to flight factors. It allows for more rapid and efficient response to pilot control.

Fuel Cell. A device which converts chemical energy directly into electrical energy. It differs from a storage battery in that the reacting chemicals are supplied continuously as needed to meet the output demands.

G. An acceleration equal to the acceleration of gravity (32.2 feet per second per second at sea level). Also used as a measurement of the force exerted on bodies undergoing acceleration such as 1 G, 2 G, or G-Forces. See ACCELERATION, GRAVITATION, GRAVITY, MASS.

Gantry. A frame structure or scaffold that stands astride the launch pad. See LAUNCH COMPLEX.

G-Force. See G.

Gimbal. A device with intersecting axes of rotation on which a rocket engine operates, giving it freedom to move in several directions, for steering purposes. See AXIS.

Gravitation. The acceleration produced by mutual attraction of two masses, directed along an imaginary line drawn between the centers of the two masses, and of a magnitude directly opposite, proportionally, to the square of the distance between the two centers of mass. See ACCELERATION, G, GRAVITY, INERTIA, MASS, WEIGHTLESSNESS.

Gravity. In earth terms, the force (attraction) imparted by the earth to a mass which is at rest, relative to the earth. See ACCELERATION, G, GRAVITATION, INERTIA, MASS, WEIGHTLESSNESS.

G-Suit. A suit that exerts pressure on the abdomen and lower parts of the body to prevent or retard the accumulation of blood below the chest during positive acceleration, as during a launch. See PRESSURE SUIT.

G-Tolerance. A tolerance in a person, organism, or piece of equipment to a force of acceleration.

Guidance System. The particular type of mechanism within a rocket vehicle or spacecraft that is used to control its direction of flight. See GYRO, INERTIA, INERTIAL GUIDANCE.

Gyro. A device which uses the spinning momentum of a rotor to sense the direction of motion at its base along one or two axes at right angles to its axis of rotation. Also called a *gyroscope*. Used in guidance systems of spacecraft and rockets. See AXIS, GUIDANCE SYSTEM, INERTIA, INERTIAL GUIDANCE.

Gyroscopic Inertia. The property of a rotor such as a gyroscope to resist any force which tends to change its axis of rotation. See AXIS, INERTIA, INERTIAL GUIDANCE.

Hardware. Term used to denote physical equipment such as rockets, spacecraft, systems, etc. Opposite: *software*—designs that exist only on the drawing board.

Heat Shield. The protective structure necessary to protect a reentry craft from aerodynamic heating. See ABLATION, AERODYNAMIC HEATING.

Hold. To discontinue a countdown and wait until an impediment has been removed so that countdown can be resumed. For example: *T minus 40 and holding*. See COUNTDOWN.

Hypoxia. Oxygen deficiency due to an inadequate physiological amount of oxygen available to or utilized by tissue without respect to cause or degree. See ANOXIA.

Inertia. Resistance to acceleration. See ACCELERATION, GRAVITATION, GRAVITY, WEIGHTLESSNESS.

Inertial Guidance. A type of control or guidance that operates by the measurement and integration of acceleration from within a craft. See GYRO, GYROSCOPIC INERTIA, INERTIA.

Insertion. The process of placing an artificial satellite or spacecraft into orbit.

Ion. An electrically charged atom or fragment of an atom.

Ionization. The process by which neutral atoms become electrically charged (plus or minus) by the loss or gain of electrons. This disturbance can cause radio blackouts during spacecraft reentry. See BLACKOUT, DROPOUT, TELEMETRY.

Jettison. To discard a material, device, or structure from a vehicle in flight.

Launch Complex. The facility for launching a space vehicle, including the launch tower (or *gantry*), pad, control center, and/or block house.

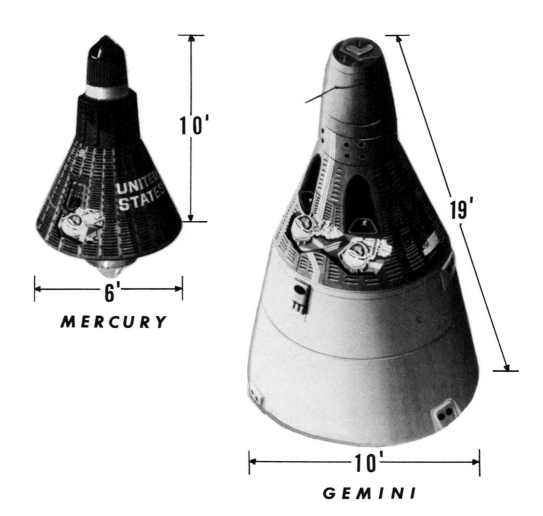

10'

6'

MERCURY

19'

10'

GEMINI

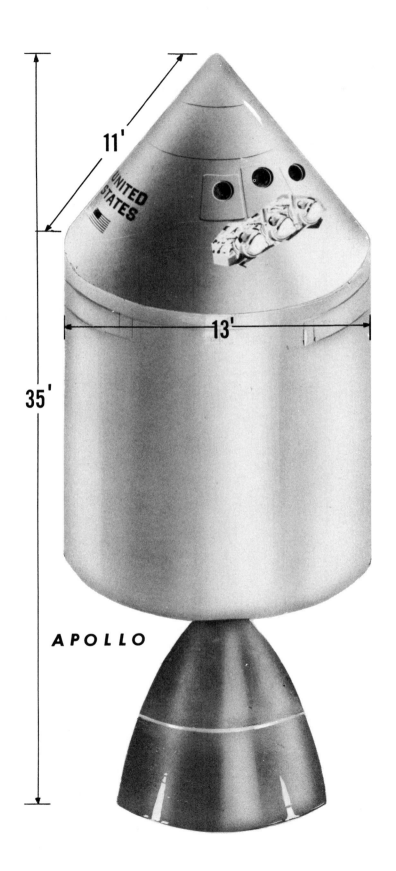

11'

13'

35'

APOLLO

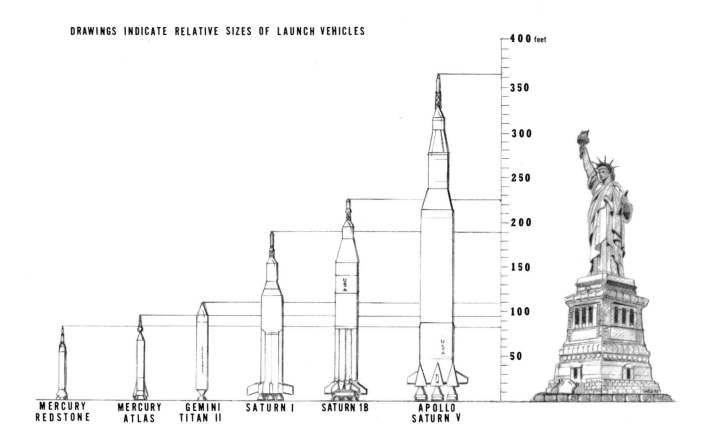

MERCURY REDSTONE   **MERCURY ATLAS**   **GEMINI TITAN II**   **SATURN I**   **SATURN 1B**   **APOLLO SATURN V**

Launch Pad. The platform which bears the rocket and from which it is launched. See GANTRY, LAUNCH COMPLEX, LIFT-OFF.

Lift-Off. The action of a rocket vehicle as it separates from its launch pad in a vertical ascent. See LAUNCH PAD.

Liquid Fuel. A rocket fuel utilized in the rocket in a liquid state. See BOIL-OFF, CUTOFF, LOX, PROPELLANT THRUST.

Lox. Oxygen supercooled to a liquid state for use as an oxydizer. See BOIL-OFF, LIQUID FUEL, PROPELLANT.

Lunar Orbiter. The name was a literal description of the unmanned probe designed to acquire photographic and scientific data of the moon while in lunar orbit. It supplemented the unmanned Ranger and Surveyor probe projects, providing lunar data in preparation for the unmanned Surveyor and later Apollo manned landings on the moon. Five flights were launched in 1966 and 1967.

Mach Number. A number used to express the velocity of a craft in relation to the speed of sound in the same environment. If the speed is twice the speed of sound, the craft is traveling at MACH 2, etc.

Mass. (Symbol: M) A quantity characteristic of a body, which relates the attraction of this body toward another body. The *mass* of a body is constant. *Weight* varies with the change in *acceleration* of that body with respect to the effects of gravity. For example the *mass* of a man is the same on the earth as on the moon, but his weight on the moon is only one-sixth of his weight on the earth since the moon's gravity is one-sixth that of earth. See ACCELERATION, G, GRAVITY, GRAVITATION, WEIGHTLESSNESS.

Meteor. The phenomena associated with the entry into our atmosphere of a *meteoroid*. The visual effect of the entry of a small body is commonly called a *shooting star*.

Meteorite. A meteoroid which has survived the meteor phase and become a geologic specimen.

Meteoroid. A body in solar orbit.

Orbit. 1. The path of a body under the influence of a gravitational force. 2. To go around the earth or other body in a closed path, as opposed to a *trajectory* which has starting and impact points. See TRAJECTORY.

Orbital Velocity. The average speed at which a satellite travels around a body such as a planet. The velocity required to attain earth orbit is 17,500 mph.

Perigee. The orbital point nearest the earth. See APOGEE, ORBIT.

Pitch. Of a vehicle, an angular displacement about an axis parallel to the lateral axis of the vehicle. A fore-to-aft rocking motion similar to the rocking of a boat traversing waves perpendicular to the bow. See ATTITUDE, ATTITUDE CONTROL, AXIS, ROLL, YAW.

Pitchover. The programmed turn from the vertical taken by a rocket as it describes an arc and proceeds down range.

Posigrade Rocket. An auxiliary rocket which fires in the direction of the vehicle's velocity. It is used, for example, in separating two stages of a vehicle.

Pressure Suit. A garment providing pressure upon the body so that respiratory and circulatory functions may continue normally, under low-pressure conditions, such as the vacuum of space. See G-SUIT.

Propellant. Any agent used for combustion in a rocket from which the rocket derives its thrust. See BOIL-OFF, CUTOFF, LIQUID FUEL, THRUST.

Purge. To eliminate a residual fluid, especially fuel or oxygen.

Radiation Belt. An envelope of charged particles trapped in the magnetic field of a celestial body. The *Van Allen Radiation Belt* girdles the earth.

Range. 1. An area in and over which rockets are fired for testing or operations. 2. The distance between two objects.

Ranger. The unmanned Ranger lunar probes were so named because of the close parallel to "land exploration activities." Their mission was to acquire and transmit, via TV cameras, detailed pictures of the lunar surface before impacting on its surface. The first US spacecraft to land on the moon was Ranger 4 in April 1962, followed by Rangers 7, 8, and 9 in 1964 and 1965. These unmanned US lunar space probes were followed by Surveyor and Lunar Orbiter.

Recycle. In a countdown, to stop the count and to return to an earlier step. See COUNTDOWN.

Redstone Launch Vehicle. The Redstone rocket was the predecessor of the Jupiter rocket and was a battlefield missile developed by the US Army. It was adapted by NASA as a launch vehicle for the suborbital spaceflights of Alan Shepard and Gus Grissom, the first and second Americans in space.

Reentry. The event occurring when a space vehicle or other object returns to the atmosphere.

Rendezvous. The event of two or more objects meeting in space and remaining stationary in relation (with relative zero velocity) to each other at a predetermined time and place.

Retropack. A rocket unit built into or strapped to a spacecraft that slows it down in order to allow reentry. See THRUST.

Retrorocket. A rocket on a spacecraft or satellite which produces thrust opposed to forward motion. See ATTITUDE, ATTITUDE CONTROL, EYEBALLS IN/OUT, PITCH, RETROPACK, THRUST, YAW.

Roll. The act of rotating a space vehicle along a longitudinal axis through the center of the body. A rolling similar to the rolling of a log. See ATTITUDE, ATTITUDE CONTROL, AXIS, PITCH, YAW.

Satellite, Artificial. A man-made object that revolves about (orbits) a spatial body.

Saturn Launch Vehicle. The later and more powerful Saturn family of rockets, the Saturn IB and the Saturn V, were developed to carry Apollo spacecraft into earth orbit and to the moon. Its developer, Dr. Wernher von Braun, is credited with naming these powerful rockets after the ancient Roman god of mythology. Saturn was the next rocket after Jupiter, the earlier rocket, which had also been developed by von Braun's team. The huge 7.5-million-pound thrust Saturn V rocket carried man to the moon.

Scrub. To cancel a scheduled rocket firing either before or during *countdown*. See Countdown, Hold, Recycle.

Sensor. The part of an instrument that converts an input signal into a quantity which is measured by another part of the instrument. Medical sensors were placed against the bodies of the astronauts. See Biosensor.

Separation. The action of a fallaway section as it is cast off from the remaining body of the vehicle or the action of the remaining body as it leaves the fallaway section behind it. See Staging.

Solar Cell. A photovoltaic cell that converts sunlight into electrical energy.

Solar Wind. The continuous expansion of the solar coronal gas into interplanetary space.

Space Medicine. A branch of medicine concerned specifically with the health of the human body in the environment of space or of a spacecraft in space.

Staging. The process during the flight of a rocket by which a stage (self-propelled separable element of a rocket vehicle) or half-stage is disengaged from the remaining body, enabling it to ignite its engine in order to be propelled along its own flightpath, as the preceding stage falls away. See Separation.

Station-Keeping. The sequence of maneuvers that maintains a space vehicle in a predetermined orbit or relationship with another vehicle or celestial body.

Statute Mile. 5,280 feet = 1.6093 kilometers = 0.869 nautical mile. Also called *land mile*.

Synchronous Satellite. An equatorial west-to-east satellite orbiting the earth at a distance of approximately 35,900 kilometers from the surface, at which altitude it makes one revolution in 24 hours *synchronous* with the earth's rotation. It will appear to remain stationary in the sky above a point on the earth. See Orbit.

Surveyor. The name *Surveyor* was chosen to designate an advanced, unmanned spacecraft series to explore and analyze the moon's surface. Surveyor I was the first US spacecraft to softland on the moon in 1966, followed by Surveyors 3, 5, and 6 in 1967 and Surveyor 7 in 1968.

Telemetry. The science of measuring a quantity or quantities, transmitting the results to a distant station and interpreting those measurements. A radio transmission of data. See Blackout, Dropout, Ionization.

Terminator. The natural boundary between sunlight on one side of a planet or satellite and the object's shadow, or dark side.

Thrust. The force developed by the firing of a rocket engine. See Cutoff, Propellant.

Titan Launch Vehicle. The Titan II rocket was the launch vehicle for Project Gemini. It was a man-rated version of the US Air Force InterContinental Ballistic Missile and adapted to manned spaceflight. Titan II was chosen as the Gemini launch vehicle because greater thrust was required to orbit the 3½-metric-ton Gemini spacecraft. Also, its storable fuels promised the split-second launch capability needed for *rendezvous* with its target vehicle. In Roman mythology Titans were a race of powerful giants who inhabited the earth before men were created.

Tracking Station. A station set up to follow the movements (track) of an object moving through the atmosphere or space, usually by means of radar or radio. These monitoring stations are located around the world (on land or sea tracking ships) and form the *Spaceflight Tracking and Data Network*.

Trajectory. Generally the path traced by a body moving as a result of an externally applied force such as a rocket in flight.

Translunar. Beyond the moon. See Cislunar.

Umbilical Cord. 1. Any of the servicing electrical or fluid lines between the ground or a tower and an uprighted rocket vehicle before launch. 2. Also the line carried by a spacewalking astronaut, connecting the astronaut to his spacecraft.

Van Allen Belt, Van Allen Radiation Belt. The zone of high-intensity particulate radiation surrounding the earth beginning at an altitude of approximately 1,000 kilometers. Composed of protons and electrons temporarily trapped in the earth's magnetic field, it was discovered by Explorer I, the first US artificial satellite, in 1958.

Viking. The Viking unmanned space probe was a larger version of the earlier Mariner spacecraft (essentially a smaller Viking Orbiter) with the addition of a robot Viking Lander spacecraft. It was programmed to automatically land itself, without direct human guidance, on the surface of Mars. The round trip radiocommunications time between Mars and the earth is 40 minutes, making remote control by radio signals impossible. It made detailed measurements of the martian environment and conducted tests for the presence of life. The first successful unmanned soft-landing on the martian surface was accomplished by Viking I on July 20, 1976, followed by Viking II a month later.

Weight. The force with which an earthbound body is attracted toward the earth. See G, GRAVITATION, GRAVITY, MASS, WEIGHTLESSNESS.

Weightlessness. 1. A condition in which no *acceleration* whether of *gravity* or other force can be detected by an observer within the system in question. 2. A condition in which *gravitational* and other external forces acting on a body produce no stress internally or externally in the body. Any object falling freely in a vacuum is weightless. See G, GRAVITATION, GRAVITY, INERTIA, MASS, WEIGHT.

Yaw. The rotational movement of an aircraft, rocket, or space vehicle about a vertical axis. A weather vane exhibits a yaw movement with the changing of the winds. See ATTITUDE, ATTITUDE CONTROL, AXIS, PITCH, ROLL.

Zero-G. Weightlessness.

DISPOSITION OF MANNED SPACECRAFT IN NASM COLLECTION

Mercury Spacecraft

MR-3	National Air & Space Museum, Washington, D.C.
MA-4	Houston Planetarium, Houston, Texas
MA-6	National Air & Space Museum, Washington, D.C.
MA-7	Japan Science Society, Tokyo, Japan
MA-8	Alabama Space & Rocket Center, Huntsville, Alabama
MA-9	Johnson Space Center/NASA, Houston, Texas

Gemini Spacecraft

GT-III	Grissom Memorial, Indianapolis, Ind.
GT-IV	National Air & Space Museum, Washington, D.C.
GT-V	Johnson Space Center/NASA, Houston, Texas
GT-VI	McDonnell Douglas Corp., St. Louis, Missouri
GT-VII	National Air & Space Museum, Washington, D.C.
GT-VIII	Armstrong Museum, Wapakoneta, Ohio
GT-IX	Kennedy Space Center/NASA, Cape Kennedy, Florida
GT-X	Swiss Museum of Transport, Lucerne, Switzerland
GT-XI	Japan Science Society, Tokyo, Japan
GT-XII	Museum of Transport, Auckland, New Zealand

Apollo Spacecraft

AS-7	National Museum of Science & Technology, Ottawa, Canada
AS-8	Chicago Museum of Science & Technology, Chicago, Ill.
AS-9	Jackson Community College, Jackson, Michigan
AS-10	Science Museum, London, England
AS-11	National Air & Space Museum, Washington, D.C.
AS-12	Langley Research Center/NASA, Langley, Virginia
AS-13	Kennedy Space Center/NASA, Cape Kennedy, Florida
AS-14	Rockwell International Space Division, Downey, Calif.
AS-15	Wright-Patterson AFB, Dayton, Ohio
AS-16	Alabama Space and Rocket Center, Huntsville, Alabama
AS-17	Johnson Space Center/NASA, Houston, Texas
Skylab 2	Naval Aviation Museum, Pensacola, Florida
Skylab 3	Japan Science Society, Tokyo, Japan
Skylab 4	National Air & Space Museum, Washington, D.C.
Apollo-Soyuz	Kennedy Space Center/NASA, Cape Kennedy, Florida

US MANNED SPACEFLIGHT CREW MEMBERS BY PROGRAM

MISSION	PRIME CREW			BACKUP CREW		
Mercury	**Command Pilot**			**Command Pilot**		
MR-3	Shepard			Glenn		
MR-4	Grissom			Glenn		
MA-6	Glenn			Carpenter		
MA-7	Carpenter			Schirra		
MA-8	Schirra			Cooper		
MA-9	Cooper			Shepard		
Gemini	**Command Pilot**	**Pilot**		**Command Pilot**	**Pilot**	
III	Grissom	Young		Schirra	Stafford	
IV	McDivitt	White		Borman	Lovell	
V	Cooper	Conrad		Armstrong	See	
VII	Borman	Lovell		White	Collins	
VI	Schirra	Stafford		Grissom	Young	
VIII	Armstrong	Scott		Conrad	Gordon	
IX	Stafford	Cernan		Lovell	Aldrin	
X	Young	Collins		Bean	Williams	
XI	Conrad	Gordon		Armstrong	Anders	
XII	Lovell	Aldrin		Cooper	Cernan	
Apollo	**Commander**	**Command Module Pilot**	**Lunar Module Pilot**	**Commander**	**Command Module Pilot**	**Lunar Module Pilot**
1	Grissom	White	Chaffee	Schirra	Eisele	Cunningham
7	Schirra	Eisele	Cunningham	Stafford	Young	Cernan
8	Borman	Lovell	Anders	Armstrong	Aldrin	Haise
9	McDivitt	Scott	Schweickart	Conrad	Gordon	Bean
10	Stafford	Young	Cernan	Cooper	Eisele	Mitchell
11	Armstrong	Collins	Aldrin	Lovell	Anders	Haise
12	Conrad	Gordon	Bean	Scott	Worden	Irwin
13	Lowell	Swigert*	Haise	Young	Mattingly*	Duke
14	Shepard	Roosa	Mitchell	Cernan	Evans	Engle
15	Scott	Worden	Irwin	Gordon	Brand	Schmitt
16	Young	Mattingly	Duke	Haise	Roosa	Mitchell
17	Cernan	Evans	Schmitt	Young	Roosa	Duke
Skylab	**Commander**	**Pilot**	**Science Pilot**	**Commander**	**Pilot**	**Science Pilot**
2	Conrad	Weitz	Kerwin	Schweickart	McCandless	Musgrave
3	Bean	Lousma	Garriott	Brand	Lind	Lenoir
4	Carr	Pogue	Gibson	Brand	Lind	Lenoir
Apollo-Soyuz	**Commander**	**Command Module Pilot**	**Docking Module Pilot**	**Commander**	**Command Module Pilot**	**Docking Module Pilot**
	Stafford	Brand	Slayton	Bean	Evans	Lousma

* Mattingly was originally assigned to the prime crew but was exposed to measles several days before launch and therefore was replaced by his backup, Swigert, on the actual flight.

Index